Advanced
GENERALIST
SOCIAL WORK
PRACTICE

DAVID S. DEREZOTES

Sage Publications, Inc.
International Educational and Professional Publisher
Thousand Oaks ▪ London ▪ New Delhi

For information:

Sage Publications, Inc.
2455 Teller Road
Thousand Oaks, California 91320
E-mail: order@sagepub.com

Sage Publications Ltd.
6 Bonhill Street
London EC2A 4PU
United Kingdom

Sage Publications India Pvt. Ltd.
M-32 Market
Greater Kailash I
New Delhi 110 048 India

Printed in the United States of America

Library of Congress Cataloging-in-Publication Data

Derezotes, David S.
    Advanced generalist social work practice / by
David S. Derezotes.
        p.   cm.
    Includes bibliographical references and index.
    ISBN 0-8039-5599-5 (cloth: alk. paper)
    ISBN 0-8039-5600-2 (pbk.: alk. paper)
    1. Social service.   2. Social workers.   I. Title.
HV40.35 .D47   2000
361.3′2—dc21   99-6726

This book is printed on acid-free paper.

00   01   02   03   04   05   06   7   6   5   4   3   2   1

Acquiring Editor:	Jim Nageotte
Editorial Assistant:	Heidi Van Middlesworth
Production Editor:	Wendy Westgate
Editorial Assistant:	Nevair Kabakian
Typesetter/Designer:	Lynn Miyata
Indexer:	Cristina Haley

Contents

Acknowledgments

There is insufficient space to acknowledge all of the people who have inspired and supported my work, but my most significant acknowledgments can be noted here. My children, Nate and Taylor, are my most important teachers. They continually remind me of the importance of community, connection, spirit, and love. I need to thank Dr. Au-Deane Cowley, James Magelby, and Dr. Tracie Hoffman, true colleagues who are whole enough to support and welcome the success of others. I acknowledge other valued mentors who believed in me and supported my own inclusive development: Florence Knopp, Dr. Roger Coulson, Reverend Jacob Weiss, and Dr. Richard Barth. Finally, I thank Dr. Charles Garvin and Jim Nageotte of Sage Publications, who believed enough in the project to give me the opportunity to complete and publish the manuscript.

To my children,
Nate and Taylor Derezotes

Preface and Introduction

The Book

This book describes an advanced generalist approach to *direct* social work practice with individuals, couples, families, and groups. The material is designed to be provided especially during the second-year MSW curriculum and thus builds upon the generalist coursework provided to students in undergraduate and first-year MSW programs. Although the focus is on direct practice, an ecological (person in environment) perspective is applied to all case situations. Text endnotes provide the reader with resources for further study.

This text uses a "top-down"[1] approach, based upon learning theory and science, that recognizes that most students master complex material by first gaining a broad understanding of the material and then specializing in selected focus areas. Applied to social work practice, top-down learning suggests that undergraduate and first-year MSW students gain a familiarity with the many methods and populations they may encounter in practice. It is hoped that by the end of the first MSW year, each student has learned basic competencies applicable to practice with all of the major social work populations at risk. In the second-year curriculum, students then gain a more in-depth understanding of practice in selected methods and populations. By the end of the second MSW year, it is hoped that students are beginning to integrate their new knowledge, skills, and values into a personal practice style that the student has learned to apply in his or her chosen specialty methods and populations.

Throughout the book, the term *clients* is used to describe the people whom the social worker serves. The spirit of the book is to view clients not as passive recipients of services but as vital partners in all social work practice situations. Used less frequently, the term *soul* describes that primary essence of a person that is recognized not only by many of the major religious and wisdom traditions of the world, but also by many of the inventors of modern psychology, psychiatry, and social work.[2] Gender bias is reduced through the alternating use of gender-related pronouns throughout the text. A Transpersonalist[3] framework is used to help incorporate biogenetic, spiritual, and environmental factors in the ecological assessment and advanced generalist intervention strategies.

An Inclusive Approach to Social Work Practice

In an era characterized by humanity's loss of connection with self, family, local and global community, and natural environment, the effective social worker needs an increasingly inclusive view of the challenges that face us today. An inclusive view expands the traditional person-in-environment perspective to also embrace the essential human need for connection with self and the world. In social work, an inclusive perspective would maximize responsible choice by enhancing the professional's ability to differentially select interventions from the universe of available methods that fit the unique ecology of each diverse case situation.

The most advanced theory is also the most inclusive; thus, inclusive social work practice is *advanced* generalist practice because the social worker values and uses both conventional generalist assessment *and* intervention strategies, as well as alternative strategies drawn from a variety of cultures and traditions. This inclusive strategy recognizes the diverse and ecological nature of human life, in that each person is influenced by his or her own intricate internal psychology, as well as by the complex social and natural environments in which he or she lives. With the hundreds of practice strategies currently available to the social worker, an inclusive practice approach is now possible that uses combinations of approaches that match the unique ecology of each case.

The inclusive perspective embraces the many seemingly opposite positions that now polarize social workers. For example, both direct practice with individuals, couples, families, and groups, as well as indirect practice with agencies, institutions, and communities, are valued as interrelated processes. Both artistic factors (e.g., intuition and relationship) and scientific factors (e.g., experiment and measurement) are used in assessment and intervention strategies. Both public and private practice settings are viewed as legitimate social work practice locations.

The inclusive approach also recognizes that both spirituality and science are legitimate ways of knowing that may be used by any populations at risk and by the social workers who serve them. Humanity's desire for connection with self and world could be conceptualized as an expression of the spiritual dimension of human development. Spirituality is viewed in this text as one of the fundamental dimensions of human development (along with the physical, emotional, cognitive, and social dimensions) and thus an important element of human diversity. Whereas a religion is a social organization with shared rituals and beliefs, spirituality is an individual growth process unique to each person.

Recently, the social work profession has rediscovered the importance of spirituality in practice. Although the social work profession had its roots in religious-based charitable organizations, the profession then largely distanced itself from spirituality as social work attempted to prove itself as a profession.

Ironically, some of the professions that social work tried to emulate (e.g., psychology and medicine) have, in the past decades, led the way in showing the empirical relationship between physical health, mental health, spirituality, and the natural environment (the body-mind-spirit-environment connection).[4]

The Council of Social Work Educators (CSWE), the leading accrediting body for social work programs in the United States, affirmed the importance of spirituality and religiosity in practice in their 1994 Curriculum Policy Statement. Accredited social work programs are now required to include spirituality and religiosity as elements of human diversity in BSW and MSW practice curricula.[5]

Spiritual development, or the lack of such development, can also be conceptualized as a key factor associated with most, if not all, biopsychosocial problems. In general, our spiritual disconnection is associated with our current imbalance of emphasis upon such life goals as power, wealth, and status rather than upon whole-person, community-of-diversity, and ecological well-being. Families, institutions, and communities that do not foster spiritual development are more likely to display such interrelated problems as poverty, mental illness, substance abuse, violence, and excessive destruction of natural resources.

Inclusive social work practice embraces the connections both within the individual and between the individual and the larger world. From this perspective, the individual's lifespan development ideally involves growth in each of the interconnected physical, emotional, spiritual, social, and cognitive dimensions. A connection is also envisioned between the health of the individual, the family, the community, and the natural environment.

The inclusive approach uses a mix of traditional social work methods as well as alternative approaches drawn from a variety of professions or traditions. As postmodern client populations continue to become more diverse, such a mix gives social workers and their clients more choices from which to draw as they seek strategies that best fit each unique case situation. More choices are surely required in a world characterized by rapid change and a new millennium of possibilities. Gender roles, marital expectations, vocational patterns, and family structures continue to evolve swiftly. The nature of local and global communities is also changing as human populations increase, economic and political realities shift, and the natural ecosystem continues to deteriorate. Finally, there is a global shift in what could be called conventional consciousness, in which increasing numbers of people are more aware of their interconnectedness with each other and the natural environment.

Thus, we live in an exciting and frightening time, one that presents us with both crises and opportunities for innovation. As a species, we are beginning to recognize the interconnectedness between our souls and the universe, just at the historical moment when not only our well-being but our very survival on an increasingly crowded, hungry, polluted, and militarized planet requires this awareness. Increasing numbers of people are calling for the co-creation of perspectives and rituals that recognize the interconnectiveness of people and the larger world. With its ecological perspective, there is no other profession that is better fitted conceptually and practically to deal with the great problems of our times than social work.

The Advanced Generalist Approach

Advanced generalist practice is both generalist and advanced.

Generalist

The generalist practice or "integrated methods" approach to social work was developed during the 1970s as social workers discovered that "clients did not fit nicely into traditional casework, group work, or community organization molds. Rather, a combination of methods might be needed to respond to the complex problems and situations these clients were presenting" (p. 28).[6] Other factors also played a role in stimulating interest in generalist practice. An explosion of new therapies demanded that social workers expand their own view of what practice is. Thus, the generalist approach is a "box" that is sufficiently large enough to include the many approaches that social workers may need in their practice today.

The first generalists recognized the ecological nature of all problems and noticed the interrelatedness of the two basic aspects of living in society: "people coping" and "environmental demands." The term *social functioning* referred to the interconnection between these two aspects.[7]

Although the generalist perspective did not formally emerge in the literature until the past two decades, the argument could be made that social work has always been a generalist discipline:

> Social work practice is inherently generalist. The profession defines itself as focusing on the person and environment in interaction, and social work practitioners attend to factors ranging from individual needs to broad social policies. The generalist perspective provides a conceptual framework that allows the social worker the versatility necessary to engage in practice of such broad scope.[8]

In summary, although there is still no agreement on the definition of generalist, an emerging consensus[9] suggests that the generalist perspective includes an eclectic base of practice, a multimethod approach, and a focus upon social justice. Thus, in a generalist curriculum, the student becomes familiar with the basic, generic knowledge, skills, and values necessary to practice with a variety of social work populations.

In this text, generalist practice is defined as an inclusive approach to practice that emphasizes the mutual responsibility of the worker/system and client/system to deal with the client's problems in the environment. The worker/system includes the social worker as a multidimensional, whole person; the worker's supports in his or her practice setting; and the other resources and supports available to the worker in the community. The client/system includes the client as a multidimensional, whole person; the client's family and other friends; and the client's local and global community. The elements of generalist practice are expanded in the text to include the following:

1. An eclectic base of practice that uses generic skills and knowledge drawn differentially from all practice paradigms to fit the unique needs of each client in environment

2. A multimethod approach that uses individual, couple, family, group, and/or community levels of practice chosen differentially to fit the unique needs of each client/system

3. A focus on social justice in which the worker/system and client/system cooperate to create and distribute resources in a balanced way that meets the interrelated needs of individuals, communities, and the natural environment

The generalist practitioner takes a broad view in assessment and is prepared to intervene in many circumstances and on many levels. Assessment and intervention strategies are used that differentially consider all environmental factors and available and appropriate approaches. For example, a worker who is helping a single parent who has been denied "workfare" benefits may combine a psychoeducational approach, which is designed to empower the parent, with a case management approach, which links the parent with child care and housing services.

The generalist perspective is useful in all social work practice settings. Rural social work requires generalist approaches; the rural social worker has to deal with a variety of increasingly complex biopsychosociospiritual problems in a locality with relatively few resources. Biopsychosociospiritual problems in urban and suburban settings require generalist practice strategies as well. Although urban and suburban social workers may be able to specialize more than their rural colleagues, their clients' problems are as "ecological" (interrelated with the environment and stemming from multiple causes) as those of rural clients. Multicultural, national, and international practice also require generalist perspectives, in which the social worker must consider many complex factors in assessment and intervention.[10]

Generalist practice can be conducted in both the public and the private sectors. Although private practice has become less fashionable in most academic circles, the private practice setting is as relevant an application of the generalist perspective as any other social work setting. The generalist social worker in private practice is likely to be effective at least in part because he or she sees each client in relationship with other people, his or her community, and the environment. The generalist social worker operates with the same principles outlined earlier, regardless of setting or target population.

Advanced

Because the most advanced theory is always the most inclusive, the advanced generalist approach is more inclusive than the generalist approach. Whereas the generalist social worker has a breadth of understanding of practice, the advanced generalist social worker is developing a more in-depth understanding of how to apply the best combinations of approaches to specific, diverse populations. Such in-depth understanding requires the social worker to use self-awareness and self-expression in a process traditionally called "conscious use of self," as well as gain a sophisticated working knowledge of the major assessment and intervention strategies.

The effective social worker needs to have the most inclusive educational preparation possible: both the broad generalist base of knowledge, skills, and values *and* an in-depth proficiency in practice using conscious use of self with selected social work methods and populations. Although social work's unique focus is on the interrelationship between the individual and the environment, the social work practitioner needs more than just generalist knowledge, skills, and values to operate in the real world of increasingly challenging and complex biopsychosociospiritual problems.

Thus, the advanced generalist social worker applies the basic elements of the generalist perspective to focused practice in three important and inter-related practice functions:

1. The worker is committed to the development and conscious use of self in cultivating helping relationships in practice (Part V in the text). The worker improves conscious use of self by fostering his or her own interrelated spiritual, emotional, physical, social, and cognitive dimensions of human development.

2. The worker uses the inclusive (or ecological) assessment of cases to inform and assess the intervention process (Part I). The worker becomes skilled at assessing the client's developmental process as well as the environmental factors (e.g., family, institution, community) that influence the client.

3. The worker employs differential selection and application of methods drawn from the paradigms of social work practice to work with each client and system served (Parts II, III, and IV). The worker becomes sufficiently familiar with the various paradigms of practice to select combinations of interventions that fit the unique ecology of each case.

Finally, throughout the book, issues of diversity are approached through an emphasis on (a) worker self-awareness through ongoing professional self-development, (b) the individual appraisal of each unique case through ecological assessment, and (c) the differential application of conscious use of self and specific intervention strategies. Thus, the effective social worker learns to recognize and use her or his own countertransference reactions to each client or population, which may include elements of prejudice such as racism and sexism.

Experiential Exercises

1. What do you think about the concept of advanced generalist practice?

2. Have the professional helpers who served you in your life (e.g., teachers, ministers, counselors) seemed to use an advanced generalist perspective? If so, or if not, what was your experience of this approach?

3. What personal and professional strengths (e.g., wisdom, life experience, compassion, etc.) do you already have that will help you practice effectively as an advanced generalist social worker?

Conscious Use of Self

There is perhaps no element of advanced generalist social work practice more vital yet more neglected today than the social worker's own conscious use of self. Conscious use of self refers to the worker's use of all of his or her own dimensions of development as a means of helping the client.[11] Relatively little emphasis is placed on fostering the multidimensional development of the social worker, which is essential in preparing the worker to use him- or herself more effectively in making assessments and interventions in any practice setting. A dichotomous, either/or perspective still exists between use of self and use of technique in direct practice.

Whereas conscious use of self is underemphasized, technique and method are overemphasized in curriculum content, classroom instruction, inservice trainings, journal publications, and case notes. What the social worker does has become vastly more important than who the worker is becoming. As a result, what the client does has also become more important than who the client is becoming. Thus, mental health has been reduced to "function," and unhealthy people are "dysfunctional."

Meta-analysis of the literature suggests that most clients attribute their own development to the quality of their relationship with the helping professional, regardless of the length of the case.[12] Current evidence indicates that the quality of this relationship is itself dependent upon the work that the helping professional does on him- or herself:[13]

> One's ability to relate to other human beings is based on one's experiences of and relationships with one's "innermost" self; and these, in turn, grow out of one's most intimate relations with other people. . . . [The professional helper has] needs, rights, and responsibilities to seek ever-richer

qualities of personal self-knowledge, self-affirmation, and active self-care . . . is generously aware of those complexities and deeply committed to taking good care of that valuable human self that presumes to counsel other selves in their own lifelong becomings. (p. 21)[14]

The importance of conscious use of self is also emphasized in the CSWE guidelines on Purpose of Education, Values and Ethics. Although the actual expression, "conscious use of self" is no longer favored by the authors of these materials, the guidelines make reference to such constructs as "professional use of self," ability to be "self critical," "personal values," and "ethical conduct."[15] Thus, CSWE appears to continue to view conscious use of self as an important component of social work education.

Multidimensional Development

Research supports the importance of multidimensional development in conscious use of self. Empirically based models have been generated to describe the cognitive,[16] affective,[17] physical,[18] social,[19] and spiritual[20] growth processes. All five dimensions have been shown to be interrelated.[21] The social worker who better understands his or her development in these dimensions will be better prepared to assess and intervene in these dimensions with clients.

Developmental science has shown that, because of complex and interrelated biogenetic and environmental factors, each person demonstrates greater development in some dimensions and less in others.[22] Therefore, we tend to develop first and most in the dimensions that are most dominant, comfortable, and enjoyable to us. As we experience success in our dominant dimension, we often are more prepared to develop in our less comfortable dimensions.

The interrelatedness of these dimensions is illustrated in Figure FM.1: Each of the leaves on the plant represents a dimension of development. The leaves often grow at different rates but are all connected together with the plant stem, which is itself rooted in a genetic predisposition and influenced by environmental conditions (e.g., rain and sunshine for the plant and parental love for a person).

Diversity

Conscious use of self enables the worker to become sensitive to client diversity so that interventions can be selected that match the unique needs of each diverse client and system. The concept of diversity implies that each client and client system is unique and requires careful, sensitive, and differential assessment. The culturally skilled counselor has developed respect for and comfort with human differences and awareness of personal values and biases.[23] Current evidence seems to suggest that there are often as many differences

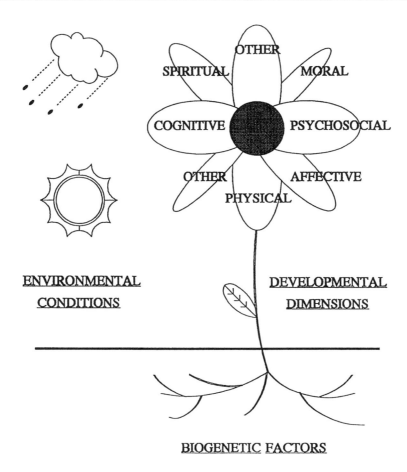

Figure FM.1. Developmental Dimensions

among members of one culture as between members of different cultures; individuals within any group defy stereotyping.[24] Thus, although the social worker should be aware of general tendencies of populations, the worker should also be aware that each client should be assessed as an individual.[25] Thus, cultural sensitivity is actually "a special form of interpersonal sensitivity and an indispensable ingredient in successful intervention with members of other cultures."[26]

Plan of Book

Inclusive (or ecological) assessment, described in Part I, involves the consideration of all intrapsychic, interpersonal, and environmental factors in the environment. The worker uses both the art and science of practice in considering these factors. Inclusive intervention, described in Part II, is based upon core social work values and draws from all of the available micro- and macrolevel paradigms. The intervention paradigms selected for each case involve the conscious use of whole self and are based upon the inclusive assessment.

The book provides resources to help students begin to develop expertise in applying interventions to most populations at risk. In Parts III and IV, students will find more detailed descriptions of the seven practice approaches first described as paradigms in Part II. Students may also further specialize in at least one population at risk through their elective course work and practicum studies.

Finally, the social worker's own professional self-development is described in Part V. Self-development is an ongoing process that builds the social worker's ability to effectively use conscious use of self in advanced generalist practice. The application of conscious use of self in working with transference and countertransference reactions is also emphasized.

Experiential Exercises

1. Recall an adult who helped you in your own life, when you were a child, adolescent, or adult. Of the following three factors, which contributed the most to your own development? Which was least important?

   ▪ a. The characteristics of the helping adult (e.g., his or her genuineness, compassion, awareness, respect, etc.)

   ▪ b. Your own characteristics at the time (e.g., your motivation, developmental readiness, openness, etc.)

   ▪ c. The techniques that the helper used to help you (e.g., reflective listening, positive reinforcement, etc.)

2. Consider which of the three factors above you value the most. Why do you think you value these? Which of the three factors above are emphasized most in universities and colleges where social work is taught? Why do you think this?

3. Consider which of your own developmental dimensions (i.e., spiritual, emotional, physical, psychosocial, cognitive) you now value the most and why.

4. Now appraise which of these dimensions were most emphasized in the environments in which you have lived, including your family of origin, educational systems, churches, and so on. How have these experiences affected the development of your dimensions?

5. On which dimension(s) do you seem to rely when you are under stress? Do you rely upon this same dimension when you work with people?

6. Consider the characteristics that others might use to describe your own unique human diversity (e.g., sexual preference, religion, culture, race,

gender, age)? If they only knew you through these characteristics, what stereotypes do you think most people would have about you?

7. In what ways do you fit those stereotypes that people would have about you? In what ways do you not fit them?

Notes

1. West, C. K., Farmer, J. A., & Wolff, P. M. (1991). *Instructional design: Implications from cognitive science.* Englewood Cliffs, NJ: Prentice Hall.

2. Coles, R. (1990). *The spiritual life of children.* Boston: Houghton Mifflin.

3. Wilber, K. (1986). The spectrum of development, the spectrum of psychopathology, and treatment modalities. In K. Wilber, J. Engler, & D. Brown (Eds.), *Transformations of consciousness: Conventional and contemplative perspectives on development* (pp. 65-159). Boston: New Science Library.

4. Worthington, E. L., Kurusu, T. A., McCullough, M. E., & Sandage, S. J. (1996). Empirical research on religion and psychotherapeutic processes and outcomes: A 10-year review and research prospectus. *Psychological Bulletin, 119,* 448-487.

5. Council on Social Work Education. (1994). Curriculum policy statement. In *Handbook of accreditation standards and procedures.* Alexandria, VA: Author.

6. Johnson, L. C. (1989). *Social work practice: A generalist approach.* Boston: Allyn & Bacon.

7. Bartlett, H. M. (1970). *The common base of social work practice.* New York: National Association of Social Workers.

8. Scheafor, B. W., & Landon, P. S. (1987). Generalist perspective. In *Encyclopedia of social work* (18th ed., p. 660). Silver Spring, MD: National Association of Social Workers.

9. Landon, P. S. (1995). Generalist and advanced generalist practice. In *Encyclopedia of social work* (19th ed.). Silver Spring, MD: National Association of Social Workers.

10. Ibid.

11. Bugental, J. F. T. (1987). *The art of the psychotherapist.* New York: Norton; Sheafor, B. W., Horejsi, C. R., & Horejsi, G. A. (1988). *Techniques and guidelines for social work practice.* Boston: Allyn & Bacon.

12. Elliott, R., & James, E. (1989). Varieties of client experience in psychotherapy: An analysis of the literature. *Clinical Psychology Review, 9,* 443-467.

13. Mahoney, M. J. (1991). *Human change processes: The scientific foundations of psychotherapy.* New York: Basic Books.

14. Ibid.

15. Council on Social Work Education. (1994). Curriculum Policy Statement. Sections B5.7 and B77.9 (p. 99), Sections B6.3 and B6.3.6 (pp. 100-101), Sections M5.7, M5.7.3, and M5.7.11 (p. 137), and Section M6.5.6 (pp. 139-140).

16. Ivey, A. W. (1986). *Developmental therapy.* San Francisco: Jossey-Bass.

17. Basch, M. F. (1988). *Understanding psychotherapy: The science behind the art.* New York: Basic Books.

18. Krueger, D. W. (1989). *Body self and psychological self: A developmental and clinical integration of the self.* New York: Brunner/Mazel.

19. Erikson, E. (1950). *Childhood and society.* New York: Norton; Mahler, M. (1973). The experience of separation-individuation through the course of life: Infancy and childhood, maturity, senescence, and sociological implications: Panel reports, American Psychoanalytic Association. *Journal of the American Psychoanalytic Association, 21,* 633; Mahler, M., Pine, F., & Bergman, A. (1975). *The psychological birth of the human infant.* New York: Basic Books.

20. Wilber (1986).

21. Cowley, A. (1992). *Multi-dimensional development.* Unpublished table, Graduate School of Social Work, University of Utah; Horowitz, F. D. (1987). *Exploring developmental theories: Toward a structural/behavioral model of development.* Hillsdale, NJ: Lawrence Erlbaum.

22. Horowitz (1987).

23. Ivey, A. E. (1991). *Developmental strategies for helpers: Individual, family, and network interventions.* Pacific Grove, CA: Brooks/Cole.

24. Lieberman, A. F. (1990). Culturally sensitive intervention with children and families. *Child and Adolescent Social Work Journal, 7*(2), 101-120.

25. Kumabe, K. T., Nishida, C., & Hepworth, D. H. (1985). *Bridging ethnocultural diversities in social work and health.* Honolulu: University of Hawaii School of Social Work.

26. Lieberman (1990).

PART I

Assessment

Effective assessment in social work practice is an inclusive process that is (a) *ecological* (considers all of the interrelated aspects of the developing client system and its evolving environment); (b) both *scientific and artistic* (uses all ways of knowing in the data collection process); (c) *sensitive to client/system diversity* (identifies the unique characteristics of every client/system); and (d) an *ongoing source of feedback* (uses data in formulating goals to appraise risk and potential, guiding interventions, and measuring the impact of interventions throughout all of the phases of a case). Therefore, the term *assessment* is used to describe the process of evaluation throughout the beginning, middle, and ending phases of each case. In this section, these four characteristics of both/and assessment are defined and developed.

CHAPTER 1

Ecological Assessment

Ecological assessment is an inclusive approach to the collection of data in practice. Simply said, the ecological model is a systematic framework that helps the social worker make the most complete investigation possible into the many interrelated factors associated with any particular case. As Carol Germain has stated: "The ecological approach to people-environment transactions is probably the most encompassing metaphor . . . an easier way of grasping the reciprocal influences of people and environments in human development and functioning" (p. 407).[1]

Social workers traditionally have applied the ecological, "person-in-environment" perspective to assessment.[2] In social work practice, assessment has essentially been a "social diagnosis" in which the client system and its environment are studied and used to develop a plan of intervention.[3] In ecological assessment, social workers can emphasize the importance of both the strengths and weaknesses (limitations or vulnerabilities) of the client system and its environment.[4]

Although "concern for persons in environment is the distinguishing feature and unifying characteristic of social work," the ecological perspective has generally "been given short shrift" (p. 407).[5] Instead, the social work literature has tended to hold a more limited perspective, emphasizing only particular aspects of the ecology of cases (e.g., measurable behaviors, cognitions, levels of social skills, knowledge). This limited perspective is consistent with this era's emphasis upon reductionistic thinking that has prevailed in modern science and philosophy.[6]

Developmental research and theory provide a useful framework for the ecological assessment model. The process of professional helping can be understood as applied developmental theory, and assessment of client development is a key element in that process.[7] Human development is well understood as a lifelong process[8] that is affected by the social environment[9] and that occurs at both the individual and group (e.g., marital, familial, community) levels.[10]

There is also evidence that human development is linked not only with the social environment, but also with other environmental factors, such as pollution and destruction of resources.[11] The assessment of the interrelationship of the client system and the environment can be understood from the standpoint of human development. In this book, the dimensions of human development are used as the framework of ecological assessment.

The Structural/Behavioral model of development assumes that observable development results from a complex structural relationship between factors on all ecological levels:

> Human behavioral development is probably, in its totality, the most complex phenomenon on this planet. The models proposed to account for the phenomenon must approximate that complexity. . . . An integrative model is needed that recognizes the multiplicity of processes and characterizations that will be needed to fully account for behavioral development. (pp. 196-197)[12]

The Structural/Behavioral model suggests that optimal developmental outcomes are directly related to the degree to which the organism is invulnerable (relatively protected from environmental trauma) and its environment is facilitative (supportive of the individual's development).

Thus, in ecological assessment, the worker assumes that individual, couple, family, and small group-level problems and challenges reflect factors in the larger environment. Similarly, the worker also assumes that local and global community-level problems and challenges are also reflected in issues that appear on the individual, couple, family, and small group levels.

Ecological Levels

Table 1.1 outlines the seven ecological levels associated with the five dimensions of human development (physical, affective, cognitive, spiritual, and social). Thus, each of the dimensions of development can be assessed at each of seven ecological levels. These levels include the "configuration of factors" that affect human development.[13] Although these levels are used here for the purpose of describing ecological assessment, it is important to note that the boundaries between them are artificial. In reality, as Ecological theory suggests, each of these levels is interrelated with all of the others.

Although the worker would ideally assess each of the developmental dimensions of the client at each of the ecological levels, in reality, workers do not have access to data in all of these 35 assessment cells. There is usually insufficient data to inform the selection of social work interventions. The ecological levels include the following:

1. *Biogenetic factors* include inherited and other physical characteristics of the individual. The family history often provides evidence of possible genetic factors and predispositions.

2. *Familial factors* include characteristics of the individual's immediate and extended family. The term *family* is defined here to include the most significant members of the client's informal support system. The immediate family may or may not include biological and other partners in living.

3. *Cultural factors* are attributes of the individual's psychosocial environment. The psychosocial environment includes the characteristics of all extra-familial individuals and groups with whom the individual has been in relationship. These may include members of the *primary* group (lovers, friends, and other relationships); the *secondary* group (those professionals who work with the individual); as well as other formal and informal support networks.

4. *Environmental conditions* are attributes of the individual's life space that affect quality of life. These attributes may be related to the natural environment as well as to man-made environments in the local and global communities.

5. *Resources and opportunities* include the safety, freedom, acceptance, wealth, power, services, and commodities available to the individual. These resources and opportunities are often associated with the tolerance, stability, policies, efficiency, and conflict resolution methodology of the local and national leadership.

6. *Patterns of self-care* are the individual's ongoing efforts to foster and nurture personal development. These patterns are associated with such internal factors as the individual's internal motivation, energy level, and level of consciousness.

7. *Current indicators of development and health* include measurable signs of developmental growth and well-being in the individual, couple, family, and community.

These ecological levels are compatible with but more inclusive than the basic PIE structure[14] used by many social workers today. Instead of considering only problems (e.g., social functioning or environmental problems), the worker also considers areas of strength at each ecological level (e.g., marital or family development). In addition, instead of considering only social, mental health, and physical health functioning, the worker considers all five inter-related dimensions of development (cognitive, emotional, social, physical, and spiritual).

Time as a Factor

Because there are always past, present, and future factors associated with any case, effective assessment requires a systematic consideration of factors across all of the dimensions of time. All factors described at each level in Table 1.1 can be predisposing, precipitating, system maintaining, and potentially influencing.

1. *Predisposing* factors include all past, long-term elements associated with the current conditions. For example, genetic characteristics are often associated with a client's level of functioning.

2. *Precipitating* factors helped to stimulate or trigger the current conditions. For example, a divorce can help precipitate various symptoms in children.

3. *System-maintaining* factors are those that have continued to help support the current conditions since the time that the condition began. For example, an aging woman, alcoholic all of her adult life, now finds that she gets more attention from her family by drinking than by being sober.

4. *Potentially influencing* factors are likely to be associated with future changes in current conditions. For example, a young couple who have poor communication skills and considerable stress in their marriage will probably be challenged further when their first child is born.

5. In addition, all cases also exist within a larger *historic time period,* during which certain political, social, and economic factors influence social definitions of health and illness.[15] For example, the many prejudices that gay and lesbian people typically have to deal with in the United States today reflect in part the extreme homophobia that characterizes the age in which we live.

Identification of Developmental Strengths and Limitations

In ecological assessment, the social worker helps each client identify which dimension(s) of development are strengths (more dominant or developed) and which are limitations (more dormant or underdeveloped). Each client will present with a unique set of developmental strengths and limitations.[16] Developmental strengths are those more dominant dimensions in which the client feels the most confidence and enjoyment. In contrast, developmental limitations are commonly those in which the client experiences minimal success and enjoyment.

TABLE 1.1: Checklist of Selected Guidelines for Ecological Assessment of Dimensions of Human Development

1. Physical development
    a. *Biogenetic factors:* race, sex, age, genetic/family history, organic factors, diseases, physical strengths, injuries, sexual orientation
    b. *Familial factors:* encouragement and modeling of physical development by caretakers or other family members
    c. *Cultural factors:* models of and norms for physical development in community, schools, churches, other organizations, and the workplace; other relevant local, state, national, and global factors
    d. *Environmental conditions:* quality of air, water, and food; availability of sunlight and green plants
    e. *Resources and opportunities:* socioeconomic status, opportunities for exercise, availability of equipment and facilities
    f. *Patterns of self-care and development:* diet, sleep, exercise, balance of work and play, use of drugs
    g. *Current indicators of development and health:* appearance, physical health, body awareness

2. Affective development
    a. *Biogenetic factors:* family history of mood disorders
    b. *Familial factors:* mirroring, acceptance, and modeling of affective development by caretakers and other family members
    c. *Cultural factors:* models of and norms for affective development in community, schools, churches, other organizations, and the workplace; other relevant local, state, national, and global factors
    d. *Environmental conditions:* quality of air, water, and food; amount of sunlight
    e. *Resources and opportunities:* socioeconomic status, opportunities for safe sharing of affect with others, availability of psychotherapists and other helping professionals
    f. *Patterns of self-care and development:* balance of social and alone time, use of drugs
    g. *Current indicators of development and health:* self-awareness of affect, self-acceptance, ability to express affect, ability to be social and alone, flexibility

3. Cognitive development
    a. *Biogenetic factors:* family history of intelligence potential
    b. *Familial factors:* acceptance and modeling of cognitive development by caretakers and other family members
    c. *Cultural factors:* models of and norms for cognitive development in community, schools, churches, other organizations, and the workplace; other relevant local, state, national, and global factors
    d. *Environmental conditions:* stimulating but not overwhelming environment
    e. *Resources and opportunities:* socioeconomic status; opportunities for intellectual discussion and exploration; availability of libraries, study areas, books, computers, and other learning materials
    f. *Patterns of self-care and development:* balance of time spent in passive activities (television) and intellectually challenging activities, use of drugs
    g. *Current indicators of development and health:* patterns of conflict resolution and problem solving

(continued)

TABLE 1.1 Continued

4. Spiritual development
    a. *Biogenetic factors:* family history of sensitivity to spiritual issues
    b. *Familial factors:* acceptance and modeling of spiritual development by caretakers and other family members, recognition of difference between religion and spirituality
    c. *Cultural factors:* models of and norms for spiritual development in community, schools, churches, other organizations, and the workplace; other relevant local, state, national, and global factors
    d. *Environmental conditions:* care of the immediate environment
    e. *Resources and opportunities:* socioeconomic status, opportunities for free discussion and exploration, availability of materials, alternative mentors
    f. *Patterns of self-care and development:* balance of time spent in reflection/meditation and more active activities, use of drugs
    g. *Current indicators of development and health:* personal life meanings, level of consciousness, attitude about life and death, states of well-being, inner peace

5. Social (psychosocial) development
    a. *Biogenetic factors:* patterns of introversion and extroversion
    b. *Familial factors:* acceptance and modeling of psychosocial development by caretakers and other family members; relative isolation of family; familial patterns of roles, models, boundaries, flexibility, and parenting
    c. *Cultural factors:* models of and norms for psychosocial development in community, schools, churches, other organizations, and the workplace; other relevant local, state, national, and global factors
    d. *Environmental conditions:* population density
    e. *Resources and opportunities:* socioeconomic status, opportunities for social interaction
    f. *Patterns of self-care and development:* balance of time spent in reflection/meditation and more active activities, use of drugs
    g. *Current indicators of development and health:* current stage of marital and familial development, patterns of assertive communication, nonviolent conflict resolution, boundaries, mutuality, respect, balance of power, balance of helping and receiving; ability to relate effectively with peers, subordinates, authority figures, human diversity; interactions as part of large groups in competition or cooperation with other cultures, nations, and ethnicities

Awareness of which dimensions are strengths and limitations will help inform the client and social worker about which developmental dimensions should be focused upon in the change process. The assessment of developmental level begins in the first minutes of the initial session and continues to be modified throughout the beginning, middle, and ending phases of practice. Clues about developmental strengths and limitations come from both history and here-and-now interactions with the client. Each of the five developmental dimensions can be analyzed on each of the seven ecological levels described above (see Figure 1.1).

Ecological levels ＼ Developmental dimensions	Physical	Affective	Cognitive	Spiritual	Social
Biogenetic factors					
Familial factors					
Cultural factors					
Environmental conditions					
Resources and opportunities					
Patterns of self-care					
Current indicators of development and health					

Figure 1.1. Developmental Dimensions and Ecological Levels of Assessment

A client can have a strength or limitation in one or more of the following interrelated dimensions.

Physical strength. Some clients seem to be dominant in physical expressions. They often experience their world and themselves primarily through bodily sensations, and may have somatic complaints. They also like to use their bodies to learn about the world and express themselves, and they may enjoy music, dance, or other physical exercise and expressions. They may express themselves physically or talk about their body during a session. They may be gifted in athletic activity and may have excelled in sports. Such clients often have a vast "physical landscape" in that they seem aware of a variety of sensations in their bodies.

For example, a father brings his son to a social worker after the school psychologist diagnosed him as having attention deficit disorder with hyper-activity. The boy does seem to have a hard time sitting still or listening to the initial discussion in the session. The worker asks if he would like to go downstairs with her and get a bottle of juice from the juice machine. He suddenly smiles broadly and eagerly runs down the stairs with her. In front of the machine, he says, "Want to see how high I can jump?" The boy jumps up and pretends to slam dunk a basketball over the juice machine. The worker understands that the boy is particularly comfortable in the physical dimension and wonders whether he may also sometimes use activity to help him avoid uncomfortable feelings and thoughts.

Physical limitation. Physical limitations might present as failure to thrive in infants, or perhaps less dramatic delays in motor functioning in childhood and adolescence. Adults and the aging can appear to lose the functioning that they once had. Adults with physical limitations may also be unable or unwilling to listen to their own bodies, and therefore be unaware of when they may need physical exercise or rest. Some people may simply be out of touch with their own bodies.

Affective strength. Some clients are emotionally dominant; they feel most comfortable experiencing and talking about their feelings about the present and past. They may often have a strong need to both share their own feelings and hear about the feelings of the social worker. They are usually aware of most of their feelings, although they may not accept them more than other people. They may easily cry or show other emotions in a session. In their relationships, they usually speak frequently and skillfully about feelings. As they mature, they tend to accept the variety of feelings that other people may have. Such clients often have a vast "emotional landscape," in that they seem to have complex and deep emotional inner worlds.

For example, an adolescent boy is referred to the school social worker after his teacher becomes concerned about his withdrawal in the classroom. Early in the assessment, when the social worker asks him about his parents, he starts to sob and talks about feeling sad. The worker asks him if his parents are still married, and he angrily replies, "No, but I wish they were . . . all they do is fight!" The worker begins to suspect that this boy may be particularly comfortable expressing his feelings.

Affective limitation. Expressions of affective limitation may include difficulties in experiencing or appropriately expressing any of the basic feelings (e.g., excitement, anger, sadness, happiness, fright). For example, many males still have difficulty experiencing and expressing sadness and are most comfortable acting as if they are angry, whereas many females have the opposite set of traits. Clients with affective limitation may present with only the ability to experience and express the "pseudofeelings" (e.g., guilt, boredom, depression, frustration, nervousness).[17]

Affective limitation may often manifest in the inability to tolerate the pain or joy of other people, which is sometimes associated with feelings of shame (or inadequacy).

Cognitive strength. Many clients are cognitively dominant; they prefer to analyze their past and present experiences rather than feel or express their emotional and physical reactions to events. These clients are often quite capable in analytical skills and may analyze themselves and others more eloquently than their social worker ever could. They are often "in their heads" in sessions and may like to lead and direct intellectual discussions. Although they are not necessarily more intelligent overall than other clients, they may have excelled in school, work, or other endeavors requiring strong cognitive skills. As they mature, they become more tolerant of alternative beliefs and views. Such clients often have a vast "cognitive landscape," in that they seem to have imaginative and profound inner worlds of thought.

For example, a 46-year-old woman comes to a family counseling clinic complaining about symptoms of depression. She is a mother of two children and is a professor at a local college. In the first session, she tells the worker, "I want you to write a letter to my physician so that he will give me a prescription for an antidepressant. From what I've read, a moderate dosage should help me get going again." When the worker asks how she has been feeling about her marriage, she replies, "Have you read that new book about how women and men are so different? Do you believe in that theory?" The worker begins to realize that his client is most comfortable relating with the world on a cognitive level. The worker is also aware that the client may be using cognitions as a coping mechanism that can help her protect herself.

Cognitive limitation. Clients who have limitations in the cognitive dimension may show a variety of symptoms. For example, some children and adolescents may show difficulties in comprehension and learning in school. Such difficulties, of course, may also be associated with biogenetic and emotional factors, and careful assessment is always necessary. Young infants may show less curiosity and responsiveness to their environment after maltreatment. Adults may show difficulty concentrating at work or the inability to tolerate people who think differently from them. Aging clients may show increased disorientation of time and space. Some clients may simply be uncomfortable talking about what they think.

Spiritual strength. Some clients may be spiritually dominant in their development. They might prefer to experience and talk about their level of consciousness; the meaning of their life; their impressions of the sacred and transcendent; or their sense of idealism, acceptance, and connectiveness with self and the world. They may or may not also be religious (sharing a particular system of beliefs, doctrines, and rituals usually associated with reverence for a supernatural creator of the universe). If they belong to a religion, they tolerate people with other viewpoints regardless of how strongly they believe in their own faith. They may talk about spiritual experiences or perceptions in sessions. They may perceive aspects of reality that others do not ordinarily notice, and they may prefer spiritual and religious explanations for their life experiences.

For example, a medical social worker visits an aging woman in her room in the oncology department. The worker asks her how she is, and the woman replies, "I am so grateful to have been granted this extra time to be with my family and friends." The worker persists, "Dr. Smith tells me you have been in a lot of pain." The woman replies, "I have been given just the right amount of pain to help me remember that I am alive." The worker discovers that the woman is a serious student of several spiritual practices and assesses that she is especially comfortable relating on the spiritual level. Such clients often have a vast "spiritual landscape," in that they seem to have resolute and profound spiritual inner worlds.

Spiritual limitation. Limitations of the human spirit may include an inability to connect with self or with the world, create a personal meaning in life, and have moments of peace of mind. Maltreatment victims may believe that the universe is unfriendly and operate from that place of fear and mistrust in every area of their lives. Young children may be afraid of God and may perceive God as having characteristics similar to an abusive parent. An abused spouse may be afraid to truly live; an aging client may be afraid to die. Limitations of spiritual development may present as the client's inability to think independently or the tendency to surrender all personal power and will to an external authority (e.g., parent, teacher, religious figure). They may also be unable to make moral decisions independent of others. Many clients may be uncomfortable talking about their spirituality.

Psychosocial (social) strength. Some clients may have psychosocial strength. They tend to emphasize interpersonal relationships in their lives. They may have well- developed communication and assertiveness skills, although they may not necessarily always use these skills to foster the highest good of themselves and others. Indeed, they may be particularly good at reading people and in getting what they want from others either "on the street" or in a service job. They may be skillfully manipulative, controlling, or quite engaging in a session with their social worker. They might be what some call streetwise—very competent at handling themselves with others out on the street. Such clients often have a vast "social landscape," in that they seem to have unusual sensitivity to their social environments.

For example, a social worker is leading a battered woman's group. Although most of the women are reluctant to talk during the first session, one of the women volunteers to respond to the questions that the worker asks. This woman also asks questions of the other women in the group. The worker realizes that this particular client is very comfortable on the psychosocial level.

Psychosocial (social) limitation. Limitations in psychosocial, or interpersonal, development may present in a variety of ways. For example, maltreated children and adolescents may become quite socially withdrawn (e.g., the young children of cocaine-addicted parents). Adults who are maltreatment victims may show an inability to relate assertively with others. Adult and adolescent perpetrators of child maltreatment are often unable to relate with adults intimately and prefer the social company of children. Other adults may need to constantly control, or be controlled by, other people. Some aging victims become quite withdrawn. However, psychosocial limitation may also manifest in the inability of a person to be alone or with others, or in the inability to recognize one's own social needs.

The concept of psychosocial development can also be expanded to include marital, familial, and community development. Psychosocial factors at each of these levels can either support or undermine the client's well-being.

Marital development. Most models of lifespan couple development suggest six life stages: (a) courtship, (b) marriage, (c) childbirth and children, (d) middle marriage difficulties, (e) weaning parents from children, and (f) retirement and old age.[18] Shorter relationships may pass through courtship, power struggle, and mutual acceptance phases. Although every couple will not navigate through every one of these stages in the prescribed order, the social worker looks at the ability of couples to move fluidly between these stages. The social worker also assesses the extent to which the client's couple relationships are healthy or unhealthy.

Familial development. Most familial models describe eight life-cycle stages of family development: (a) establishment stage (no children); (b) first parenthood (children under 3); (c) family with preschool children (oldest child 3-6); (d) family with school child (oldest child 6-12); (e) family with adolescents (oldest 13-20); (f) family as launching center (leave-taking of children); (g) family in middle years (empty nest); and (h) family in retirement ("breadwinners" in retirement).[19] Again, the order and experience of these stages will vary, but the worker assesses the ability of the family to flexibly adapt to the changes in life. The worker assesses the strengths and limitations of the family structure(s) in which the client may be involved.

Local community development. Peck[20] suggests that there are several predictable stages in the development of a community. In the initial stage of "pseudocommunity," members often pretend to be more friendly and intimate than they are. A period of chaos may follow, in which members begin to feel safe enough to show more of their feelings and thoughts and to reveal differences. However, true community cannot develop until individual members become willing to look at their own issues that may be obstacles to real dialogue and cooperation. This model suggests that there is a strong relationship between intrapsychic work (e.g., being willing to be more self-aware and integrated) and interpersonal work. The worker assesses the strengths and limitations of the local and global communities in which the client lives.

Global community development. Social workers may become more consciously involved in the evolution of our global human community. One view of the developmental process of the global community is as follows.

Premodern, ancient societies, like indigenous societies that still exist today, were relatively simple and isolated, and they tended to provide clear "psychic anchors" for people. These psychic anchors may have included fairly narrow definitions of what the roles of women and men should be. Premodern people knew who they were, what they believed, and what their lives were about.[21] They had strong connections with the earth, the seasons, and the cosmos that established an order and rhythm to life.

The *modern* societies that followed were much more complex, urban, and mobile, and they were also more alienated from their source (e.g., the earth, the seasons, the cosmos). People became increasingly aware that they shared the planet with billions of other people. Perhaps in response to a need or longing for simplicity, modern intellectual (or Enlightenment) thinking stressed rationality and order and the axiom that only one answer existed for any question. It was comforting to make order out of the chaos; it was comforting to believe that Truth was out there and could be found. Modern thinking is objectivist, that is, reality can be known through an empirical strategy of knowing. Psychoanalysis can be understood as an extension of Enlightenment thinking; based upon reason, psychoanalysis became another belief system in an ultimate truth. Ironically, although one of the basic objectives of psychotherapy was individual integration, the profession itself became increasingly fragmented as more and more competing paradigms of practice were developed.[22]

Today, we in the United States live in a *postmodern* society, characterized by the growing realization that one truth will not suffice for every person. Our era is characterized by an accelerating awareness of the complexities of human nature and the interdependency of humanity and the environment. Advances in theory and technology have helped us to appreciate our complex inner selves as well as the diversity and commonness of humanity as a whole. Advances in communication and travel have created a growing appreciation of the complex interrelationship between every aspect of the universe.

Recent advancement in the hard sciences has demonstrated how certain and complex reality is. Physicists exploring quantum theory have made discoveries that "shattered traditional notions of causality," "showed that our knowledge of nature is fundamentally limited" (p. 22), and demonstrated that observation often alters the outcome of experiments.[23] Because of such discoveries, postmodern people increasingly realize that they live in a participatory universe, which each individual helps co-create. Thus, "a society enters the postmodern age when it loses faith in absolute truth—even the attempt to discover absolute truth" (p. 22).[24] Postmodern thinking is constructivist; human beings themselves invent or construct reality.[25]

Ego States \\ Level	Parent (P)	Observing Self (OS)	Child (C)	All
Prepersonal	Undeveloped	Undeveloped	Dominant	(P) (OS) (C)
Personal	Dominant	Undeveloped	Suppressed	(P) (OS) (C)
Transpersonal	Developed	Dominant	Developed	(P) (OS) (C)

Figure 1.2. Ego States in Multidimensional Development

A Model of Multidimensional Developmental Assessment

The advanced generalist social worker may consider using Wilber's[26] three basic levels of development of consciousness as a foundation framework for assessing each client's multidimensional development. Wilber's model is Transpersonal (an inclusive paradigm described later in the text) and thus considers all five dimensions of human development. In social work assessments, all three levels—the prepersonal, personal, and transpersonal—are equally valued. Each has advantages and disadvantages in human functioning.

Figure 1.2 illustrates from a Transactional Analysis[27] (TA) perspective how the three levels of transpersonal development can be linked to the relative strength of the parent, observing self, and child ego states. As can be seen, at each level, there is one ego state that tends to dominate or regulate the personality.

Table 1.2 summarizes how the three levels of transpersonal development can be linked to client characteristics (physical, emotional, cognitive, spiritual, psychosocial) and goals for client, others, and environment. Although the

TABLE 1.2:   Three Levels of Multidimensional Development

Level[a]	Current Developmental Dimensions	Immediate Developmental Goals
Prepersonal (dominant child)	1. Self underdeveloped 2. May show signs of autism, psychosis, or *DSM* Axis II disorders 3. Black and white thinking 4. Poor social skills and generally uses people 5. Underdeveloped superego (little conscience) 6. Relatively disconnected from emotion, mind, body, and environment	1. Create stable self-structure 2. Avoid harming self, others, environment 3. Develop superego
Personal (dominant parent)	1. Stable self now developed 2. May show signs of depression and/or anxiety 3. Conflicted thoughts and feelings 4. Ego often overwhelms id (personal needs ignored and over-emphasizes caretaking of others) 5. Struggling to reconnect with body and mind, but still hungry for spirit connection	1. Integrate mind, body, and emotions 2. Develop balanced response-ability for self/others/community
Transpersonal (dominant observing self)	1. Evolving beyond self 2. Working to disidentify from mind, emotion, body, and external possessions	1. Let go of self 2. Develop spiritual path of service to self/others/community

a. Three levels based upon Wilber.[28]

client may perceive a natural hierarchy with the three levels, the worker can help the client value all three equally and is aware that a client may shift back and forth between each of the three over time. In fact, as will be described further, all three levels have advantages and disadvantages. Therefore, healthy functioning may be redefined as the ability to move from one level of development to another with *conscious fluidity*. Conscious fluidity can be thought of as the ability to choose to function at one developmental level for as long as the person wishes.

Prepersonal level. At the prepersonal level, the client is primarily operating from a childlike personality state, often because she has not yet developed a constant self with "conscious and unconscious mental representations that pertain to one's own person" (p. 12).[29] The client may exhibit frequent and often dramatic personality changes. From a TA perspective, the client has a strong "inner child" but only a weak "inner parent" to manage the child's impulses. The client usually has little "observing self" to monitor and manage the other two ego states. The key developmental goals at the prepersonal level are to try to develop a stable self (by developing an internal parent) and to avoid causing harm to self, others, or the environment. The client is not yet ready to work on personal or transpersonal developmental goals, and there is danger of "infanticitus" as the client tends to ignore the needs of others and focus upon meeting personal needs. Clients and their workers may become confused in assessment because prepersonal functioning is often rewarded with such cultural success indicators as wealth, status, and power.

Wilber's term, *prepersonal,* may be replaced with "child ego state dominance." All of us function at the child ego state from time to time. If we could not function from a child state, we would be unable to play and enjoy ourselves and the world. Conversely, if someone is *always* functioning at the child ego state, she would be unable to exert any impulse control.

For example, a worker sees a young man who has been caught for shoplifting. His parents brought him to counseling against his wishes. It turns out that this client has a serious addiction to the over-the-counter cough syrup he was stealing. When the worker asks the client to talk about himself, the client is unable to express his feelings. The young man was previously in an inpatient drug treatment program, and he left 6 months ago against medical advice. He has made several suicidal gestures. The worker assesses the client as operating primarily at the prepersonal level.

Personal level. At the personal level of functioning, the client has developed enough of a stable self to now become concerned with a new set of goals. The client now has enough strength to be aware of uncomfortable feelings and thoughts and personal limitations. From the TA perspective, the client is now capable of becoming more "response-able" for other people and the environment. However, the client's inner child may now be overcontrolled by an increasingly powerful inner parent. Thus, there is a danger of "responsibilititus" as the client tends to abandon self-needs and focuses upon meeting the needs of others. The observing self is beginning to develop but may not be strong enough to help balance the personality structure. The client is striving to balance caretaking of other people and the environment with self-care.

Wilber's term, *personal,* may be replaced with "parent ego state dominance." All of us need to function at the parent ego state so that we can delay gratification to pay our bills, go to school, and so on. Conversely, if someone is *always* functioning at the parent ego state, he would be unable to ever behave spontaneously and joyfully.

For example, a worker sees a 40-year-old housewife who complains of moderate depression. She has been married more than 20 years and has six children. Although at first she reports that she is happy in her marriage, the worker learns from her that her husband has beaten her and that she has tried unsuccessfully to hide this fact from her children. The worker assesses the client as operating primarily at the personal level.

Transpersonal level. At the transpersonal level of functioning, the client has consciously chosen to try to disidentify from (become less attached to) such aspects of self as possessions, social roles, beliefs, symptoms, and feelings. This process can be differentiated from the prepersonal level, where the client has not yet developed a persona (or self) and thus cannot consciously choose to disidentify. From a TA perspective, the balance established between the inner child and parent can now be upset by the new expansion of the observing self. The client may be interested in developing a path of service to herself, others, and the environment. However, there is a danger of "egoitis" as the client's observing self occasionally regresses and clings to such personal anchors as self-importance, status in a spiritual community, or financial gain.

Wilber's term, *transpersonal,* may be replaced with "observing-self ego state dominance." The observing self is able to reflect upon internal conflicts between the inner child and parent. The observing self state also allows a person to go into meditative and other altered states of consciousness. However, if a person is *always* functioning at the observing self level, he may be unable to relax and play or to complete the everyday tasks necessary to survive independently in the larger society.

For example, a worker sees a 50-year-old man who reports in the first session that he thinks he is having a midlife crisis. The man went through a divorce 2 years ago and now lives with his three children in an apartment downtown. Recently, he has found that he no longer gets satisfaction from his job as an attorney and partner in one of the city's biggest law firms. He states that his employers are "just a bunch of money-hungry fools." The man has been experimenting with meditation and is frightened that he may soon find himself "out of work, unemployable, and just interested in meditating." The worker assesses the client as operating primarily at the transpersonal level.

Experiential Exercises

1. Review Figure 1.2 and Table 1.2. Describe a person you know who seems to be living primarily at the prepersonal level of development (protect that person's confidentiality when necessary). Do the same exercise at the personal and transpersonal levels of development.

2. At which level in Figure 1.2 and Table 1.2 do most people in your community seem to operate? Why do you think this is? At which level do most social workers seem to operate?

3. Where would you see your own multidimensional development in terms of this model? What would you see as the next developmental steps in your own life?

CHAPTER 2

The Art and Science of Assessment

Two premises are developed in this section. The first premise is that successful assessment in social work practice involves many ways of knowing, because neither the scientific nor artistic ways of knowing are sufficient in themselves to do an adequate job. The second premise is that, although social workers currently underutilize and undervalue the art of practice, we do not do an adequate job of using either the science or the art of practice in our assessments.

The science of social work practice includes the use of ideas, axioms, ethical principles, theoretical orientations, and practice models based upon knowledge derived from the scientific method. The art of practice includes the use of relationship, creativity, energy, judgment, and personal style and is often based upon alternative ways of knowing.[30] Social work practice continues to hold a dualistic position related to art and science in which the importance of art is deemphasized.[31]

The scientific method used in social work is rooted in that branch of epistemology called logical positivism.[32] During most of its history, social work has largely followed the positivist tradition, an outgrowth of modern empiricism that applied the scientific method to psychosocial problems. Empiricism itself grew in opposition to mainstream rationalism. Many rationalists believed that we can understand reality only through reason and not by means of our senses. In contrast, "empiricists argue that while sense information may not be entirely certain, these data are important and ought to be collected and considered" (pp. 125-126).[33] One of the most intensely debated principles of logical positivism is that "a proposition is meaningful if and only if it can be empirically verified with sensory observation and experience" (p. 127).[34]

Science has helped modern people to distinguish between what is false and what is true. Without science, we might still be living under the manacles of ancient dogma and other biases. Yet science itself is limited and creates its own dogma. Although successes in other disciplines have demonstrated that science in itself can solve some of our modern problems and challenges (e.g., we have smart missiles, vaccinations, and home computers), social scientists now recognize that biopsychosociospiritual problems are more challenging:

> Human behavioral development is probably, in its totality, the most complex phenomenon on this planet. The models proposed to account for the phenomenon must approximate that complexity. . . . An integrative model is needed that recognizes the multiplicity of processes and characterizations that will be needed to fully account for behavioral development. (pp. 196-197)[35]

Unfortunately, we simply do not yet have the knowledge or ability to put together models that can adequately predict human behavior. Thus, our scientific ways of knowing and our present scientific knowledge bases are useful but still too limited to inform practice alone.[36]

Even physicians, those practitioners whom many social workers have emulated most, admit that science must often take a back seat to the practical needs of the client:

> My orientation is and always has been to treat patients. . . . If it works, I don't care if I understand it. That's the way clinical medicine is. We have to be sure we don't harm the patient, so we have to understand it well enough to know what the risks are, but to do experiments to know exactly what's happening before ever going into the patient—there would be lots of people dying or dead by the time you did. (p. 387)[37]

Our artistic ways of knowing are also both useful and limited. Intuition, the primary artistic way of knowing, often provides the most helpful practice insights. However, intuition often works best when accompanied by the use of simple methods of observation and deduction.

There is no reason to believe that the science and the art of practice are mutually exclusive. Social work, as well as all of the other helping professions, traditionally has been understood as involving both science and art.[38]

Unfortunately, there is still very little in the literature that supports the inevitable and necessary marriage of science and art, and even less on exactly *how* social workers might use both in assessment and research.[39]

Experiential Exercises

1. With which way of knowing are you most comfortable, and why (scientific or artistic)?

2. What obstacles, both internal and external, seem to be in the way of your using the way of knowing that you value the least? Internal obstacles may included old biases, fears, or blind spots. External obstacles may include the prejudices of others around you and the policies of your work or school setting.

3. How could you better value the diversity of ways of knowing that are available to yourself and others?

Measurement in Direct Practice

Although social work has become increasingly committed to accurate, empirically based evaluation of practice, there is still insufficient integration of basic, empirically based research concepts into direct practice.[40]

This lack of integration can be attributed at least in part to narrow definitions of measurement that include the following: (a) defining measurement only in terms of counting, which restricts available options; (b) using methodology that is useful only in measuring behavioral interventions; and (c) the observation of only the client's changes, rather than also the change of the client's system and the worker/system.[41] These definitions are unnecessarily restrictive, because most social workers are eclectic, and relatively few can use in their practice the narrowly defined research methods they were taught in social work programs.

Measurement in social work assessment can be viewed as "a process that results in the consistent assignment of properties of people or objects so they can be classified, ordered, or counted" (p. 27).[42] This process includes the development of (a) an idea to be measured, (b) an indicator of that idea, (c) an operational definition of the necessary data, (d) ordered information that can be arranged into a variable, and (e) the reliability and validity of the variable. Although measurement techniques cannot be used in every case situation, incorporating these "measurement concepts and principles into direct practice is not only possible but necessary" (p. 23).[43]

By conceptualizing and operationalizing human characteristics, the social worker can probably measure just about any factor considered in the ecological assessment of a case. Conceptualization is the process of specifying precisely what any particular characteristic is. For example, in order to measure the client's religiosity, the worker needs to understand exactly what she means by religiosity. Operationalization is the process of creating definitions for each concept in terms of operations by which observations will be categorized. Thus, for example, the worker might decide to define religiosity simply as the number of days per year (the "operation") that the client goes to church meetings.

As the worker implements interventions, he continues to assess the client-system. Two ways that the worker can estimate client improvement is by considering the clinical (practice-relevant) significance and the statistical (mathematical) significance of improvement.[44] Nonstatistical (clinically significant) procedures that can be used to evaluate progress are (a) interviews of client, (b) worker's observations of client, and (c) observations of client from others.

Statistical significance often may not be measured because many social workers have quite limited knowledge of formal measures of clinical practice. Although most social workers will not specialize in doing formal assessments, there are practical reasons why they should be at least familiar with some of the most common assessment tools. Workers might evaluate their own effectiveness by using some of these tools. Workers might also need to interpret or use the scientific findings of others. For example, social workers who see victims of maltreatment are often asked to prepare verbal or written reports for a probation officer, court hearing, or a protective service worker. In preparing such reports, the worker can draw upon the results of various measures that have been given by other practitioners.

Bloom and Fischer[45] particularly recommended the use of single-system designs in evaluating practice. A single-system design is a study of one case in which the worker repeatedly observes the client/system over time, usually before and after a specific intervention has been given. Often, the worker analyzes the data with the help of simple charts or other visual methods.

Journey Analysis

A particularly useful framework for measurement in social worker practice with individuals, couples, families, and groups is Journey Analysis.[46] Journey Analysis is probably the most inclusive of existing frameworks because it incorporates all forms of measurement. A strong value is an emphasis upon two key social work practice values: (a) service to the client (sometimes called *action research*) and (b) the ecological perspective. Room is left to each group of clients and social workers to use the "journey" metaphor in creative ways that work for them. The application of Journey Analysis to assessment means an emphasis on (a) client-worker dialectic (interactions), (b) historical perspective (client's experience), (c) contextual emphasis (person-in-environment), and (d) in-flight corrections (openness to changing methods and conclusions).

The emphasis on *client-worker dialectic* means that assessment is not a vertical process in which the expert social worker defines the client's problems and progress. Rather, the worker views the client as the expert consumer and engages in an evolving relationship with the client. Rather than holding to any particular fixed diagnosis, goal, or cure, the assessment is an alive and open process that continually evolves as the client teaches the worker how to help.

The *historical perspective* involves an emphasis upon the client's experience of her own journey. The worker listens to the client describe how she arrived at the current situation and where she is going, through various key challenges and turning points. The *contextual emphasis* means that the worker and client always view the changing historical situation from an ecological perspective. Finally, *in-flight corrections* are changes in perspective that the client and worker make as the case continues across time. Thus, as immediate challenges and obstacles are considered and resolved, new learnings are used to inform the next intervention steps. Assessment is thus used immediately to help inform the process of improving the client's welfare. Any number of in-flight corrections may be used in the assessment process.

A brief example of an application of journey analysis to assessment in practice may be offered. A social worker is conducting therapy with adolescent sex offenders at an outpatient treatment center. The worker asks the adolescents individually and collectively to describe what they think would help them. The consensus seems to be that the teens want help in avoiding reoffending and feel that their own impulses are the biggest obstacles to changing. The worker designs a curriculum with the teens that involves meditation and other relaxation techniques. Each week, they meet and discuss how the treatment is working. During the second week, the teens suggest to the worker that the treatment also include some kind of more active physical activity. The midflight correction during the third week is to include in the interventions some exercises drawn from the yoga and aikido disciplines. Later, during the fourth week, the social worker also uses some single-subject designs and his intuition (described in the next section) to help inform the teens, their parents, and himself in the ongoing work.

Experiential Exercises

1. Explore your own feelings and beliefs regarding scientific measurement. Where did they come from? How do they help or limit your assessment in practice?

2. How have the professional helpers who have helped you the most (e.g., teachers, counselors, etc.) used scientific measurement? What did you like or dislike about their approach to this process?

3. How much do you use scientific measurement in your practice? In your life? How could you value the diversity of ways that people may use such methods to help guide their lives?

4. Do a journey analysis of how your life led you into social work as a career. Identify key turning points in the process and any in-flight corrections you may feel are necessary now in your own professional journey.

Intuition

Of all of the artistic factors in social work assessment, probably the most used, yet least recognized, is intuition. The profession currently tends to hold a dualistic position on the subject, preferring to either ignore or deemphasize the role of intuition in social work practice. Very little can be found in the area of intuition in the social work literature:

> Until recently intuition has been treated like an employee who, forced to retire, keeps going to work because he is indispensable. . . . Some people don't know he exists, some downgrade his contributions as trivial, some revere him privately while trying to keep his presence a secret. (p. 15)[47]

Increasingly, however, science supports the efficacy of intuition in assessment. Evidence exists that intuition plays a major role in learning.[48] Many well-respected psychologists believe that intuition is an essential tool of the professional helper.[49] The business world has long recognized the importance of intuition in making correct decisions.[50] According to his own accounts, Albert Einstein used his intuition to develop his mathematical theories and was often quoted as saying, "The really valuable thing is intuition."

The literal meaning of the word intuition is "to see within." "Intuition can be understood as the mind turning in on itself and apprehending the result of processes that have taken place outside awareness" (p. 137).[51] Intuition is an inner way of knowing that is different from what could be called an "outer," or scientific, way of knowing based upon experience and observed external phenomena.[52]

From the ecological perspective, intuition is a way of knowing that is not in dualistic opposition to rational thought but often works in concert with reasoning. Thus, intuition can contribute to reason, and reason can help prepare for intuition. The vital importance of intuition in higher functioning has been long recognized, for example, by senior business managers: "The higher you go in a company, the more important it is that you combine intuition and rationality, act while thinking, and see problems as interrelated" (p. 81).[53] The intuitive process in social work practice has three components: (a) preparation, (b) enhancing awareness, and (c) additional confirmative evaluation.

Preparation for intuition begins with the worker. The social worker identifies which dimensions of development she uses in the intuitive process. Some workers may make particular use of the physical dimension; for example, they may rely on a "gut" (intestinal) or heart experience. Other workers may place more trust in mental (cognitive) or emotional (affective) experiences. Other workers may use a combination of experiences. Social workers can practice using intuition in workshop, supervisory, or classroom settings. Preparation for intuition also includes the reduction of common internal (intrapsychic) and external (other psychosocial) obstacles to intuition. *Internal* obstacles to intuition may include the following:[54]

- The worker does not believe that intuition exists or can be accurate.

- The worker's emotions may interfere with the intuitive process. For example, the new knowledge being intuited may be emotionally painful to the worker. A new breakthrough in knowledge often is accompanied by anxiety when that knowledge is somehow threatening or disturbing to the worker. Sometimes, the worker may confuse desire with intuition; if the worker wants something to be true very much, he may become convinced that it is true.

- The worker is excessively self-critical about his ability to accurately intuit. Many social workers lack confidence in their own intuitive process.

- The worker has excessive standards of detail or proof in assessment. Intuition often provides a new perspective on a case. The particulars of that new perspective often have to be filled in later. The worker may unrealistically expect to have overwhelming collaborating evidence in support of intuited knowledge.

- The worker may confuse intuitive knowing with ideas based more upon impulsiveness, image making, or rebelliousness.

- The worker currently suffers from various life stressors, such as fatigue, illness, and life transitions that interfere with knowing.

External obstacles to intuition may include the following:

- The worker is afraid of censure by agency, institution, or other external authority. Social workers may lack the support from colleagues and supervisors that is necessary so that the intuitive process can be explored and cultivated openly and safely. Such workers may need to develop alternative informal or formal support networks.

- The client or client/system is unfamiliar or uncomfortable with the intuitive process. For example, a mother may not be willing to accept the worker's intuition that her child is angry. Social workers should not, of course, insist that the client accept any intuitions. Sometimes, the worker can help the client develop more trust of the client's own intuitive process.

Preparation also includes the cultivation of various personal characteristics that help foster intuition. Intuition cannot be ordered up at will, but it is more likely to occur when a person has what Goldberg[55] called "conceptual flexibility." Conceptual flexibility includes the following:

- An attitude of detachment from expectations of result
- A desire or passion for the truth
- A willingness to take the risk to be called wrong
- A tolerance for complexity in reality
- A willingness to play with and enjoy imagination
- An openness to question assumptions of self or others

Enhancing awareness includes relaxation and focusing techniques to help the worker become more conscious of intuitions. The quality of intuition is related with higher consciousness, or the ability to focus attention inward at the deeper levels of the mind. Research suggests that the higher consciousness necessary for intuition is associated with mental clarity, inner calm, and quiet surroundings.[56]

The social worker can use any relaxation technique to foster awareness of intuition. All such techniques tend to make the worker more calm and alert, and they also involve four elements: a quiet environment; mental concentration (upon a phrase, image, or concept); a passive (open and receptive) attitude; and a comfortable body position.[57]

Relaxation techniques may be used before or after work with a client, can be quite simple, and may include (a) visualization exercises, (b) breath work, (c) meditation techniques, or (d) yoga. Other activities that may help foster intuition include[58]

- Brainstorming possibilities
- Using word associations (e.g., words that describe my client)
- Using sentence completion (e.g., my client reminds me of _____)
- Considering specific goals and objectives for client
- Reviewing all sources of information about the topic
- Consulting personal dreams
- Using physical activity/stretching
- Writing or drawing in an intuition journal
- Clarifying personal resistances (e.g., fear of censure, failure, authority, or anything new; self-criticism; disbelief in intuition)

Each social worker may use any of these techniques to enhance her intuition in a given situation.

Additional confirming evaluation. Intuition, however powerful, need not bear the whole burden of assessment. The social worker has other means of measuring reality as well, and she can use these other methods to further substantiate, modify, or challenge the initial intuition about a client/system. In seeking further confirmation of intuition, social workers can use any of the sources of information available at the various ecological levels, including

- Informal questioning of client(s) or others in client system (e.g., significant others, parents, teachers, etc.)

- Informal observation of the client and client/system

- Use of formal measurement instruments

- Observation of whether interventions based upon intuition help further the process of the client and client/system.

An example of the intuitive process in practice can be described here. A Child Protective Service (CPS) social worker is assigned a voluntary case. A single father has two young sons, ages 6 and 9. He identified himself as being at risk of losing his temper with his children. The immediate assessment issue is to determine if the children are indeed at risk for maltreatment.

The social worker suspects that her client is not sure that intuition belongs in practice, so she does not try to force her intuitions on him, nor does she even discuss them with him. This worker tends to experience intuitions about clients in her body, particularly in her stomach. Last year, the worker requested a transfer to a CPS unit that has a supervisor with a reputation for being open to working with all ways of knowing in practice.

The worker's own preferred method of relaxation and focus is a simple form of meditation she learned in college. She usually meditates for a few minutes before and after her workday. When the worker visits the father, she realizes that she has a gut feeling that his temper is severe when he is under considerable stress in his life, but also that he is sincere in wanting to protect his children from his temper. The worker wants to be as sure as possible that her intuition is accurate, so she discusses the case with her supervisor. Her supervisor encourages her to both trust her initial intuition and do more assessment of the family. The worker interviews the children, the neighbors, and other adults in the children's lives. She discovers that there is no evidence that this father has ever physically or psychologically abused his sons.

Experiential Exercises

1. Explore your own feelings and beliefs regarding intuition. Are they more positive or negative? Where did they come from? How do they help or limit your assessment in practice?

2. How have the professional helpers who have helped you the most (e.g., teachers, counselors, etc.) used intuition? What did you like or dislike about their approach to the intuitive process?

3. How much do you use intuition in your practice? In your life? How could you value the diversity of ways that people may use intuition in their lives?

CHAPTER 3

Issues in Advanced Generalist Assessment

Sensitivity to Client/System Diversity

The strategy that most social worker educators use today to foster sensitivity to diversity in their practice is to teach the characteristics of the various populations they serve. Knowledge of common characteristics of people of a particular gender, age, sexual preference, race, or culture can, of course, help a worker understand the possible strengths and limitations of a client. Unfortunately, even the well-intentioned worker can make errors in assessment by assuming that any unique client has the characteristics that the textbook says the client has. For example, one student was taught in school to never look directly in the eyes of people from a particular ethnic minority population. He tried to avoid eye contact with all members of this population until one of his clients was offended because the worker was always staring at the floor when they met.

In reality, there is usually as much diversity *within* particular populations as there is between them. Particularly in our evolving postmodern society, every individual who belongs to one population has unique characteristics that may not fit all of the statistical norms. For example, a social worker can make some generalizations about how men are different from women (e.g., men are competitive, women are relational). The worker must use such generalization with caution, however, because there are as many differences between men as there are between men and women. For example, the worker may see a couple in which the woman may be relatively more competitive than her boyfriend and the man more relational than his girlfriend.

Overcoming Common Obstacles to Sensitivity to Diversity

An additional strategy designed to foster the social worker's sensitivity to diversity is to help the worker overcome the obstacles that typically hinder the worker's sensitivity and conscious use of self. There are many potential obstacles to making sensitive ecological assessments, and these obstacles may be created by the individual social worker, the service setting, the culture, and/or the profession. Examples of obstacles in each of these levels are described below.

Individual social worker. The worker may have blind spots in his or her practice that are usually associated with personal values, developmental limitations, or countertransferences. The worker may, for example, be quite sensitive to the client's observable behaviors but tend to neglect the feelings of the client or the impact that the client's family has on his functioning. Usually, such insensitivities are related to similar insensitivities that the worker has developed in his personal life. Thus, a social worker who is relatively unaware of her own cultural heritage may also tend to be insensitive to the impact of culture upon clients. In general, the social worker's blind spots often can hinder sensitivity to client diversity. For example, a social worker who currently neglects her personal spiritual development may tend to neglect the importance of spiritual development of clients.

Social workers often share some common biases. There is evidence that professional helpers generally prefer not to work with clients who are relatively poorer, less intelligent, less attractive, and less verbal than most other people.[59] Because social workers tend to give more guarded prognoses to these clients, special sensitivity may be required when assessing clients who may fit these less desirable categories.

In general, the most effective tool to combat individual and shared obstacles to sensitivity is the worker's own self-awareness and self-acceptance (see Parts I and V). The most effective social worker strives to be aware of and accept his own unique obstacles and the unique characteristics of each case. The worker endeavors to understand the most likely characteristics of each element of diversity. For example, when preparing to work with straight, white, male Iowans, the worker becomes familiar with typical characteristics of this group. However, the effective worker also realizes that each straight, white, male Iowan will be unique and needs to be approached with an open-minded strategy of assessment.

Although social workers are often taught today to use theory-based practice, the most effective social worker does not let existing theories excessively color ecological assessment. For example, although a worker might believe that all sex offenders have been molested as children, he must remain open to discovering that there are exceptions to that rule every time he begins a new case. Beginning social workers may legitimately need to cling to a theory of human behavior like a sailor holds on to the life raft, because the seas of practice can often be quite stormy indeed. However, in time and with support, the worker can gradually learn to be more open to discovering that each new case may present unique challenges to cherished or currently fashionable theories of human behavior.

Ecological assessment thus requires the developmental maturity necessary to accept what is discovered in the investigation process. "Accurate assessment requires consideration of alternative explanations" (p. 180).[60] Without awareness and acceptance of self and openness to accepting what is discovered, social workers may be easily influenced by the biases of self, setting, profession, and society. Unconscious ego attachment to particular viewpoints will create obstacles to discovering new perspectives in the assessment of a case.

Service setting. The social worker's assessments may be influenced by the characteristics of the service setting in which she works. For example, some service settings may particularly emphasize the assessment of some aspects of a case (such as observable behaviors, level of social skills, etc.) and deemphasize the assessment of other aspects of a case (such as psychodynamic history, current family dynamics, or cultural aspects). When social workers see clients in settings that use the medical model approach, such as in many psychiatric hospitals, the biopsychosocial aspects of functioning may be overemphasized and affective and spiritual functioning underemphasized. Social workers who see their clients only in professional offices will, of course, have no opportunities to observe the client/system in his or her natural environments (e.g., school, home, work). The prognosis of cases may also be influenced by setting characteristics. For example, a particular agency administrator may tend to be pessimistic about the ability of abusive husbands to change and may overtly or covertly influence clinical social workers to ignore the possibility of positive change in such client/systems.

Ideally, in a healthy work setting, the administrators and supervisors continually strive to analyze and question their own assumptions about practice and to accept the diversity of the workers they supervise. At such a setting, social workers are not only allowed to question the underlying assumptions found at the work setting, but they are also encouraged to actively explore alternative explanations of human behavior as they conduct assessments.

Social workers in positions of leadership may need to analyze not only their own personal assumptions, but also the assumptions of top administrators, colleagues, and on-line workers. Ideally, each social worker should feel free to express personal perspectives on human behavior and the social environment without having to fear any negative consequences. The workers also ideally feel safe enough to talk with their supervisors about the countertransference reactions they experience with their clients.

Culture. The culture in which the social worker lives and works often influences assessment as well. Culture can be understood as a "general set of shared meanings held by a specified group of people and other social units and serves as a foundation for their organized way of life" (p. 72).[61] As postmodern theory suggests, reality is socially constructed and can be created on both the local and societal levels. The norms for role performance in our American society may vary within any cultural group on variables such as social class, sex, age, and the physical and social environment.

Prevailing notions in some communities may be expressed overtly or covertly. For instance, a woman who is considering divorce might be accepted and supported in some local cultures and severely judged in others. In another example, the Child Protective Service worker located in an isolated rural area may be influenced by a locally held belief that government should not interfere with the father's right to treat his children (or wife) the way he chooses. In this example, the social worker may respond in one of two opposite extremes; he may tend to look for maltreatment when there is no evidence of it, or he may shy away from seeing maltreatment unless it is so dramatic that it cannot be ignored.

Cultural influences may also come from the larger society. Society is the "most dominant, inclusive, and self-sufficient of all forms of social organization . . . composed of a specified group of people and other social units who share a common culture" (p. 72).[62] As is every social organization, society is interrelated with a larger "suprasystem," the global family of all human beings. For example, many individuals within the United States still tend to value the ideal of the nuclear family (father at work, mother at home with 2.3 children), despite its increasing scarcity. This bias may influence the way we assess people living in nontraditional family systems.

No matter where they live, social workers may need opportunities where they can safely meet together, identify the realities constructed within the local and broader societal cultures, and process what it is like to work in such conditions. Most of us become particularly susceptible to social pressure from time to time, and in such situations, a social worker may also need to take the time to reconnect with who she is. When we reconnect with ourselves, we rediscover what we think and feel. This process may be facilitated by a therapist, supervisor, or through recreation (re-creating).

Social work profession. Our profession collectively holds positions on practice that may limit ecological assessment. These positions are linked to a number of current trends that influence assessment, including (a) short-term or brief treatment, (b) accountability, (c) professionalism, and (d) science in social work. Clearly, today there is an increased emphasis upon short-term treatment (or brief intervention[63]) and accountability (or quality assurance[64]). Economic and political factors associated with these trends have been documented in the literature. Since 1980, there have been fewer dollars available for services to populations at risk; social welfare expenditures did not rise to deal with the dramatic shift of resources away from the poor and to the rich.[65] Both short-term treatment and accountability are, of course, realities that, in themselves, are neither good nor bad. Short-term treatment may often be very useful and appropriate in some cases, and often, practitioners must strive to become more accountable in order to survive.

However, the emphasis upon short-term treatment and accountability may create obstacles to effective assessment in social work practice. As postmodern theory suggests, the most important question is, Do such trends ultimately serve the client? Short-term treatment methods will not serve every client's best interests. For example, short-term strategies may limit the aspects of ecological assessment that are considered. If a social worker has only 4 weeks to see students at a campus clinic, she may tend to ignore those deeper issues that do not respond quickly to interventions, regardless of the importance of such factors in any particular case.

Accountability also may not serve the best interests of the client. The emphasis is often more upon accountability toward the funding source rather than accountability toward the client. Efforts to enhance productivity and reduce costs can result in a lowered quality of service to clients.[66] Social workers, under pressure to demonstrate increased productivity, may focus upon the behaviors that they can attempt to change quickly and ignore the importance of other dimensions of human development that seem more difficult to assess and affect.

Similarly, calls for increased professionalism and science in social work may lead to less effective assessment. Although both of these goals have contributed to social work, they can also reinforce certain insensitivities. For example, emphasis upon professionalism has led to continued focus upon new practice frameworks that have "distracted social workers from their unique focus on the person-environment interaction" (p. 661).[67] Social workers who are taught to be more professional may tend to relate to clients in a "vertical" or disrespectful manner. Emphasis on only scientific ways of knowing can lead to the exclusion of intuitive ways of knowing.

Inclusive and ecological assessment puts the needs of the client/system first and resists taking on any dualistic or exclusive positions that may reduce practice effectiveness. In every era, the full implications of current trends in practice must be analyzed if obstacles to sensitivity are to be avoided.

Client as Supervisor

In making assessments of diverse client/systems, the effective social worker is aware that the client can be her best supervisor. The client is usually the leading expert in her own developmental strengths and in the biopsychosociospiritual problems with which she lives every day. The client can help guide the social worker in making initial assessments, "midcourse evaluations," and final case evaluations.

In initial assessments, the worker invites the client to begin talking first and listens to what the client presents. The client's statements give clues about what is going on in the client's own experience as well as in the client's environment. For example, a client may come into the office and say, "Man, what a mess it is outside today! There was a bus stuck in the snow down the street and the plows have not even gone down Main Street this morning!" The worker's supervision for the meeting today may be that the focus should be, at least in part, on the difficulties that the client is having in navigating through his life.

In the middle phase of a case, the client is asked to help the social worker make any necessary midcourse corrections in the direction that the work is going. For example, after a social worker has been seeing a single mother and her troubled daughter for several weeks, the worker asks them to evaluate the first three sessions. The daughter says, "When are we going to start talking about Billy hitting me?" The social worker then learns for the first time that the girl's brother has been bullying her for months. The mother, daughter, and worker agree to refocus the next sessions on the problem with Billy.

Finally, evaluations in the ending phase of practice should include client feedback when possible. Clients can give feedback directly to the worker and can also give information indirectly through paper-and-pencil questionnaires or through other formal or informal measurement instruments. It is hoped that clients can also be given opportunities to tell their stories to groups of social workers in agency meetings, classrooms, seminars, and other educational settings.

Experiential Exercises

1. Describe a situation when elements of your own unique diversity were stereotyped by a professional (e.g., your race, age, gender). Why do you think the professional viewed you incorrectly? What was this experience like for you?

2. What obstacles seem to get in the way of your own ecological assessment of diverse populations (e.g., personal, setting, cultural)? How can you best overcome such obstacles?

The Fourth Edition of the *Diagnostic and Statistical Manual of Mental Disorders (DSM-IV)* and Ecological Assessment

Social workers often include a *DSM-IV* diagnosis[68] in the assessment of a case. *DSM-IV* diagnoses are used in many clinical, research, and educational settings; are often used to communicate case information with clients and other professionals; and are often essential in the process of receiving third-party payments for social work services. A working knowledge of the *DSM-IV* is thus essential to the advanced social work practitioner.

When possible, *DSM-IV* diagnoses should be included as a part of the larger ecological assessment. The *DSM-IV* uses a system of categorization that is based upon state-of-the-art theory, clinical observation, research, and professional dialogue, but should not be given more importance than the assessment of client strengths and relevant environmental factors. The *DSM-IV* diagnosis looks at pathology, or client limitations, as defined by psychiatry and/or society.

The advanced generalist social worker recognizes that the client's strengths include those associated with each *DSM-IV* diagnosis. The social worker may also reframe the processes described by the *DSM-IV* diagnosis as an attempt by the organism to cope and heal and grow rather than only as a symptom of illness that must be eliminated. Symptoms that are called mental disorders in the Western medical tradition may be regarded from other perspectives (e.g., holistic medicine or Jungian psychology) as a sign that something is working rather than that something is broken.

For example, a worker considers the possibility that the ADHD symptoms in a young boy she is seeing may actually also reflect some strengths in him. The worker discovers that this boy (who was described as "spacey" and "hyper" by his teacher) can also be seen as having a great deal of energy, creativity, and enthusiasm for life. The boy appears to be gifted in visual arts, poetry, and dance. The worker notes these client strengths in the final report.

In another example, a man who has experienced a divorce and the death of both of his parents in a 3-month period might be expected to have some symptoms of depression. This man's depression can be viewed as his soul's way of letting him know that he needs to grieve the losses he has experienced and become more whole. Indeed, in some psychological traditions, the mental disorders are viewed as signs of health, as attempts by the soul to communicate something important to the self.[69] Healing means wholing, going through loss with all the parts of the self intact, including the emotional, cognitive, physical, social, and spiritual dimensions of self. If the social worker conceptualizes all symptoms only as things to eliminate, medicate, or otherwise cure, then opportunities for healing and growth may be diminished.

Experiential Exercises

1. Describe a time in your own life when you felt that you were not viewed as a unique person, but rather stereotyped (e.g., as a man, as an aging person, as a mainstream person). What was that experience like?

2. Which stereotypes do you find that you tend to make about other people (e.g., all Democrats are radical liberals, all homeless people are lazy, etc.)? How could you be more open to diversity in this area?

3. What *DSM-IV* diagnosis fits you the best? What would you be afraid that other people would automatically think of you if they knew you had that diagnosis?

4. Is there a particular *DSM-IV* diagnosis about which you might tend to make stereotypes (e.g., schizophrenics are all dangerous)? How could you be more open to client diversity in this area?

Assessment as an Ongoing Source of Feedback

Assessment is an ongoing source of feedback. It is ongoing in that assessment continues through the planning, beginning, middle, ending, and follow-up phases of treatment. Assessment (often described as taking place only in the planning and beginning phases of treatment) is sometimes conceptualized as a process distinct from evaluation (often described as occurring in the termination phase of treatment). However, both assessment and evaluation are processes that continue throughout treatment and use intuition and measurement. Thus, assessment is a source of feedback in that it uses data in both formulating goals to guide interventions and measuring the impact of those interventions. A model of practice flow can be designed that describes evaluation and intervention movement through the phases of treatment (see Figure 3.1). In initial assessment, the worker identifies client developmental strengths and limitations. In the beginning phase, the worker works with the developmental strengths of the client (primary interventions), which maximizes probability of success. These initial interventions are evaluated, and further primary interventions may be necessary. Then, secondary intervention strategies are implemented, in which secondary interventions target the developmental limitations. In the ending phase, these secondary interventions are evaluated, and further interventions are implemented when necessary.

Assessing for Risk and Acting to Protect

Any discussion of assessment must emphasize the worker's responsibility to act to protect clients and other people when safety and/or well-being is at risk. Many populations that social workers serve are populations at risk; many of our clients may become victims and/or victimize others. The word *responsibility* can be understood to mean "able to respond." In other words, therapists

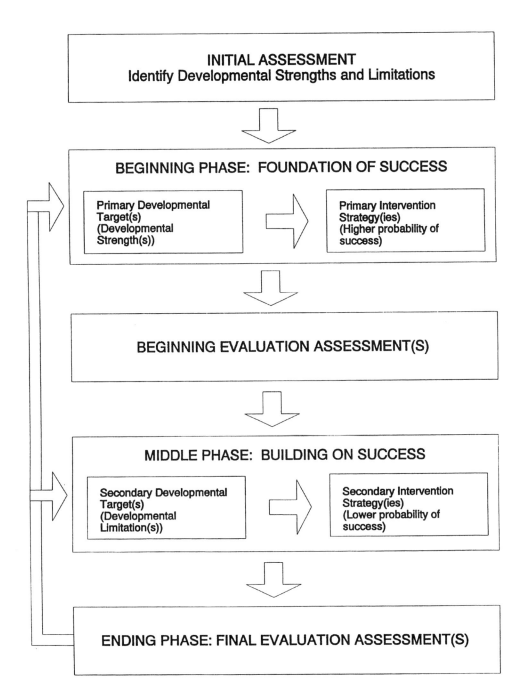

Figure 3.1. Practice Flowchart

respond to safety and protective concerns to the extent to which they are able. In every meeting with a client or family, and particularly in the first session(s), the worker always assesses for possible risk of danger to her client, the client's family, herself, or anyone else identified in the casework process. Examples of such risks include, but are not limited to, the following:

1. Maltreatment of a child or adolescent

2. Maltreatment of an adult spouse or partner

3. Maltreatment of a vulnerable adult (including the physically or mentally handicapped)

4. Maltreatment of an aging person

5. Threat of suicide (or other self-destructive behavior)

6. Threat of homicide (or other dangerous, outer-directed behavior)

7. Loss of a person's access to resources to meet essential needs (e.g., income, food, housing, health care)

The most effective and appropriate response to such threats to safety and well-being will vary according to the individual circumstances of each case. The specific laws that protect people from harm vary from state to state, and workers must keep informed as to the current various reporting and protection laws, mental health statutes, and protective service mandates and guidelines. In many situations, workers must immediately report safety and protective issues to various authorities, including those in law enforcement and the state protective services.

Social workers should always act to protect when there is reasonable concern that there are safety issues. Assessment of safety and protective issues should always begin in the first session with the client and client/system and should continue throughout the work with the client. Social workers can consult with law enforcement and protective service experts, as well as with supervisors and colleagues, when in doubt about the appropriate response to indications of any threat to safety.

Most social workers are well aware that they are themselves increasingly at risk of civil lawsuits. Unfortunately, workers are quite vulnerable to being held fully responsible for situations in which their ability to respond may be limited.[70] Because workers can potentially lose their malpractice insurance, their livelihoods, and even personal possessions, there is pressure on them to take actions that would serve to protect themselves (but that may or may not protect the client).

It does not appear that practicing social workers can ever completely avoid some risk of being unreasonably blamed. Workers themselves can also take actions to reduce this risk,[71] but these self-protective actions should not serve to increase the risks of harm to others. Unfortunately, some workers take extreme precautions to protect themselves from such risk, and these precautions ultimately may endanger clients more, such as avoiding maltreatment cases altogether, warning clients not to disclose information, and overreporting information to authorities.

Risk factors are factors in the ecology of a case that are likely to be associated with danger to the safety and well-being of clients and other people. Although knowledge of risk factors can be helpful in making assessments and interventions with maltreatment cases, social workers cannot be certain initially which factors might be associated with any particular cases.

Social workers are encouraged to consult with local protective service and law enforcement professionals (e.g., Child Protective Service social workers, police) before they try to do any initial, in-depth interviewing of maltreatment victims. Social workers should make themselves aware of the guidelines and procedures for interviewing of victims in each administrative area and be ready to refer victims quickly to interview specialists when appropriate (e.g., in many larger communities, trained police investigators or trained hospital social workers and physicians).

Although a complete discussion of risk factors is outside the scope of this book, all social workers should be aware of basic and common factors that may suggest that a danger exists. Maltreatment is most likely to occur in families where there is the greatest power differential.[72] Abusive family members seem to be particularly likely to maltreat when they believe that they are losing or have lost power and personal empowerment. Dominant husbands can become violent when their wives begin to assert themselves. Parents who have lost physical health or economic security can become more likely to maltreat their children or aging parents. Research has identified risk factors for potential child sexual abuse victims, such as when the child is female, the parents are in conflict, a stepfather is in the family, the child has a poor relationship with a parent, the mother has employment outside the home, and the natural father is outside of the home. In addition, there is evidence that male child molesters tend to have had a history of past sexual trauma, heightened sexual arousal to children, difficulty relating to adult females, low impulse control, and abuse of alcohol.[73]

Both victims and perpetrators of couple maltreatment tend to have violence in their own backgrounds, dysfunctional learned responses to stress and violence, and unrealistic beliefs about marriage and relative male and female power.[74] Whereas aging victims of maltreatment tended to be female; average 80 to 84 years of age; and have lived with a family member for 10 years or more, the abusers tended to be family members; male (particularly sons and, less often, aging husbands); and under considerable outside stress. Other risk factors involved in the abuse of the aging include histories of intergenerational conflict; functional dependency of the victim; and histories of alcoholism, retardation, or psychiatric illness in either caretaker or victim.[75]

There is an extensive and growing literature on risk factors associated with suicide. Risk factors in all areas of the client/system ecology have been identified, including biological, psychological, cognitive, and environmental factors. Biological factors include associations with clinical depression, various genetic traits, and the male gender. Males are two to five times more likely to commit suicide. Psychological risk factors are feelings and behaviors that contribute to suicide, including depression, hopelessness, helplessness, low self-esteem, and poor coping skills. Cognitive risk factors include rigid, dichotomous, and narrowly focused thinking. Environmental factors include negative family experiences, loss, other negative traumatic life events, and the availability of weapons and other means of self-destruction.

Various triggering events may or may not be associated with every suicide attempt.[76] Some mental disorders have been found to be associated with risk for suicide, including schizoid-asocial, avoidant, passive-aggressive-negativistic, borderline-cycloid, dysthymia, psychotic thinking, and psychotic depression.[77]

Social workers can use a variety of formal or informal methods of evaluating risk factors for suicide. A survey of suicide instruments used by practitioners in assessing adolescents at risk identified 29 well-established instruments.[78] A study of suicidal adolescents and young adults indicated such risk factors as distress, poor coping skills, hopelessness, depression, hostility, and low confidence in their ability to improve their lives.[79]

Risk factors for homicide also can be considered to include factors across the ecology of the client/system. These factors include substance abuse; low impulse control; poor school, work, or military records; prior history in the deaths of others; and various organic elements.[80] Depression has been linked to homicidal behavior in adolescents.[81] Risk factors that have been found to be associated with homicide with battered women include elevated frequency and severity of battering, proximity of firearms, sexual abuse (marital rape), substance abuse, history of violence outside the home, perpetrator's need to control partner, battering during pregnancy, history of child abuse, suicide threats, minority group membership, poverty, and youthfulness.[82]

Experiential Exercises

1. Have you ever been (or was someone close to you) at risk of suicide or in danger from others? How, if at all, did others either help or make the process more difficult? What would have been most helpful?

2. Have you or any other social worker you know ever been sued by a client? What was that experience like? What was learned, and what needed to be changed (if anything) in practice?

3. Have you (or someone you know) ever had to call an authority regarding child maltreatment, suicidal or homicidal ideation, or another protective issue? What was that experience like? What was learned?

Notes

Chapter 1

1. Bloom, M. (1992). A conversation with Carol Germain on human development in the ecological context. In M. Bloom (Ed.), *Changing lives: Studies in human development and professional helping* (pp. 407-411). Columbia: University of South Carolina Press.

2. Meyer, C. H. (1988). The eco-systems perspective. In R. A. Dorfman (Ed.), *Paradigms of clinical social work* (pp. 274-294). New York: Brunner/Mazel.

3. Northern, H. (1987). Assessment in direct practice. In National Association of Social Workers, *Encyclopedia of social work* (18th ed., Vol. 1, pp. 171-183). Silver Spring, MD: National Association of Social Workers.

4. Compton, B. R., & Galaway, B. (Eds.). (1979). *Social work processes* (2nd ed.). Homewood, IL: Dorsey; Pincus, A., & Minahan, A. (1973). *Social work practice: Model and method.* Itasca, IL: F. E. Peacock.

5. Bloom (1992).

6. Maslow, A. (1966). *The psychology of science.* New York: Harper & Row; Needleman, J. (1975). *A sense of the cosmos.* Garden City, NY: Doubleday; Polanyi, M. (1959). *Personal knowledge.* Chicago: University of Chicago Press; Rosak, T. (1978). *Person/planet: The creative disintegration of industrial society.* New York: Anchor.

7. Ivey, A. E. (1991). *Developmental strategies for helpers: Individual, family, and network interventions.* Pacific Grove, CA: Brooks/Cole.

8. Nemiroff, R. A., & Colarusso, C. A. (Eds.). (1990). *New dimensions in adult development.* New York: Basic Books.

9. Bloom (1992); Thomas, R. M. (1992). *Comparing theories of child development.* Belmont, CA: Wadsworth.

10. Chess, W. A., & Norlin, J. M. (1988). *Human behavior and the social environment.* Boston: Allyn & Bacon.

11. Macy, J. R. (1983). *Despair and personal power in the nuclear age.* Baltimore: New Society Publishers; Rosak (1978).

12. Horowitz, F. D. (1987). *Exploring developmental theories: Toward a structural/behavioral model of development.* Hillsdale, NJ: Lawrence Erlbaum.

13. Bloom (1992).

14. Karls, J. M., & Wandrei, K. E. (1994). *Person-in-environment system: The PIE classification system for social functioning problems.* Washington, DC: National Association of Social Workers.

15. Gambrill, E. (1990). *Critical thinking in clinical practice.* San Francisco: Jossey-Bass.

16. Horowitz (1987).

17. Hendricks, G., & Weinhold, B. (1982). *Transpersonal approaches to counseling and psychotherapy.* Denver: Love.

18. Sperry, L., & Carlson, J. (1991). *Marital therapy: Integrating theory and technique.* Denver: Love.

19. Hill, R. (1986). Life cycle stages for types of single parent families: Of family development theory. *Family Relations, 35,* 19-29.

20. Peck, M. S. (1987). *The different drum: Community making and peace.* New York: Simon & Schuster.

21. O'hara, M., & Anderson, W. T. (1991, September/October). Welcome to the postmodern world. *Networker,* pp. 19-25.

22. O'hara and Anderson (1991).

23. Horgan, J. (1992). Quantum philosophy. *Scientific American, 267,* 94-101.

24. O'hara and Anderson (1991).

25. Watzlawick, P. (1984). *The invented reality: Contributions to constructionism.* New York: Norton.

26. Wilber, K. (1986). Treatment modalities. In K. Wilber, J. Engler, & D. P. Brown (Eds.), *Transformations of consciousness* (pp. 127-160). Boston and London: New Science Library/Shambhala.

27. Berne, E. (1961). *Transactional analysis in psychotherapy.* New York: Grove.

28. Wilber (1986).

29. Hamilton, N. G. (1992). *Self and others: Object relations theory in practice.* Northvale, NJ: Jason Aronson.

Chapter 2

30. Scheafor, B. W., Horejsi, C. R., & Horejsi, G. A. (1988). *Techniques and guidelines for social work practice.* Boston: Allyn & Bacon.

31. Siporin, M. (1988). Clinical social work as an art form. *Social Casework, 69*(3), 177-183.

32. Reamer, F. G. (1993). *The philosophical foundations of social work.* New York: Columbia University Press.

33. Reamer (1993).

34. Reamer (1993).

35. Horowitz (1987).

36. Garfield, S. L., & Bergin, A. E. (1986). *Handbook of psychotherapy and behavior change: An empirical analysis* (3rd ed.). New York: John Wiley; Meares, P. A. (1990, October). *Research on treatment and outcome of depression in children and adolescents.* Paper presented at the Conference on Child and Adolescent Mental Health, University of California, Berkeley.

37. Radetsky, P. (1991). *The invisible invaders: The story of the emerging age of viruses.* Boston: Little, Brown.

38. Rapoport, L. (1968). Creativity in social work. *Smith College Studies in Social Work, 38*(3), 139-161.

39. Reamer (1993).

40. Blythe, B. J., & Tripodi, T. (1989). *Measurement in direct social work practice.* Newbury Park, CA: Sage.

41. Meyer, C. H. (1989). Integrating research and practice. *Social Work, 29,* 323.

42. Blythe and Tripodi (1989).

43. Hillman, J. (1975). *Re-visioning psychology.* New York: HarperColophon.

44. Hillman (1975).

45. Bloom, M., & Fischer, J. (1982). *Evaluating practice: Guidelines for the accountable professional.* Englewood Cliffs, NJ: Prentice Hall.

46. Lawson, H. (n.d.). *Journey analysis.* Unpublished manuscript, Graduate School of Social Work, University of Utah.

47. Goldberg, P. (1983). *The intuitive edge: Understanding and developing intuition.* Los Angeles: Jeremy P. Tarcher.

48. Bruner, J. (1961). *The process of education.* Cambridge, MA: Harvard University Press; Bruner, J., & Clinchy, B. (1971). Toward a disciplined intuition. In J. Bruner (Ed.), *The relevance of education* (pp. 82-100). New York: Norton; Clinchy, B. (1968, February). The role of intuition in learning. *National Education Association Journal,* pp. 33-37.

49. Allport, G. (1929). The study of personality by the intuitive method. *Journal of Abnormal and Social Psychology, 24,* 14-27; Berne, E. (1977). *Intuition and ego states.* New York: Harper & Row; Jung, C. J. (1971). *Psychological types.* Princeton, NJ: Princeton University Press; Maslow (1966).

50. Mintzberg, H. (1976, July/August). Planning on the left side and managing on the right. *Harvard Business Review,* pp. 49-58.

51. Goldberg (1983).

52. Shallcross, D. J., & Sisk, D. A. (1989). *Intuition: An inner way of knowing.* Buffalo, NY: Bearly Limited.

53. Isenberg, D. J. (1984, November/December). How senior managers think. *Harvard Business Review,* pp. 81-90.

54. Goldberg (1983).

55. Goldberg (1983).

56. Goldberg (1983).

57. Benson, H. (1975). *The relaxation response.* New York: Avon.

58. Goldberg (1983).

Chapter 3

59. Schofield, W. (1964). *Psychotherapy: The purchase of friendship.* Englewood Cliffs, NJ: Prentice Hall.

60. Northern, H. (1987). Assessment in direct practice. In National Association of Social Workers, *Encyclopedia of social work* (2nd ed., Vol. 1, pp. 171-183). Silver Spring, MD: National Association of Social Workers.

61. Chess, W. A., & Norlin, J. M. (1988). *Human behavior and the social environment.* Boston: Allyn & Bacon.

62. Chess and Norlin (1988).

63. Gustafson, J. P. (1986). *The complex secret of brief psychotherapy.* New York: Norton.

64. Coulton, C. J. (1987). Quality assurance. In National Association of Social Workers, *Encyclopedia of social work* (18th ed., Vol. 1, pp. 443-445). Silver Spring, MD: National Association of Social Workers.

65. Ginsberg, L. (1987). Selected statistical review. In National Association of Social Workers, *Encyclopedia of social work* (18th ed., Vol. 1, pp. 256-288). Silver Spring, MD: National Association of Social Workers.

66. Coulton (1987).

67. Scheafor, B. W., & Landon, P. S. (1987). Generalist perspective. In National Association of Social Workers, *Encyclopedia of social work* (18th ed., Vol. 1, pp. 660-668). Silver Spring, MD: National Association of Social Workers.

68. American Psychiatric Association. (1994). *Diagnostic and statistical manual of mental disorders* (4th ed.). Washington, DC: Author.

69. Hillman, J. (1975). *Re-visioning psychology.* New York: HarperColophon.

70. Besharov, D. (1985). *The vulnerable social worker.* New York: National Association of Social Workers.

71. Besharov (1985).

72. Finkelhor, D. (1986). *A sourcebook on child sexual abuse.* Beverly Hills, CA: Sage.

73. Finkelhor (1986).

74. Finkelhor (1986).

75. Hudson, J. E. (1988). Elder abuse: An overview. In B. Schlesinger & R. Schlesinger (Eds.), *Abuse of the elderly: Issues and annotated bibliography* (pp. 67-89). Toronto: University of Toronto Press.

76. Stillion, J. M., & McDowell, E. (1991). Examining suicide from a life span perspective. *Death Studies, 15,* 327-354.

77. Hull, J. S., Range, L. M., & Goggin, W. C. (1992). Suicide ideas: Relationship to personality disorders on the MCMI. *Death Studies, 16,* 371-375.

78. Garrison, C. A., Lewinsohn, P. M., Marsteller, F., Langhinrichsen, J., & Lann, I. (1991). The assessment of suicidal behavior in adolescents. *Suicide and Life-Threatening Behavior, 21,* 217-229.

79. Simonds, J. F., McMahon, T., & Armstrong, D. (1991). Young suicide attempters compared with a control group: Psychological, affective, and attitudinal variables. *Suicide and Life-Threatening Behavior, 21,* 134-150.

80. Stern, T. A., Schwartz, J. H., Cremens, M. C., & Mulley, A. G. (1991). The evaluation of homicidal patients by psychiatric residents in the emergency room: A pilot study. *Psychiatric Quarterly, 62,* 333-343.

81. Malmquist, C. P. (1990). Depression in homicidal adolescents. *Bulletin of the American Academy of Psychiatry and the Law, 18,* 23-36.

82. Campbell, J. C. (1986). Nursing assessment for risk of homicide with battered women. *Advances in Nursing Science, 8*(4), 36-51.

PART II

Advanced Generalist Approach Interventions With Individuals, Couples, Families, and Groups

In this section, a universal framework of advanced generalist social work practice with individuals, couples, families, and groups is forwarded. The basic premise in this framework is that the most effective advanced generalist interventions are (a) ecological, (b) inclusive, (c) differentially eclectic, (d) relational, and (e) ethical. In this section, each of these five interrelated elements is further described. The seven paradigms of advanced social work practice introduced in this section are more fully described in Parts III and IV.

An inclusive definition of *intervention* is applied here, which includes the cooperative efforts of the worker/system and the client/system to foster the physical, affective, spiritual, psychosocial, and cognitive development of individuals and to improve the collective welfare of couples, families, groups, and the local and global communities. The advanced generalist practitioner recognizes that most of the changes that occur in human and system development are not achieved directly by social workers but by the people whom social workers strive to help. Thus, clients are viewed as equal partners with the social worker in the co-creation and analysis of assessments and interventions.

CHAPTER 4

A Practice Framework

Ecological Intervention

Fostering Interrelatedness and Stewardship

In ecological intervention, the overall goal of all advanced generalist social work practice includes both individual and collective well-being, because the two are always ecologically interrelated. The social worker recognizes how the well-being of the individual client is interrelated with the collective well-being of the client/system. The term *client/system* refers not only to the client's family, local community, and natural ecosystem, but also to humanity, the international community, and the global ecosystem.

The social worker understands that the developing, self-actualizing individual tends to become more "response-able" for both personal well-being and the well-being of the client/system. The converse is also true; as the client becomes more responsible for herself and her environment, the client's personal development tends to be fostered. The worker thus models and encourages stewardship of both himself and the client/system.

Ecological intervention is consistent with ecological, or eco-systems theory, which emphasizes the interdependence of all elements of a system.[1] The goal of ecological intervention is also consistent with many traditional models of social work practice. For example, in the Reciprocal Model[2] of group work, the worker encourages clients to build a "mutual aid system" in which they work toward both individual and societal goals, and the worker mediates between systems. More recent theories also support ecological intervention. For example, ecological intervention is consistent with deep or transpersonal ecology, which suggests an interconnectiveness between human psychology and ecology.[3] Radical Feminist Therapy suggests a strong interconnection between personal empowerment and societal oppression.[4] Even the way we talk in our postmodern world reflects the shift toward ecological thinking; information-processing metaphors no longer describe linear (stimulus and response) operations but rather those more simultaneous (parallel) and interdependent.[5]

This ecological perspective extends beyond the client's interrelationship with the family, local community, and even the nation to the globalization of her everyday life. The advanced generalist social worker needs to develop interventions that help the client relate to global reality:

> We therefore live in a globalizing social reality, one in which previously effective barriers to communication no longer exist. . . . Accordingly, if we want to understand the major features of contemporary social life, we have to go beyond local and national factors to situate our analysis in this global context. (pp. 1-2)[6]

As all of these theories suggest, the effective social worker strives to help the client become a more responsible steward of both herself and the world and recognizes the interrelatedness of self-help and helping others: "We work on ourselves, then, in order to help others. And we help others as a vehicle for working on ourselves" (p. 92).[7] Thus, the goals of ecological intervention strategy include the stewardship of both (a) the client's multidimensional individual development, and (b) the client/system.

Stewardship of Multidimensional Individual Development

The worker strives to help the client become a steward, or caretaker, of his own development. All social work practice can be conceptualized as being applied developmental theory,[8] and all interventions can be understood as attempts to directly or indirectly foster human development in the affective, physical, spiritual, cognitive, and psychosocial dimensions. The specific developmental dimensions targeted will vary, of course, from case to case. However, the fostering of human development can be conceptualized as having four interrelated phases: (a) an understanding and acceptance of current multidimensional development; (b) a building upon existing developmental strengths; (c) development of the less developed, or "shadow," dimensions; and (d) evaluation.

Understanding and acceptance of current multidimensional development. During the assessment process, the worker strives to help each client understand and accept those personal dimensions of self that are currently most developed and those that remain relatively underdeveloped.

For example, a sex offender referred to an agency might tell his social worker that he thinks he might have been molested when he was a child. It may turn out that this man's cognitive dimension is his dominant (most developed) dimension, that is, he is most comfortable discussing these past issues intellectually. He also happens to be quite uncomfortable experiencing and expressing his feelings about these events (affective dimension).

In another example, an aging client may seem to want to reminisce about her past, and she likes to talk about her life events from a spiritual perspective.

However, she is not as developed in her physical dimension, no longer takes care of how she eats and exercises, and does not yet accept the natural changes in her body.

A woman might need help in leaving an abusive lover. She is quite intelligent (cognitive dimension) but has difficulty being assertive (psychosocial) or expressing anger (affective).

Finally, an adolescent wants to learn how to deal with his test anxiety and make more friends. He is a skilled athlete (physical dimension) but is less developed in the cognitive and psychosocial dimensions. In all four examples, the worker tries to help the client become aware of and accept these areas of strength and limitation.

Building upon existing developmental strengths. The identification and acknowledgment of the dominant and underdeveloped dimensions of self-development prepare the worker and client to begin the second phase, which is building on the client's existing strengths. The worker and client strive to recognize both the goal and the process of the work. The ultimate goal is integrity, or wholeness; the client wants to move toward her developmental potential in all dimensions. However, the process of achieving this goal includes a solid foundation of success. Success in development in one dimension often breeds further success in the other dimensions. The client is most likely to work willingly and effectively in the developmental dimension in which she feels most comfortable.

Using the same examples introduced above, the sex offender (who is cognitively dominant) may initially be most comfortable intellectualizing about his life. The aging client who is very spiritual can be asked at first to talk about the meaning of life. The woman with the abusive lover may feel comfortable attending a psychoeducation workshop about domestic violence. The adolescent with test anxiety and no friends may respond well to a worker who initially plays catch with him in the agency parking lot and encourages him to try out for the football team.

Development of the less developed, or shadow, dimensions. After the dominant developmental dimension is recognized and further enhanced, the client is more prepared to begin the third step of the process. This involves working in the less developed dimension(s). The social worker strives to help the client make progress in those most difficult areas.

For example, the sex offender begins to feel what happened to him, to mourn his losses. The aging client is supported in taking better care of her body. The woman with the abusive lover may start to rehearse and practice assertiveness with others. The adolescent with test anxiety learns to relax and do his best in his examinations.

Usually, clients respond best when the worker has a patient attitude and encourages reasonable approximations toward goals. Approximations are small degrees of change in the desired direction. For example, a young gang member who wishes to get her high school diploma may need to identify all of the steps she needs to take toward that goal, and then concentrate on taking them one step at a time.

Sometimes, the most effective way to foster self-development is to practice *convalescence*. Many clients need to take sufficient time and rest to grow strong again. Any biopsychosociospiritual healing process may require a certain amount of time and rest before wellness can fully return. The amount of rest and time may vary from individual to individual, from family to family, and from culture to culture. For example, the length of bereavement over the loss of a loved one may vary, as may the length and extent of recovery from the experience of rape.

Although the literal meaning of convalescence is "to grow strong," today we reserve the use of the term primarily to refer to the care and maintenance of the very ill (as in a convalescent home for the aging). It was not that long ago, however, that people took the time to convalesce, to gradually grow strong and well, after a physical or psychosocial trauma. Now, most people have the expectation that most trauma can, and should be, cured quickly. For example, with the proliferation of antibiotic medications, workers and students are expected to take little (if any) time off. With the increased pressure to provide short-term treatment (or what some call "fast-food social work"), social workers are expected to cure their clients' psychosocial problems just as quickly. The most effective social worker resists such pressures in order to support each client's individual needs for true convalescence.

Evaluation. The fourth step involves the evaluation of progress so far, and future planning. The client and worker assess the client's successes and map out together the next developmental steps that lie ahead. Because an emphasis on accountability is a reality in most practice settings today, effective social workers are always looking for ways to demonstrate the outcomes of their interventions. The most effective evaluation process is client centered, strength oriented, and individualized.

Client-centered evaluation involves both client and social worker in the process of setting goals, tasks, and evaluation plans. The client is encouraged to participate to the degree that he is developmentally ready.

In strength-oriented evaluation, the worker emphasizes the strengths and successes of the client. The client's limitations are also reviewed honestly but are reframed as positively as possible, as future goals on which to focus.

Finally, evaluation is individualized when the worker considers the unique characteristics of the client and client/system, and resists pressure to use only certain standards when they do not fit a unique case. For example, in many practice settings, social workers are required to use particular *DSM-IV* diagnoses in assessment summaries. The effective social worker realizes that although such diagnoses may be useful in communicating about mental disorders, they are quite limited in describing client strengths and successes in the stewardship of herself and the client/system. The worker realizes that she needs to use additional language when evaluating social work practice. The client's success is measured not so much by the extent to which the system has changed, but by how the client's behaviors, attitudes, and feelings have expanded.

Stewardship of the Client System

All biopsychosociospiritual problems, including the most common concerns (i.e., those regarding intimacy, empowerment, openness to human relationships, and self-forgiveness[9]), involve both individual and collective factors. In other words, problems are more likely to be resolved when the client attends to the many factors in both the inner self and the outer world. Stewardship of the client/system means that, as the client works to develop himself, he also begins to take more responsibility for the well-being of others in the community and for the protection and enhancement of the natural ecosystem.

Community may include the client's closest associates, family members, individuals in support systems, and neighbors, as well as the housing, transportation systems, work settings, recreational facilities, and other human-made structures in the local and global communities. Most clients have at least some ability to care for other people in their community. For example, an 11-year-old boy might want to help his younger sister with her homework. A college student might volunteer to help rebuild a hiking path near the river in town. An 80-year-old woman might want to read to her neighbor who has lost his eyesight.

The natural ecosystem includes the land, water, and atmospheric systems, and the living things that share those systems with the human inhabitants. Most clients are at least somewhat aware of the natural ecosystem around them and are at least somewhat concerned about the health of that system. A grade school boy might write letters with his class to the governor, asking him to take a stand on an environmental issue. An adolescent girl might want to join a group of teens that plants trees in the inner city. A working mother might help raise funds for a new park to be constructed for young children and their mothers near her neighborhood.

Stewardship of the client/system also means that the client works with the social worker and others in developing social justice within the client/system. Social justice requires the ongoing co-responsibility for and co-creation of a community environment where all diverse members have equal access to opportunities, resources, status, and the power and freedom necessary to develop their full potential.

The effective social worker realizes that the individual well-being of any client is always related to the extent to which there is social justice in the local and global communities in which the client lives. Most clients can be helped to become more aware that any social justice issues can affect them directly; that when social justice for anyone is reduced, social justice for all community members is also threatened. When a client works for any social justice issue, the client is helping herself. When a client works against social justice, the client hurts himself.

A key assessment challenge in making social justice interventions is making an accurate appraisal of the level of social responsibility for which each client and client/system is developmentally ready. Every client is uniquely able to respond to the environmental conditions in which they find themselves. The worker therefore needs to avoid setting expectations for social responsibility that are either too low or too high.

Avoiding expectations that are too low. Each person needs to feel that he or she is successful at making a valuable contribution to family and community. Recognition of such contributions help people feel that they are successful. The worker will notice that many clients have never felt that they had anything of value to contribute to their family or communities. In many cases, the worker can help clients identify their unique gifts, stimulate their own empowerment, and increase their social responsibility.

For example, in a men's group, one very talented but depressed straight white male ("Bill") expressed hostility toward gay men. He told the group how he fired a gay man at his workplace. It turns out that one of the other men in the group ("Bob") is gay, and this second client tells Bill about his sexual preference. The group helps Bill to see how his attacks on gay men are, in part, an unsuccessful attempt to build himself up. Bill learns to respect Bob and eventually helps him get a job working at a company in town. In the group, Bob helps Bill get more in touch with his feelings.

Avoiding expectations that are too high. If the expectations for contributions to others is unrealistic (either because the client is developmentally unprepared or because the environment is too stressful or unfriendly), then the worker needs to help the client reduce those expectations to manageable levels.

Thus, for example, a worker is assigned to provide workfare services to an unemployed single mother. The client has four children and lives in a one-bedroom apartment. The worker recognizes that this mother is already stretched to her limit, not because of her personal developmental limitations but because of the many demands upon her time. She does not need to have additional social responsibilities at this time because she requires all of her energy to effectively mother her children. The worker is able to postpone the workfare deadlines for the mother so that she can have 12 extra months of services (to help better meet needs for income, child care, transportation, and housing) before she is required to work for income.

A second key assessment challenge in making social justice interventions is the discovery process that the client and worker go through to co-determine exactly what social justice is in each unique situation. Although the social work profession has a code of ethics, these guidelines are not extensive enough to guide decisions in all real-life situations. Usually, each worker and client has at least slightly different values about a given situation, and it is the worker's responsibility to facilitate an ongoing dialogue between the worker and clients about their values concerning social justice issues.

For example, a worker is facilitating a group of former welfare mothers who are meeting as "family experts" to help guide the training of future Child Protective Service (CPS) social workers. The group is discussing the problems that clients have in not being treated in a friendly manner by CPS workers. The worker realizes that the group has many different feelings about this issue, and she asks the group to take the time to discuss the issues involved. Eventually, several core suggestions emerge from the discussion on which everyone can agree.

The stewardship metaphor supports an inclusive, both/and approach to practice instead of the dualistic, either/or concepts of micro and macro practice. The specialty areas of micro- and macrolevel practice were perhaps necessary steps in the development of social work practice theory. The human mind tends to separate complex material into more easily digestible units, and social workers have separated practice into micro (clinical direct practice) and macro (administration, community planning) levels. However, as awareness of the ecological nature of practice has increased, social workers have realized that the micro, mezzo, and macro levels of practice are always interrelated.[10] Stewardship of the client/system thus includes the caretaking of all local and more global levels of that system.

Stewardship of the client's *local* client/system means that the client becomes a guardian of family, friends, co-workers, and local community and ecosystem. The client does not give up herself in taking on this responsibility, but rather strives to maintain an equilibrium, a symmetry of focus between the needs of the internal and external worlds. The client increasingly recognizes that, just as a muscle has to be exercised to grow, all developmental dimensions also need to be exercised in service to both self and others. The client is only responsible (able to respond) to the community and local environment to the extent that she is developmentally capable. Stewardship does not mean that the client owns the local community, but rather that the client is a temporary caretaker of that community.

Stewardship of the client's *global* client/system also means that the worker encourages the client to become a keeper of the broadest community/environment. As will be described further in Part IV, there are global-level factors associated with all biopsychosociospiritual problems on the individual, couple, family, and small group levels. There is evidence that people are healthier when they are able to do something to improve their environment (e.g., help clean up the local highway or contribute to an organization that is working to reduce the proliferation of nuclear weapons).[11] Stewardship also means that the client does not own the local or global community, but rather is a temporary caretaker of those communities. In this era of workfare, it is important to note that stewardship does not apply only to those who may need to receive welfare services, and who may be viewed by some as lazy. The healthiest community is one where all people (e.g., rich and poor, young and old) are participants in its welfare.

For example, a case of sexual abuse in a family in a small midwestern town may be associated with such large-scale social factors as the unequal distribution of wealth and power and Western attitudes toward children, women, and men.[12] The adult who was sexually victimized as a child may be further empowered by joining a study group on men's and women's issues and contributing to an organization committed to fighting oppression of women and children.

Thus, the process of fostering the client's stewardship of the environment includes several stages: (a) maximizing the client's awareness of his interdependence with community and environment; (b) preparing the client to interact more responsibly with community and environment at a reasonable level of individual and/or collective involvement; (c) fostering the client's commitment to developmentally appropriate stewardship of community and living environment; and (d) evaluating the client's awareness, responsibility, and balance in stewardship.

Maximizing the client's awareness of her interdependence with community and living environment. Each client has a unique relationship with community and environment. In our postmodern society, however, many clients are relatively unaware of the nature of that relationship. In our culture, we still tend to think of our community and environment as systems that are separate from us.

Social work, more than any other discipline, emphasizes ecological thinking. The social worker strives to help the client understand how the community and living environment interact with his life. As will be illustrated further in Part IV, social workers can often help clients to gain such awareness by giving them opportunities to be in and enjoy nature. Social workers also may encourage clients to provide meaningful service to others and to provide positive role models for community responsibility. For example, in working with a suburban adolescent, the social worker realizes that the young man feels that he has been ignored and abandoned by family and traditional institutions. He feels an affiliation only with his gang, but even that affiliation is characterized by fear and power rather than mutual acceptance and support of empowerment. The young man also seems quite alienated from his environment. He has an ambivalent attitude toward the city in which he lives. He views this environment as his territory, yet he does not feel the need to protect or enhance its beauty. He takes what he can get from his community and his environment and feels no responsibility to give anything back. The worker does not judge the young man (make him wrong) but also does not support his behavior and thinking. Instead, the worker strives to help him understand how his life is interconnected with his environment. The worker discovers that the young man wants to coach basketball and finds him a job opportunity to be mentored by a successful coach.

Preparing the client to begin to take more responsibility for community and living environment at a reasonable level of individual and/or collective involvement. Responsibility involves both individual and/or collective *response* and developmental and environmental *ability.*

Social workers recognize that clients cannot become responsible to the community and living environment until they feel and express their own heartfelt *response* (unique, personal passion) about their community and environment. Healthy responsibility is internal (comes from inside the person) rather than external (comes from an outside authority, such as a religious leader, politician, or author). The social worker strives to help clients (regardless of their age or diagnostic category) become more aware of how they really feel inside about their community and living environment. The client is asked with which aspect of community he is most motivated to work.

For example, a young woman living in a poor urban area tells the social worker, "I hate this neighborhood and all the hoodlums that live here!" The worker replies, "I don't blame you for feeling that way. If I were you, I would probably feel the same way you do . . . and want to do something about it." Or, a gang member in the same neighborhood tells his probation officer (a social worker) that he "used to want to be in college until I realized there was no way." The worker might reply, "You might not know that there is a scholarship and work-study program that you could apply for."

Often, as in the examples above, clients identify their passions by first alluding to what they are hurt and angry about; often, dreams seem to build upon the initial awareness of negative feelings. Generally, the worker strives first to help clients become more aware of what they do not like or want (their "no") and then more aware of what they do like or want (their "yes"). For example, the young woman mentioned above might eventually be able to describe the kind of community she would like to help co-create for herself and her future family: "I would like a neighborhood where people know each other and look out for each other. I would like a neighborhood where people of different races and religions live close together and respect each other's differences."

As emphasized above, effective involvement in community can be either collective or individual in focus.[13] Most clients will have their own personal preference for either individual or group involvement strategies. The social worker helps the client discover which kinds of involvement work best at any given time.

The client's *ability* to make behavioral changes often requires in part the development of new beliefs. As the client works toward improving community and environment, she may also need to develop hope and personal empowerment, as well as an alternative consciousness.

There are many potential obstacles to increasing social responsibility. Many clients are likely to feel discouraged and disempowered in their ability to make a difference in improving community and environment.[14] There may be

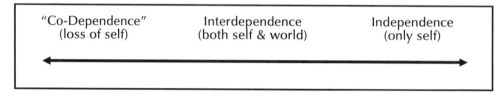

Figure 4.1.

political implications involved in encouraging clients to become more active in their communities, and social workers and their clients may become understandably afraid of angering politically powerful people.

The worker can help the client overcome such obstacles. As will be discussed further in Part IV, there are ways to affect even the largest, most global problems through small-sized interventions. The social worker may need to encourage and help empower the client. Community and environmental work requires, in part, a change in human consciousness, in the way we collectively think about ourselves and our postmodernist world.[15] In fact, human beings are some of the most adaptable animals on earth, and there is evidence that rapid social change is possible when human consciousness has shifted.[16] Social workers can help foster consciousness by teaching and modeling ecological awareness, critical thinking, and adaptability to change.

For example, the young woman mentioned above may still believe that there is nothing that can be done to change the way things are in her neighborhood. The social worker may choose to challenge and modify this way of thinking and help her brainstorm about her choices.

Fostering the client's commitment to stewardship of community and living environment. There is substantial evidence that commitment to a cause larger than the self is associated with increased mental and physical health.[17] In this context, commitment involves a pledge to work toward creating a healthy community and living environment. The most effective social workers encourage their clients to become committed stewards of their community and living environment.

The social worker strives to help the client keep this commitment in balance with the real demands and issues present in the client's life. Many clients may be already overextended in helping others. They may choose to take better care of their own needs before they can address larger issues. However, other clients are overinvolved in their own life dramas and may need to refocus more energy outside of themselves. Thus, there is a continuum of possible ways that the client can balance care for self and care for the world (see Figure 4.1). The most healthy or optimum position on the continuum is a middle position, where the client balances care for both herself and the world.

The social worker best fosters stewardship in the client by modeling stewardship. For example, the worker can become active in promoting social policies that help mitigate the kinds of problems that clients face. The worker might invite the participants in a support group to attend a community-organizing event with her or him. The worker could take two homeless parents to a town meeting or bring a children's group out to the park, where they pick up trash together. A social worker might have a delinquent adolescent client join in distributing Christmas gifts to children in the oncology unit at the local hospital.

Evaluating the client's awareness, responsibility, commitment, and balance in stewardship. The social worker works with the client to help evaluate progress in these areas. Again, the most effective evaluation process is client centered, strength oriented, and individualized.

Experiential Exercises

1. Consider a current challenge or problem in your own life (e.g., being in a graduate program, depression). How is this challenge or problem interrelated with the rest of your world? Describe how the collective well-being of your local and global communities may be interrelated with your challenge or problem.

2. Consider a current problem in your local or global community (e.g., pollution, inflation, war). How is this problem interrelated with your own life right now?

3. How do you see yourself as a steward of yourself, your immediate family or friends, your local community, and the global community? Describe the benefits and costs of this stewardship. Describe how you might overcome any internal (e.g., fear, limited time, energy) and external (e.g., distance, mistrust) obstacles to your stewardship.

4. How well balanced are your own commitments to self and to your community at this point in your life?

CHAPTER 5

The Inclusive Toolbox

Developing All of the Tools for the Job

An inclusive strategy uses the universe of available interventions, which may be divided into seven interrelated direct practice paradigms: the Four Forces[18] of psychology—psychodynamic, cognitive/behavioral/communications, experiential/humanistic/existential, and transpersonal[19]—as well as case management,[20] biopsychosocial,[21] and local[22] and global[23] community. Each of these practice paradigms employs individual-, couple-, family-, and group-level interventions. All of these paradigms are described in more depth in Parts III and IV.

Reciprocal connectiveness exists between the paradigms; each paradigm deals with parts of a greater whole. The First Force, psychodynamic theory, emphasizes increasing client insight into past events and related internal dynamics. The Second Force, cognitive/behavioral/communications theory, emphasizes changing the way clients think and act in the here and now. The Third Force, experiential/humanistic/existential theory, highlights the client's awareness of and responsibility for feelings and experiences as he grows in the here and now. The Fourth Force, transpersonal theory, emphasizes the individual's spiritual development. Case management stresses the linking of the client to informal and formal networks of support in the client/system. Biopsychosocial theory features the enhancement of the client's care for her body. Finally, local community work emphasizes the stewardship of the local community and ecosystem, and global community work emphasizes the enhancement of global consciousness and perspective (spiritual connectiveness) in the client.

All five dimensions of development can be fostered through the use of interventions drawn from any one of the seven practice paradigms. However, each paradigm especially emphasizes work with one or two specific dimensions of human development (see Table 5.1). Thus, spiritual development is empha-

TABLE 5.1: Developmental Dimensions Most Emphasized in Each of the Practice Paradigms

Practice Paradigm	Developmental Dimensions
Psychodynamic	Cognitive social
Cognitive/behavioral/communications	Cognitive social
Experiential/humanistic/existential	Affective
Transpersonal	Spiritual
Case management	Social
Biopsychosocial	Physical
Local and global community	Social spiritual

sized in the Fourth Force (transpersonal) and community paradigms. Cognitive development is emphasized in the Second Force (cognitive/behavioral/communications) and First Force (psychodynamic) paradigms. Social development is emphasized in the First Force, Second Force, case management, and community paradigms. Physical development is emphasized in the biopsychosocial paradigm. Affective development is emphasized in the Third Force (experiential/humanistic/existential) paradigm.

The inclusion of all of these paradigms in advanced generalist practice is consistent with ecological theory and social work's person-in-environment perspective.[24] Because every human problem is related to many intrapsychic, interpsychic, and other environmental factors (see Part I), the most effective intervention strategies must be flexible enough to target any of those factors. For example, one depressed woman may respond to a strategy that includes aerobic exercise (biopsychosocial), replacement of thinking errors (Second Force), Gestalt group work (Third Force), referral to a career counselor (case management), and meditation (Fourth Force).

In addition, the many factors in the ecology of a case are always interrelated. Research supports the notion of reciprocal connectiveness of the paradigms; there is increasing evidence that each characteristic in the client and client/system is related to all other characteristics. For example, "research has documented . . . that knowing and experiencing processes are influenced by some of the same things mainstream cognitive science has systematically ignored (such as feelings, mood, context, culture, and history)" (p. 67).[25]

Inclusiveness maximizes *choice:* The worker and client can select from any or all of the interventions currently available. The inclusive intervention strategy is consistent with the postmodernist perspective that there is no one Truth that describes reality. The inclusive intervention strategy is consistent with generalist social work and eclectic theory, which suggests that the most effective helping strategies must draw upon the full spectrum of available models. Choice is no longer limited by either/or positions, which overemphasize the usefulness of some interventions and minimize the usefulness of others. Choice will, however, always be limited by other factors, including worker/system characteristics (e.g., training, experience, agency rules) and client/system characteristics (e.g., motivation, opportunity).

Because clients are multidimensional beings, they require multidimensional interventions that include many strategies of change. An exclusive overemphasis on any one of the seven paradigms can be potentially harmful to clients. Inclusive intervention assumes that any paradigm that the worker uses is always part of a larger practice picture.

For example, intervention that is focused on symptom reduction without structural (personality) change (or vice versa) may be harmful to a client population. As described in Part V, the emphases that currently exist in general social work practice are on cognitive-behavioral goals, application of technique, and short-term treatment. These emphases are most likely to be effective when they are part of a larger practice framework that also includes the potential for longer treatment using the other goals and interventions as differentially required. The inclusive intervention strategy reflects changes occurring in the way postmodern professionals view human change:

> There are many indications that we are now in the midst of sweeping conceptual shifts that mark a clear turning point in the history of human understanding. . . . The discipline of psychology has already moved through a conceptual spiral remarkably similar to that exhibited in the overall history of ideas . . . from an initial focus on the inner person, through a long period of exclusive focus on ostensibly external factors (behavior-environment relations) and then to a more distributed balance that still leans toward the insides of the organism (as in the cognitive revolution and the modern resurgence of phenomenology). (pp. 48-49)[26]

Evidence exists that there is currently more convergence than divergence of opinion between professionals who represent the different models. In their review, Saltzman and Norcross[27] found much more consensus than contention between psychotherapists, particularly in three key content areas: patient characteristics, therapeutic relationships, and clinical strategies. They also noted that more research is needed to demonstrate the process of integrating the various models, as well as the outcomes of such integrative approaches: "Clinicians and researchers both have critical roles to play in documenting the applicability and efficacy of integrative models of practice" (p. 249).

An inclusive approach to practice is not universally supported. As they prepare to take licensing examinations, many social workers are still warned to avoid using an eclectic theoretical base in front of their board. Instead, they are often encouraged to formulate an orientation based on the work of a well-known therapist, such as Rogers, Satir, or Ellis, or on an established framework, such as ego, structural, or cognitive psychology. Eclectic workers

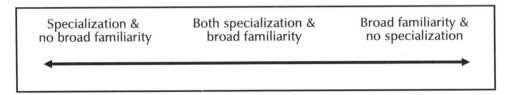

Figure 5.1.

are sometimes characterized negatively as renaissance workers and viewed with suspicion as "jacks of all trades and masters of none."

However, the social worker's effectiveness is limited when she develops either specialization without broad familiarity or broad familiarity without specialization. Specialization without broad familiarity may lead to the application of one model in cases where the model is not useful to the client/system. Broad familiarity without any specialization may lead to an incomplete application of models in cases that require more in-depth skill and knowledge. The alternative to these exclusive positions is the inclusive, both/and position, which involves the gradual incorporation of in-depth specialty areas within a continuing context of broad familiarity (see continuum in Figure 5.1).

Current adult learning theory supports the use of an inclusive intervention strategy, suggesting that most professionals learn most effectively from a top-down or whole-to-part strategy.[28] This strategy suggests that social workers first develop a broad but simplified understanding of the many existing intervention models. As time goes on, each worker develops a more in-depth understanding of one or more practice paradigms. Gradually, workers will identify and study intervention models that (a) fit who they are, (b) seem to be effective with the populations with which they work, and (c) are appropriate in the practice setting in which they work. Although few, if any, professionals are equally familiar and comfortable with every model, most can gradually incorporate more interventions into their practice throughout their professional development.

Seven Paradigms for Direct Social Work Practice

In this section, selected models from each of the paradigms of practice are briefly introduced and referenced for further study. In Parts III and IV, key interventions from each of the paradigms are detailed. The models are introduced here to faciliate the reader's top-down, whole-to-part learning.

In each of the four practice modes (individual, group, couple, and family work), a therapist can use models drawn from one or more of the Four Forces of psychology (Tables 5.2-5.5); from case management and biopsychosocial theory (Table 5.6); or from the local community and global community paradigms (Table 5.7). Each model considers one or more of the dimensions

TABLE 5.2: Four Forces of Psychology and Practice With Individuals

Four Forces	Selected Models
1. Psychodynamic	1. Freudian[30]
	2. Jungian[31]
	3. Adlerian[32]
	4. Transactional analysis[33]
	5. Object relations[34]
	6. Self psychology[35]
2. Cognitive/behavioral/communications	7. Paradoxical[36]
	8. Rational emotive[37]
	9. Reality therapy[38]
	10. Cognitive therapy[39]
3. Experiential/humanistic/existential	11. Client centered[40]
	12. Gestalt[41]
	13. Peoplemaking[42]
4. Transpersonal	14. Hendricks and Weinhold[43]

of human development and may draw upon theory and interventions from other models. For example, although rational emotive therapy[29] (or RET, Table 5.2) emphasizes work in the cognitive dimension of development, the approach also considers affective and interpersonal development, and it uses interventions consistent with both Second and Third Force psychology.

Tables 5.2 through 5.5 contain practice models drawn from the four Forces of psychology. They are similar because each of the Four Forces can be used in social work with individuals, groups, couples, and families. Table 5.2 shows selected models of theory and intervention for practice with individuals. Table 5.3 describes selected group work models, Table 5.4 has selected couple work models, and Table 5.5 has selected family therapy models. Table 5.6 provides an outline of some selected case management and biopsychosocial models. Table 5.7 describes selected models of the local and global community paradigm.

Social Work Practice With Individuals

Interventions drawn from the models described in Table 5.2 can all be used with individual clients. Key interventions from each paradigm are described in detail in Parts III and IV. A very brief description of some key differences between the models follows.

Psychodynamic models with individuals. The Freudian, or psychoanalytic, model uses such techniques as free association and interpretation to help clients resolve internal conflicts that arose in their early psychosexual stages of development. The Jungian model emphasizes the archetypal aspects of internal dynamics and consciousness, whereas Adlerian psychology broadened the client's review of the past to include the impact of siblings and other life experiences. Transactional analysis provides a convenient mechanism for working with the ego states of consciousness (parent, adult, and child). Object relations offers a well-developed theory of how the client's patterns of intimate relating developed. Self-psychology uses empathic interventions to help clients understand and modify their relationship patterns.

Cognitive/behavioral/communications models with individuals. Paradoxical interventions essentially prescribe the client's symptom in order to help the client let go of that symptom. Rational emotive therapy helps clients change their thinking in order to help them relieve difficult emotions and change unwanted behaviors. Reality therapy emphasizes the consequences of behaviors. Cognitive work focuses on changing the underlying beliefs that are associated with the client's problems.

Experiential/humanistic/existential models with individuals. Client-centered interventions are nondirective; the worker offers empathy, warmth, and genuineness to the client. Gestalt interventions are more directive, and the worker strives to help the client own and express all of his "parts." The people-making approach uses a blend of techniques to help foster effective communication and client growth.

Transpersonal models with individuals. Hendricks and Weinhold offered one theoretical framework of transpersonal practice. There are currently fewer models of practice in the transpersonal paradigm than in the other three forces of psychology, although widespread and growing public interest in these areas will probably stimulate further model development.

Social Work Practice With Groups

Psychodynamic models with groups. The Freudian, or psychoanalytic, model tends to use individual techniques within a group context to help clients resolve internal conflicts that arose in their early psychosexual stages of development. Adlerian groups offer clients opportunities to uncover the impact that such past experiences as birth order had on their lives. Transactional analysis can be used in group settings to help clients understand and modify the way they relate with others from their own ego states (i.e., the inner child, adult, and parent).

Cognitive/behavioral/communications models with groups. Paradoxical interventions use indirect methods to help relieve symptoms. Cognitive interventions challenge and replace thinking errors to relieve symptoms. Behavioral approaches

TABLE 5.3: Four Forces of Psychology and Practice With Groups

Four Forces	*Group Work Models*[a]
1. Psychodynamic	1. Psychoanalytic[a]
	2. Transactional[a]
	3. Adlerian[a]
2. Cognitive/behavioral/communications	4. Paradoxical[a]
	5. Cognitive[a]
	6. Behavioral[a]
	7. Reality therapy[a]
	8. Rational emotive[a]
3. Experiential/humanistic/existential	9. Client centered[a]
	10. Psychodrama[a]
	11. Gestalt[a]
4. Transpersonal	11. Process oriented[44]

a. Identified by Corey.[45]

help clients develop, maintain, and generalize new behaviors. Reality therapy is used to help group members take responsibility for the consequences of their behaviors. Rational emotive therapy is used to help clients change their thinking in order to help them relieve difficult emotions and change unwanted behaviors.

Experiential/humanistic/existential models with groups. In client-centered groups, the worker is nondirective but offers the core conditions of growth (empathy, warmth, and genuineness). In a psychodrama intervention, group members act out internal experiences and life events. Gestalt interventions may involve the use of empty chairs, which group members use to express different parts of themselves to each other.

Transpersonal models with groups. Process-oriented psychology provides a theoretical framework for thinking about spiritual development. There are currently fewer models of practice in the transpersonal paradigm than in the other three forces of psychology.

Social Work Practice With Couples

Psychodynamic models with couples. The classical psychoanalytic model uses individual techniques within the couple-work context to help clients resolve internal conflicts that arose in their early psychosexual stages of development. Object relations theory offers a way to understand how clients developed their

TABLE 5.4: Four Forces of Psychology and Practice With Couples

Four Forces	Couple Work Models
1. Psychodynamic	1. Classical psychoanalytic[a]
	2. Object relations[a]
	3. Self-psychology[a]
2. Cognitive/behavioral/communications	4. Cognitive/behavioral[a]
	5. Strategic[a]
	6. Structural[a]
	7. Systemic[a]
3. Experiential/humanistic/existential	8. Client centered[46]
	9. Gestalt[47]
4. Transpersonal	10. Hendricks and Weinhold[48]

a. Identified by Sperry and Carlson.[49]

patterns of intimate relationships. Self-psychology interventions are empathic and may help clients "walk in the shoes" of their partners.

Cognitive/behavioral/communications models with couples. Cognitive behavioral interventions challenge and replace thinking errors in each partner and then support the development of new behaviors that would strengthen the relationship. Strategic interventions use strategies to help clients change the way they act with each other. Structural interventions focus upon changing the boundaries (structures) in the relationship so that the couple can become either less enmeshed or disengaged with each other. Systemic work helps the clients view their relationship problems from a systems theory perspective.

Experiential/humanistic/existential models with couples. In client-centered work with couples, the worker offers the core conditions of growth (empathy, warmth, and genuineness) and helps the partners attend to each other. In a Gestalt approach, the worker is more directive and encourages honest feedback and communication in the relationship.

Transpersonal models with couples. Hendricks and Weinhold offer a theory of intervention that includes the fostering of spiritual development in practice. There are currently fewer models of practice in the transpersonal paradigm than in the other three forces of psychology. Examples of transpersonal couple work are provided in Part III of this book.

TABLE 5.5: Four Forces of Psychology and Practice With Families

Four Forces	*Family Work Models*
1. Psychodynamic	1. Psychoanalytic[a]
	2. Group[a]
2. Cognitive/behavioral/communications	3. Behavioral[a]
	4. Communications[a]
	5. Strategic[a]
	6. Structural[a]
3. Experiential/humanistic/existential	7. Experiential[a]
4. Transpersonal	8. Hendricks and Weinhold[50]

a. Identified by Nichols.[51]

Social Work Practice With Families

Psychodynamic models with families. Psychoanalytic interventions with families use individual techniques with parents and children to help them resolve internal conflicts and develop healthier family relations. The group model is an early model of family intervention that also used psychodynamic techniques.

Cognitive/behavioral/communications models with families. Behavioral family therapy uses behavior modification techniques to change the behaviors of targeted family members. Communications family therapy assists parents and children to become more aware of and improve their communication patterns. In strategic family therapy, the worker uses strategies of change, such as paradoxical and reframing techniques, to change behaviors. Structural family therapy attempts to modify the boundaries, coalitions, and other family structures to promote behavioral change.

Experiential/humanistic/existential models with families. Experiential family therapy focuses on helping family members become more aware of and express their emotions. The worker models effective listening and provides the core conditions of growth (empathy, warmth, and genuineness).

Transpersonal models with families. Hendricks and Weinhold provide a theoretical framework of practice that can be used to support the spiritual development of family members. There are currently fewer models of practice in the transpersonal paradigm than in the other three forces of psychology. Additional examples of transpersonal family work are provided in Part III of this book.

Case Management Models

System linkages are the worker's efforts to connect clients with services, resources, and opportunities in the community. Environmental structuring

TABLE 5.6: Case Management and Biopsychosocial Paradigms of Practice With Individuals, Couples, Families, and Groups

Practice Theories	*Practice Models*
5. Case management[52]	System linkages
	Environmental structuring
	Coaching[53]
6. Biopsychosocial[54]	
	Psychopharmacology
	Diet
	Exercise
	Bodywork
	Relaxation/stress reduction

involves the worker's attempts to modify the client/system (e.g., housing, employment, school). Coaching includes the provision of encouragement and the teaching of social skills by the worker.

Biopsychosocial Models

Psychopharmacology involves the use of medication, prescribed by a physician, to relieve unwanted symptoms. Diet and exercise may help clients improve mental and physical health. A variety of bodywork interventions may be used to help clients become more aware of their bodies and to help move body energy. Relaxation and other stress reduction techniques can help clients recover from trauma and improve their physical and mental health.

Local and Global Community Models

Community development involves the organization of clients to act to improve the community in which they live. Community social work empha- sizes the empowerment of individual clients and collective community change. Community making is the organization of clients to act to create new commu- nities that will better meet their needs. In this book, individual-, couple-, family-, and group-level interventions that help enhance healthy community development will be considered. In this book, I will introduce "community stewardship," in which the client and worker strive toward fostering commu- nity well-being.

Deep ecology provides theory on the interconnection between the indi- vidual's well-being and the well-being of the natural ecosystem. Transpersonal ecology emphasizes the relationship between individual spiritual development and the individual's connection with the natural ecosystem. Global family

TABLE 5.7: Local and Global Community Paradigm

Practice Theory	*Practice Models*
7. Local community paradigm	Community development[55]
	Community social work[56]
	Community making[57]
	Community stewardship
	Deep ecology[58]
	Transpersonal ecology[59]
	Global family therapy[60]
	Personal power[61]
	Global consciousness

therapy provides theory on how family therapy methods may be used to help resolve global problems and how global problems may be considered in family therapy. Personal power refers to theory that links individual empowerment and hope with the global threat of nuclear war. In this book, I will introduce "global consciousness," in which the client and worker view and deal with problems and challenges from not only a global perspective, but also from the perspective of universal time and space.

Most social workers now recognize that an orthodox or fundamentalist approach to practice (which uses only one approach for all client situations) is quite limited and less effective, given the increasingly complex and varied problems and challenges encountered in postmodernist society: "One of the major challenges facing modern psychology is to move beyond such self-handicapping internal schisms and paradigm rivalries. . . . I do not believe such a movement requires the elimination of diversity in psychological theory and practice" (pp. 61-63).[62]

Experiential Exercises

1. Based upon what you have read, to which of the seven paradigms of practice are you personally most attracted at this point in your own professional development? Why do you think this paradigm(s) is particularly attractive to you? Which paradigm would seem most likely to help you if you were the client? Is it the same one you identified above?

2. To which of the paradigms are you least attracted? Why do you think these paradigms are particularly unattractive to you? Consider which paradigm would seem most unlikely to help you if you were the client.

3. If your goal was to become proficient at using all seven paradigms, how would you strive to achieve this goal? What do you see as primary obstacles to this goal? How might you eventually overcome them?

CHAPTER 6

Differential Eclectic Practice

Differential eclectic practice uses interventions drawn from all seven paradigms of inclusive practice, across all of the modes of intervention. The modes of intervention include individual, couple, family, small group, and large group. It is hoped that the interventions that are chosen reflect the specific elements of diversity present in each unique client/system. Thus, differential eclectic interventions are both selective and integrative.

Selective means discriminating and particular; the social worker chooses interventions that fit the unique and ever-changing requirements of each practice situation. Specifically, the effort is to determine "*what* treatment, by *whom*, is most effective for *this* individual with *that* specific problem, and under *which* set of circumstances" (p. 118).[63]

There are three elements of selective social work practice. The first element of selective practice is that the worker chooses the intervention(s) that best fits (a) the client system,[64] (b) the helping process,[65] and (c) the social worker system.

The *client system* includes the unique developmental dimensions of the client(s) as well as the other environmental factors (e.g., family, culture, natural environment) that the worker considers when making an ecological assessment of the case. Wilber's[66] model of development of consciousness suggests that clients who have "prepersonal" disorders of development often respond best to structured, Second Force, and case management interventions. Clients with "personal" disorders may also respond to uncovering work from the First and Second Forces. Finally, clients with "transpersonal" disorders may respond best to Fourth Force interventions.

The *helping process* refers to exactly where the client and worker are in the beginning, middle, and ending phases of the work. In the beginning phase, for example, a worker may find that many high-functioning clients respond well to a humanistic (Third Force) approach, in which the worker is genuine, warm, empathic, and relatively nondirective and unstructured. Case management interventions may also be used to assist clients with immediate and practical needs.

During the middle phase, the worker may also draw from First Force interventions to build deep insight, as well as from Second Force interventions, which tend to help the client change thoughts and behaviors. Community-level interventions may help the client reconnect with her environment during the middle phase.

During the ending phase, the worker may use Third Force interventions to assist the client with the feelings of termination, as well as case management interventions in facilitating referrals and follow-up work.

The *social worker system* includes the characteristics of the worker(s) involved in the case, as well as of the practice location. Some practice locations emphasize or even mandate the use of particular assessment and intervention strategies. Because each worker has unique strengths and interests, it makes sense for her to use those strengths and interests in her practice, unless they bring harm to her clients.

For example, a worker who is especially comfortable and skilled in Gestalt therapy may use Gestalt techniques with clients who may benefit from them. In another example, social workers who are asked by their agencies to use short-term treatment models may tend to draw upon Second Force, cognitive-behavioral interventions, which tend to be simple and require less time than First, Third, and Fourth Force interventions.

A second element of selective practice is that the worker chooses the blend of both art and science of practice that best fits the unique needs of each case. The science of social work practice includes the use of interventions supported by scientific method, study, or practice and may include related concepts, precepts, ethical principles, theoretical orientations, and practice models. Artistic factors in social work include the use of intuition, relationship, creativity, energy, judgment, and personal style.[67]

The science of practice is still emphasized in the social work literature, although most social work practitioners realize that the artistic factors are equally important:

> An age of superstitions is a time when people imagine that they know more than they do. In this sense, the twentieth century was certainly an outstanding age of superstition, and the cause of this is an overestimation of what science has achieved—not in the field of comparatively simple phenomena, where it has, of course, been extraordinarily successful, but in the field of complex phenomena, where the application of the techniques which prove so helpful with essentially simple phenomena has proved to be very misleading. (p. 176)[68]

Integrative means that the worker usually consolidates many different interventions in his practice. A growing majority of professional helpers use an eclectic strategy, in which they carefully integrate a variety of clinical approaches in their practice. These helpers find that the use of multiple approaches with the same client/system is usually more effective than the exclusive use of only one approach.[69]

Multiple approaches may be used across various time spans, ranging from one 30-minute session to a case lasting years. Some modes are quite complementary to each other and can often be used in concert. For example, a worker is seeing a 40-year-old man who was sexually traumatized as a young boy by his mother. In one session, the worker may ask the man to first reflect on a specific event that occurred when the man was 12 years old (First Force intervention). Then, the worker may ask the client to process the angry and sad feelings he has about this past traumatic event (Third Force). Finally, the worker may suggest new ways of thinking and acting (e.g., "I can recover from this molestation" and "I will be more assertive with my girlfriend") that the client can implement the next week (Second Force).

Multiple approaches may also be multimodal (i.e., use individual-, couple-, family-, group-, and/or community-level interventions). For example, a family is referred to a clinic by the local police after the father is arrested for domestic violence. The workers at the agency determine that the father could benefit from both individual treatment at the clinic and from a men's group on violence at a local church. The mother is referred to the local YWCA for a battered women's group. The two adolescent children are seen individually. Finally, marital and family therapy is initiated only after the cycle of violence has been stopped.

A third element of selective work is what could be called "mid-course corrections." The worker constantly strives to adjust to and even anticipate the changing needs of the client and changing conditions in the client/system. Regardless of whether the case is short term or of longer duration, as problems and challenges are dealt with, the client, couple, family, or group often presents with new problems and challenges.

For example, a social worker may begin working with a man who initially complains of depression. The worker focuses initially on helping the client realize that his depression is related to unhappiness about his marriage and job. After 3 months, the man decides to separate from his wife. In response, the worker changes the focus of their work to helping the man deal with his newly emerging economic, legal, and emotional needs. The focus of the work shifts again in another month as the client's mother is diagnosed with cancer. His mother's illness reactivates the client's memories of loneliness and neglect in his own childhood that are parallel with memories he had of his marriage. The focus of the work shifts again to an analysis of the client's psychosocial history.

Linking the Seven Paradigms to the Developmental Dimensions

In eclectic practice, the social worker differentially selects intervention strategies from each of the seven paradigms of practice that are likely to help further client and client/system development. In Parts I and V, the five dimensions of human development are described in detail. Table 6.1 provides a summary of key intervention strategies that might be used in each paradigm of practice and across the five dimensions of development.

Experiential Exercises

1. Describe the process that you seem to use when you select methods of intervention with clients. To what extent is this process artistic, and to what extent is it scientific? Describe why you think you prefer either the art or science of practice. How could you better use a blend of both art and science in selecting interventions?

2. Why do you think that increasing numbers of social workers are using an eclectic approach to their practice today? How do you feel about the eclectic philosophy? Why?

TABLE 6.1: Key Intervention Strategies for Each Development Dimension by Paradigm

Paradigm	*Developmental Dimension*				
	Emotional	*Spiritual*	*Physical*	*Social*	*Cognitive*
First Force	Uncovering of repressed feelings	Do spiritual history	Uncover physical trauma	Understand history of love[a]	Insight into past patterns and internal dynamics[a]
Second Force	Modify cognitive antecedents to emotions	Challenge thinking errors about soul and world	Modify beliefs about body	Dialoging, problem-solving, and assertiveness skills[a]	Identify and replace thinking errors[a]
Third Force	Awareness and expression of feelings[a]	Awareness of feelings about soul and universe	Express emotions through movement	Develop emotional intimacy	Awareness of feelings about beliefs
Fourth Force	Social worker works on personal emotional shadow	Foster spiritual development[a]	Develop body-mind-spirit connection	Develop spiritual intimacy	Create more helpful myths about universe
Case management	Refer client to growth experiences	Connect client with religious group	Refer to services that provide basic needs	Teach client how to use resources[a]	Refer to educational resources
Biopsychosocial	Locate and express feelings in body	Circle dance to make connection	Practice bodywork, suggest exercise[a]	Develop sexual intimacy	Create more positive body image
Local community	Process feelings about self in community	Community dialogues between diverse traditions	Create community recreation programs	Develop skills that support community[a]	Community support for improved education
Global community	Process feelings about self in universe	Develop connectedness with universe[a]	Relate to ecosystem with body	Enhance connectiveness with humanity and the earth	Reframe excessive wealth and power as immoral

a. This developmental dimension particularly emphasized in paradigm.

CHAPTER 7

The Helping Relationship
Integrity, Use of Self, Reciprocity, Mutuality, and Multidimensionality

As described in earlier sections, there is substantial evidence that the helping relationship between the worker(s) and client(s) is the most important factor related to success in practice. Most clients attribute their progress to the quality of the relationship they have with their professional helper.[70]

In addition, "the existing literature is consistent in its suggestions that therapeutic techniques and theoretical orientations are much less powerful predictors of change than are client and therapist characteristics . . . combined with the quality of the human relationship that they develop" (p. 314).[71] The effective helping relationship begins with the social worker's integrity; uses conscious use of self; and is reciprocal, mutual, and multidimensional.

When the worker brings *integrity* to the helping relationship, she practices with wholeness, with her whole self. The worker with integrity recognizes and accepts all of her parts (including the developmental dimensions) and acts in congruence (harmony) with those parts.

The advanced generalist social worker may integrate many methods of assessment and intervention into practice but never loses sight of the central importance of integrity. Because every social worker is unique, each social worker eventually develops his own unique style of practice. Like any process of development, the social worker's development of a personal style of integrity may well take many twists and turns as the worker has varied personal, educational, and professional experiences. The worker may choose to try various aspects of practice that he may learn about from books, mentors, and other sources. Some of these are integrated into personal style, whereas others are discarded. Gradually, a style develops, although minor modifications may continue across the professional life span.

Conscious use of self (see Parts I and V) in the effective helping relationship means the use of all interrelated aspects of self, including the worker's own personality and spirit. When the worker is thus authentic or genuine, the helping process becomes more effective. This is because the worker is modeling an example of self-awareness, acceptance, and creative expression for the client to follow.

The worker is aware and accepting of his personality, which may be conceptualized here as the mask that every worker wears in social relationships. Although the worker realizes that she is more than just a personality, the worker also realizes that the personality is an important tool to use in the helping relationship. When the worker relates from personality, the worker enjoys her own mask and plays that role in company with the client. The worker's authentic expressions of personality may help the client feel more comfortable with his own personality. For example, a female Adult Protective Services worker goes out to visit an older man who has been depressed following the death of his wife. The client happened to be watching a football game on television. The worker happens to be a football fan herself, and she sits down on the couch and cheers on the home team. They talk about the various teams in the league. The worker consciously uses her interest in football as an aspect of personality that helps her relate with the client. The worker also continues to strive to develop her own personality in all of the dimensions (e.g., to become more effective in work and more capable of recreation, intimacy, self-care, and responsibility to others).

The worker is aware and accepting of his spirituality, which may be conceptualized here as that aspect of self that seeks connection with the innermost self and the universe. Because spirituality provides an integrating function, it is often expressed through activities that link body, mind, spirit, and environment. The interconnection of human events with everything else in our universe is supported by the chaos theory of postmodern physics, which suggests that human change is often nonlinear, cannot be predicted by deterministic models, and can result in unexpected connections.[72]

For example, a school social worker is running a support group for grade school children whose parents are in dysfunctional marriages. In one session, the social worker plays some popular music and starts to drum and then dance. He invites the children to participate. The worker soon has the children all interacting together in a circle. In another example, a worker leading a women's growth group might have her clients lay on the grass outside in a circle. The worker might begin by showing the clients a drawing she made of how she relates with the earth. Then, she provides art supplies to the group so that they can also draw pictures as they wish. The worker also strives to develop her connection with and expressions of soul in her everyday life.

In other examples, before or after each session, a social worker might choose to silently pray for her clients. Or, a worker might focus on projecting loving energy toward the client during a session. The worker also strives to continue to develop his connection with and expressions of spirit in everyday life.

In a reciprocal relationship, the client and worker share co-responsibility for the work process. The worker also fosters what Satir[73] called a horizontal relationship with the client, in which the worker and client view themselves as essentially equals who are working together for the good of the client/system. In addition, the worker and client co-create the practice goals, objectives, and tasks (to the extent that they are developmentally able to do so):

> Clients have a right (indeed responsibility) to express their preferences in terms of which concerns are most important to them at that time and what their hopes and expectations are regarding the services they will receive. . . . Some individuals want reassurance and encouragement. Some want assessments, diagnoses, or explicit training in coping skills. Most seek some form of self-understanding . . . and many are interested in self-exploration. . . . [The helper] respects those desires, is flexible enough to deal with a wide range of them and to adjust his or her services to each client's current concerns, and is professional enough to refer clients elsewhere when referral is in their best interest. (p. 208)[74]

In a reciprocal relationship, the worker shows the client not only personal strengths, but also her personal limitations. The client does not need a perfect social worker, but the client does need a social worker to be aware and accepting of his own imperfections. This is because the client is also imperfect and needs a model of how to relate to those imperfections in a healthy way (e.g., with awareness and acceptance).

In a *mutual* relationship, the social worker fosters an attitude of bilateral respect and trust between worker and client. The worker gives the client an opportunity to model and practice mutuality within the helping relationship so that the client can eventually generalize mutuality in the client system. For example, a social worker might first help a client define and develop mutual respect and trust in the helping relationship, and then encourage her or him to develop those same elements of mutuality in other relationships within the family or community.

A mutual relationship is thus a small community of diversity, inasmuch as interdependence and confirmation of otherness[75] are practiced between members. Interdependence means that both worker and client recognize that the welfare of all people is interconnected. Confirmation of otherness means that every person affirms the unique characteristics and value of herself and others.

In a multidimensional relationship, interactions may occur on all of the dimensions of human development. The worker has integrity, which means he is a whole person who is open to relating with the client on the affective, cognitive, spiritual, physical, and social dimensions of development. The worker does not force relating on any level upon the client, because every client has a different set of developmental strengths and limitations. However, the worker strives to be prepared to deal with any dimension that may facilitate the helping process.

The worker models integrity for the client to support the client's own development of increased integrity. Thus, in the multidimensional relationship, the goal is not so much to help the client change but to help the client move toward healing or "wholing" (or having all of her parts). As she goes through the inevitable losses in life, the client strives to not lose her parts, but rather becomes more of herself. The client works to integrate all dimensions of development:

The affective dimension is a vital element in the helping relationship. Our emotions are what move us:

> There are . . . no more important communications between one human being and another than those expressed emotionally, and no information more vital for constructing and reconstructing working models of self other than information about how each feels about the other . . . during the course of psychotherapy. . . . It is the emotional communications between a patient and . . . therapist that play the crucial part. (pp. 156-157)[76]

Many clients are comfortable relating on the cognitive dimension. For that reason, social workers often begin casework sessions with simple cognitive relating. For example, the social worker may discuss what depression is with an intelligent client before attempting to get into the spiritual or emotional aspects of depression. To be effective on the cognitive level, the social worker does not have to be brilliant but does need to be capable of listening and learning, and must be willing to do so.

Some clients may be very comfortable relating on the spiritual dimension. Such relating often includes talking about the meaning that the client gives to both everyday experiences and life in general. As when working in any other dimension, the social worker is careful to honor the diversity of spiritual paths, beliefs, and related rituals that will be encountered in client populations.

Some clients need to relate on the physical dimension, at least initially. For example, a worker may be seeing a 10-year-old boy who has been labeled as having attention deficit disorder by his school teacher. It turns out that the boy is very kinesthetic and enjoys most sports. On the first session, the worker wisely takes the boy outside and shoots some baskets with him on the court across the street from the clinic.

The social dimension can also be a useful vehicle for the helping relationship. Some clients, for example, feel safest in a group situation. The social worker may want to see such clients in group therapy sessions when possible. Worker who are skilled at small talk may find it useful to help some clients initially relax by engaging them in such communications.

Experiential Exercises

1. How were you taught to define integrity? How is it different from the definition used in this chapter? How do you feel about applying either definition to social work practice?

2. If you were a client, would you prefer that your social worker was reciprocal or not reciprocal (i.e., preferred to take all responsibility for the outcome)? Why?

3. As a client, on what developmental dimensions would you prefer to be related by your worker? Do you tend to relate with clients on these same dimensions? How might you expand the dimensions that you use to relate?

CHAPTER 8

Ethics as Love, Connection, Awareness, Nonabusiveness, and Justice

In an ethical helping relationship, the social worker is loving, connective, nonabusive, and committed to social justice.

Loving means that the social worker cares about the welfare of the client and client/system. A loving attitude is inclusive; all of the client's parts are accepted. It has become unfashionable to talk about love in the context of professional social work. Perhaps this reluctance speaks more to the need of social workers to protect themselves than the need to protect their clients. When a worker is loving, he is certainly more vulnerable to emotional pain than when he closes off his heart. However, when a worker is loving, she also becomes more effective; without love, the intervention techniques employed by the worker are empty therapeutic rituals: "Techniques per se are inert unless they form an integral part of the therapist as a person" (p. 314).[77] The client needs to know that the worker cares about her.

Love for the client includes the elements of commitment, intimacy, awareness, acceptance, and energy. The social worker is committed to promoting the increasing welfare of the client and client/system. The worker is willing and able to be intimate with the client. Here, intimacy refers to the ability to share even the most private and innermost emotions and thoughts in the helping relationship for the purpose of furthering the client's welfare and development. Awareness means that the worker strives to understand and take responsibility for his own self, particularly those shadow aspects of self activated in countertransference reactions (see Part V). Awareness also means that the worker strives to understand all of the dimensions of the client as well. As the social worker becomes more aware of herself and the client, the worker also strives toward increasing acceptance and forgiveness of herself and the client (see Part V).

A loving relationship goes beyond unconditional acceptance of the client, however. The most loving relationship is characterized by dialogue and confirmation of otherness.[78] Dialogue can occur only when there is mutual respect, safety, and honesty. Confirmation of otherness means that the worker is able to not only accept the client's own uniqueness, but also accept and (as appropriate) express her own uniqueness.

For example, a worker might be seeing a young man who has battered his wife repeatedly. The man states, "She deserved to be hit." The worker may first respond by saying, "I can understand why you may feel and think that way, given what you told me about your own life story." However, the worker may also add, "I need to also tell you where *I* am coming from. I personally believe that being violent with your wife will never get you what you want, and that there are much more effective ways for you to communicate to her how you feel and what you think."

Connective means that the worker not only cares about the welfare of the client and client/system, but also demonstrates that caring. In connecting with a client, the social worker shows empathy and compassion (see Part V). Sometimes, being too loving in the context of professional social work has been labeled "unhealthy." Social workers have been labeled co-dependent and sometimes viewed as overly idealistic do-gooders who want to save the world. Certainly, in being helpful, a worker can become out of touch with the needs of the client and the self. However, perhaps this concern about co-dependency speaks more to the need of social workers to protect themselves rather than clients. When a worker is connected with the client, the worker is more vulnerable to feeling pain. Although clients can sense whether a social worker really cares about them, clients usually need to have that love demonstrated to them. When a worker uses therapeutic techniques in a loving manner, the client is more likely to respond with healing and growth.

There has also been increasing concern about setting adequate boundaries between social workers and clients. Certainly, workers are unlikely to help clients when they force kisses, hugs, and other expressions of affection on clients. However, there are certainly many clients who can benefit from simple verbal and physical expressions of affection. The effective worker can first determine with the client whether she or he is comfortable with any particular expression. For example, a worker is listening to an adolescent talk about his father's death. The worker asks, "May I hold your hand?" The boy replies, "I guess so."

A social worker who is connected with the client is willing and able to be present with that client in all of the dimensions of development. Thus, the worker is in his body (physical), is emotionally available, is spiritually open (to share souls), is socially available, and is mentally open to having creative and new experiences with other human beings.

Nonabusive means that the social worker does not try to get her own needs met by taking advantage of the unequal power that usually exists between worker and client in the helping relationship. Forms of client abuse may include emotional, physical, sexual, economic, spiritual, and physical neglect. However, nonabusive also means that the helping relationship is not a distant relationship, with rigid, unnecessary boundaries between the social worker and the client. In a nonabusive relationship, the social worker works

> within the healing paradoxes of the therapeutic relationship—cultivating equality in a hierarchical relationship, mutuality in an inherently non mutual relationship, empowerment in a power-imbalanced relationship. The therapist who sees himself as an all-knowing expert . . . is much more likely to abuse his power than the therapist who sees herself as an accountable coequal in therapy and her client as a person with an inherent wisdom that guides the therapeutic process. (p. 52)[79]

Social justice means that the social worker is committed to developing environments in which all people have equal access to opportunities, resources, status, power, and freedom to develop their full potential. The goals of social justice apply to all of the levels of the client/system, including couples, families, groups, institutions, and communities. As suggested above, the worker encourages the client to share in the responsibility to help make the client/system more socially just. The social worker models a commitment toward social justice for the client, which is one of the most unique qualities of the social worker as a professional helper. The concept of social justice fits nicely with advanced generalist theory because the concept encourages the social worker to look at the whole ecology of a case.

For example, when a social worker in private practice sees a competent father who is depressed because he has lost custody of his children following a sudden and painful separation and divorce, the worker may wish to link broader social justice issues with the more personal and interpersonal issues in this man's life. In addition to working with the man in terms of his failed marriage and future plans, the worker might also want to help involve the father in making educated and responsible changes in social myths and policies that still denigrate the importance of fathering. The worker may educate the client about the literature on joint custody, legal issues, and children's mental health. The worker may refer the father to a local men's group that is active in supporting fathers and reforming the legal system.

Social justice also means that the social worker is committed to protecting the safety of vulnerable people in the client/system. There can be no social justice when there is violence, because violence tends to silence the voice of the victim. As discussed in Part I, the social worker has a responsibility to act to protect clients and other people when their safety and/or well-being is at risk. That responsibility is, of course, limited by many factors, including the worker's precise knowledge of the risk and ability to respond, available community resources, and various client characteristics (such as developmental level, motivation, and cooperation).

When potential protective issues are identified, the social worker prioritizes protective issues in the case. The social worker acts as quickly as possible to intervene. The process of selecting appropriate interventions is often immensely complex. The worker seldom has full and precise knowledge of the risk and often has only limited data available in the assessment. There may also be a danger that well-intended interventions meant to protect could increase the risk of other problems for people in the client/system. The worker must balance all of the risks involved. In general, when time permits, the worker may wish to consult with supervisors or other colleagues.

Social workers themselves are increasingly at risk of becoming victims of psychological, physical, sexual, and economic violence. If the social worker is under attack or feels threatened, his effectiveness can be severely limited. In general, social workers should give themselves permission to take reasonable steps to reduce the risk of violence. A variety of strategies of self-protection are available to social workers. A general assessment of risk should be made; when the social worker works with others, this risk assessment should be made collectively and periodically. Clients and client/systems that are particularly dangerous should be identified, and alternative methods of practice may need to be identified and implemented. Incidents of violence should be reported, and a written policy for safety should be developed and kept current. Social workers need to develop support systems for help in planning for and dealing with violence. Models of safety risk are available that quantify risk for each social work case.[80]

The social worker becomes a victim of economic violence when a party in the worker or client/systems tries to influence the worker by threatening to harm the worker's livelihood or career. For example, a client may hint that she will sue a worker if he does not write a letter to the court supporting her custody case. Or, a supervisor may threaten to give a student a poor grade in practicum if she does not keep silent about a particular issue at the practicum setting. Workers who are victimized by such threats need not deal with them alone, nor do they need to give in to the demands of those who wish to influence them. For example, the worker described above who was threatened by the client wanting a supportive custody letter could seek support and counsel from a supervisor or from the state NASW office. The student mentioned above could discuss her difficulties with her school advisor.

As described in Part I, the social worker should be familiar with legal definitions of maltreatment, child and adult reporting laws, and protection guidelines in the state in which he is practicing. Procedures for notifying authorities of suspected maltreatment may also vary from community to community. The worker should be aware that laws also vary with regard to maltreatment in marriage and other relationships between adults. In addition to reporting suspected maltreatment as appropriate, the worker may need to take additional steps to protect children or vulnerable adults in a particular client/system.[81]

The social worker should also be familiar with legal requirements that may apply when risk of suicide and homicide is identified in a case. In certain cases, the social worker may have a legal and ethical responsibility to act to protect potential victims of suicide and homicide. In addition to making any legally required interventions (e.g., hospitalizing the client, notifying potential victims, calling the police), the social worker may often want to follow up with other interventions (e.g., making a suicide agreement, discussing the issues in therapy, making referrals).[82]

Experiential Exercises

1. What do you think love is? How important is it to helping others?

2. How do you tend to show your clients that you love them? What obstacles seem to get in the way of you loving your clients? How could you overcome those obstacles?

3. What makes you feel very connected with another human being? Can such connection occur between a social worker and a client? Should it occur?

4. In what ways might you be at risk for becoming abusive with a client? What do you need to do to better protect future clients and yourself from that happening?

5. Some people think that clinical social workers are not concerned enough with social justice, particularly those in private practice settings. Others suggest that the same danger exists for social workers whose practice is research, administration, or community organization. What do you think? How can both clinical and nonclinical social workers better integrate social justice issues into their practice?

Notes

Chapter 4

1. Meyer, C. H. (1988). The eco-systems perspective. In R. A. Dorfman (Ed.), *Paradigms of clinical social work* (pp. 274-294). New York: Brunner/Mazel.

2. Papell, C. P., & Rothman, B. (1966). Social group work models: Possession and heritage. *Journal of Education for Social Work, 2,* 66-78.

3. Fox, W. (1990). *Towards a transpersonal ecology.* Boston: Shambhala.

4. Burstow, B. (1992). *Radical feminist therapy: Working in the context of violence.* Newbury Park, CA: Sage.

5. Mahoney, M. J. (1991). *Human change processes: The scientific foundations of psychotherapy.* New York: Basic Books.

6. Beyer, P. (1994). *Religion and globalization*. London: Sage.

7. Dass, R. (1993). Service: The soul of community. In C. Whitmyer (Ed.), *In the company of other: Making community in the modern world*. New York: Jeremy P. Tarcher/Perigee.

8. Ivey, A. W. (1986). *Developmental therapy*. San Francisco: Jossey Bass.

9. Mahoney (1991).

10. Meyer (1988).

11. Macy, J. (1983). *Despair and personal power in the nuclear age*. Philadelphia: New Society.

12. Gil, D. (1987). Maltreatment as a function of the structure of social systems. In M. R. Brassard, R. Germain, & S. N. Hart (Eds.), *Psychological maltreatment of children and youth* (pp. 159-170). New York: Pergamon.

13. Flynn, J. P. (1995). Social justice in social agencies. In National Association of Social Workers, *Encyclopedia of social work* (19th ed., Vol. 3, pp. 2173-2179). Silver Spring, MD: National Association of Social Workers.

14. Macy (1983).

15. Ornstein, R., & Ehrlich, P. (1989). *New world new mind: Moving towards conscious evolution*. New York: Doubleday.

16. Ornstein and Ehrlich (1989).

17. Macy (1983).

Chapter 5

18. Maslow, A. H. (1971). *The further reaches of human nature*. New York: Viking.

19. Sperry, L., & Carlson, J. (1991). *Marital therapy: Integrating theory and technique*. Denver: Love; Corey, G. (1990). *Theory and practice of group counseling*. Pacific Grove, CA: Brooks/Cole; Fenell, D., & Weinhold, B. (1989). *Counseling families: An introduction to marriage and family therapy*. Denver: Love.

20. Vourlekis, B. S., & Greene, R. R. (Eds.). (1992). *Social work case management*. New York: Aldine; Rothman, J. (1991). A model of case management: Toward empirically based practice. *Social Work, 36*, 520-529.

21. Johnson, H. C., Atkins, S. P., Battle, S. F., Hernandez-Arata, L., Hesselbrock, M., Libassi, M. F., & Parish, M. S. (1990). Strengthening the "bio" in the biopsychosocial paradigm. *Journal of Social Work Education, 26*, 109-123.

22. Manning, G., Curtis, K., & McMillen, S. (1996). *Building community: The human side of work*. Cincinnati, OH: Thompson.

23. Institute for World Order. (1981). *Peace and world order studies: A curriculum guide*. New York: Author.

24. Gordon, W. E. (1965). Toward a social work frame of reference. *Journal of Education of Social Work, 1*(2), 19-26.

25. Mahoney (1991).

26. Mahoney (1991).

27. Saltzman, N., & Norcross, J. C. (Eds.). (1990). *Therapy wars: Contention and convergence in differing clinical approaches*. San Francisco: Jossey-Bass.

28. West, C. K., Farmer, J. A., & Wolff, P. M. (1991). *Instructional design: Implications from cognitive science*. Englewood Cliffs, NJ: Prentice Hall.

29. Ellis, A. (1962). *Reasons and emotion in psychotherapy*. New York: Lyle Stuart.

30. Freud, S. (1932). New introductory lectures. In E. Strachey (Ed.), *Standard edition of the complete psychological works of Sigmund Freud* (Vol. 22). London: Hogarth.

31. Jung, C. J. (1954). *The collected works of Carl Jung* (Vol. 17). Princeton, NJ: Princeton University Press.

32. Adler, A. (1958). *The practice and theory of individual psychology.* Patterson, NJ: Littlefield, Adams.

33. Berne, E. (1961). *Transactional analysis in psychotherapy.* New York: Grove.

34. Hamilton, N. G. (1990). *Self and others: Object relations theory in practice.* Northvale, NJ: Jason Aronson.

35. Mahler, M., Pine, F., & Bergman, A. (1975). *The psychological birth of the human infant.* New York: Basic Books.

36. Haley, J. (1973). *Uncommon therapy: The techniques of Milton H. Erickson.* New York: Ballantine.

37. Ellis, A., & Grieger, R. (1978). *RET: Handbook of rational emotive therapy.* New York: Springer.

38. Glasser, W. (1965). *Reality therapy: A new approach to psychiatry.* New York: Harper & Row.

39. Persons, D. (1989). *Cognitive theory in practice: A case formulation approach.* New York: Norton.

40. Rogers, C. (1951). *Client-centered therapy.* New York: Houghton Mifflin.

41. Perls, F. S. (1969). *Gestalt therapy verbatim.* Moab, UT: Real People.

42. Satir, V. (1988). *The new peoplemaking.* Mountain View, CA: Science and Behavior Books.

43. Hendricks, G., & Weinhold, B. (1982). *Transpersonal approaches to counseling and psychotherapy.* Denver: Love.

44. Goodbread, J. H. (1987). *The dreambody toolkit.* London: Routledge and Kegan Paul.

45. Corey, G. (1990). *Theory and practice of group counseling.* Pacific Grove, CA: Brooks/Cole.

46. Rogers (1951).

47. Perls (1969).

48. Hendricks and Weinhold (1982).

49. Sperry and Carlson (1991).

50. Hendricks and Weinhold (1982).

51. Nichols, M. (1984). *Family therapy: Concepts and methods.* New York: Gardner.

52. Vourlekis and Greene (1992).

53. Ivey (1986).

54. Johnson et al. (1990).

55. Rothman, J., & Tropman, J. E. (1987). Models of community organization and macro practice perspectives: Their mixing and phasing. In F. M. Cox, J. L. Erlich, J. Rothman, & J. E. Tropman (Eds.), *Strategies of community organization: Macro practice* (pp. 3-26). Itasca, IL: F. E. Peacock.

56. Darvill, G., & Smale, G. (1990). Introduction: The face of community social work. In G. Darvill & G. Smale (Eds.), *Partners in empowerment: Networks of innovation in social work* (pp. 11-28). London: National Institute for Social Work.

57. Whitmyer, C. (1993). *In the company of others: Making community in the modern world.* New York: Jeremy P. Tarcher/Perigee.

58. Rosak, T. (1978). *Person/planet: The creative disintegration of industrial society.* Garden City, NY: Anchor Press/Doubleday.

59. Fox, W. (1990). *Towards a transpersonal ecology: Developing new foundations for environmentalism.* Boston: Shambhala.

60. Gould, B. B., & Demuth, D. H. (1994). *The global family therapist: Integrating the personal, professional, and political.* Boston: Allyn & Bacon.

61. Macy (1983).

62. Mahoney (1991).

Chapter 6

63. Paul, G. L. (1967). Strategy of outcome research in psycho-therapy. *Journal of Consulting Psychology, 32,* 118.

64. Beutler, L. E. (1986). Systematic eclectic psychotherapy. In J. C. Norcross (Ed.), *Handbook of eclectic psychotherapy* (pp. 94-131). New York: Brunner/Mazel.

65. Sheafor, B. W., Horejsi, C. R., & Horejsi, G. A. (1988). *Techniques and guidelines for social work practice.* Boston: Allyn & Bacon.

66. Wilber, K. (1986). Treatment modalities. In K. Wilber, J. Engler, & D. P. Brown (Eds.), *Transformations of consciousness* (pp. 127-160). Boston and London: New Science Library/Shambhala.

67. Sheafor et al. (1988).

68. Hayek, F. A. (1979). Law, legislation, and liberty. In *The political order of a free people* (Vol. 1). Chicago: University of Chicago Press.

69. Norcross, J. C., & Saltzman, N. (1990). The clinical exchange: Toward integrating the psychotherapies. In N. Saltzman & J. C. Norcross (Eds.), *Therapy wars: Contention and convergence in differing clinical approaches* (pp. 1-14). San Francisco: Jossey-Bass.

Chapter 7

70. Elliott, R., & James, E. (1989). Varieties of client experience in psycho-therapy: An analysis of the literature. *Clinical Psychology Review, 9,* 443-467.

71. Strupp, H. H. (1978). The therapist's theoretical orientation: An overrated variable. *Psychotherapy: Research and Practice, 15,* 314-315.

72. Robertson, R. (1995). Chaos theory and the relationship between psychology and science. In R. Robertson & A. Combs (Eds.), *Chaos theory in psychology and the life sciences.* Hillsdale, NJ: Lawrence Erlbaum.

73. Satir, V. (1972). *Peoplemaking.* Palo Alto, CA: Science and Behavior.

74. Mahoney (1991).

75. Friedman, M. (1974). *The confirmation of otherness in family, community, and society.* New York: Pilgrim.

76. Bowlbey, J. (1988). Attachment theory. In *A secure base.* New York: Basic Books.

Chapter 8

77. Strupp (1978).

78. Friedman (1974).

79. Greenspan, M. (1995). Out of bounds. *Common Boundary, 13*(4), 51-58.

80. Griffin, W. (1995). Social worker and agency safety. In National Association of Social Workers, *Encyclopedia of social work* (19th ed., Vol. 3, pp. 2293-2305). Washington, DC: NASW Press.

81. Hampton, R. L., Gullotta, T. P., Adams, G. R., Potter III, E. H., & Weissberg, R. P. (Eds.). (1993). *Family violence: Prevention and treatment.* Newbury Park, CA: Sage.

82. Ivanoff, A., & Riedel, M. (1995). Suicide. In National Association of Social Workers, *Encyclopedia of social work* (19th ed., Vol. 3, pp. 2358-2372). Washington, DC: NASW Press; Morales, A. (1995). Homicide. In National Association of Social Workers, *Encyclopedia of social work* (19th ed., Vol. 3, pp. 1347-1357). Washington, DC: NASW Press.

Intervention Paradigms:
The Four Forces of Social Work

Advanced generalist social work practice is inclusive because the universe of available interventions is used. These interventions can be organized into seven paradigms. In this section, the Four Forces[1] of psychology, introduced in Part I, are described in detail as the first four paradigms of social work: (a) psychodynamic, (b) cognitive/behavioral/communications, (c) experiential/humanistic/existential, and (d) transpersonal.[2]

Interventions drawn from these Four Forces deal with the "organism" and "microsystem" levels of the client/system,[3] or what are now commonly called the "micro" and "meso" systems.[4] That is, the Four Forces include interventions that were generally designed for direct work with individuals, couples, families, and small groups. The other three paradigms, described in Part IV, deal with methods of direct practice that consider either the physical body or larger ("exosystem" or "macro") systems.

As described in Part II, each paradigm in advanced generalist social work practice includes models that share the basic theoretical elements of the paradigm. Each of these models also has a number of interventions. The general goal of all interventions is to further the developmental process and well-being of both the client and the client/system.

A complete description of all of the models and interventions in each paradigm is beyond the scope of this book (or any reasonably sized text). The advanced generalist social worker recognizes that the learning of these paradigms is a career-long task that only begins (or is fostered) in graduate school. Key concepts and introductions are introduced, and case examples are used to illustrate basic intervention concepts. In Parts III and IV, there is a focus on 13 key elements in each paradigm:

1. Major focus of paradigm

2. Dimensions of development primarily targeted in paradigm

3. View of health (of individual client and/or client/system)

4. View of pathology (of individual client and/or client/system)

5. Art and science (what we know about efficacy of paradigm)

6. Relationship (between worker and client and/or client/system)

7. Strengths of paradigm

8. Limitations of paradigm

9. Fit of paradigm in advanced generalist practice

10. Key intervention strategies with case examples

11. Work with couples, families, and groups

12. Experiential exercises to enhance conscious use of self

13. Impact on individual, family, and local and global community

Because advanced generalist practice is eclectic, interventions drawn from all seven paradigms can be used in practice. The advanced generalist worker recognizes that the most effective interventions often use a blend of interventions differentially selected to meet the unique and diverse client and client/system needs of each case. Many of the case examples in Parts III and IV will be additive, in that they will demonstrate ways to include interventions drawn from many paradigms for use in a single case.

CHAPTER 9

Psychodynamic Paradigm

Key Elements

Focus. Psychodynamic social work interventions focus on the impact of past experiences upon present intrapsychic (internal dynamic) and interpsychic (social) functioning. The core of the work is the healing of the trauma of past experiences and the resolution of related inner conflicts so that the individual can learn to love and be loved.

Developmental dimensions. The emphasis is on cognitive development (insight into the relationship between the past and the present) and psychosocial development (developing loving relationships in which both or all people get their needs met).

View of health. The client is aware of her internal dynamics (all of her parts). The client has become individuated (has a self), experiences that self as good enough, and is able to get his personal needs met well enough in an imperfect world. There is a balance of power and ongoing dialogue between the three ego states of the psyche: the parent, observing self, and child.

View of pathology. The client's childhood was unfriendly and may have included maltreatment and other trauma. To protect herself, the client developed childhood coping mechanisms that are now dysfunctional. Because the client is also unaware (unconscious) of her internal conflicts (between personal needs and negative views of herself and world), these conflicts continue to limit the client's ability to love and be loved.

Art and science. The empirical base is limited. Many core theoretical concepts remain untested or unproven (e.g., the unconscious, psychosexual stages), and the relative effectiveness of various interventions is uncertain. Practitioners can select psychodynamic interventions based upon empirical research, theory, and worker and client intuition.

Relationship. A more vertical (rather than horizontal) relationship is used between worker and client. Although the worker does not take responsibility for the client's decisions, she is the expert who often provides interpretations and leads the client in the exploration of self.

Strengths. Psychodynamic work is "depth psychology"; the client explores deep-seated internal dynamics. Therefore, psychodynamic interventions may have longer lasting effects on intrapsychic functioning than other, less deep, intervention strategies.[5] Because there are many different psychodynamic models that reflect the different diagnostic groups of clients upon whom they are based, the social worker can choose a model that is most helpful to the specific case or population with whom he is working.[6]

Limitations. Psychodynamic work can be time-consuming. Clients can become focused primarily upon the past and ignore current or future issues. Some clients gain insight but make little other change in intrapsychic or interpsychic functioning. Clients who have not yet developed a self, who still primarily operate on the prepersonal level of functioning,[7] may not be able to tolerate psychodynamic work. Some clients may place excessive blame on parents or other past figures for their own problems.

Social workers can use psychodynamic theory but still be cautious about taking psychodynamic concepts to represent literal truth. For example, although most professionals and laypeople alike today believe that each persona has an unconscious, there is still no evidence of the nature of that unconscious, or even that it really exists. Thus, various models are equally acceptable and should be considered when working with people.

For example, Jung[8] believed that we all share in a collective unconscious that connects all people together. Some have suggested that this collective unconscious extends past humans to other life forms and even all matter in the universe. Hayek[9] has suggested that instead of an unconscious, there is a "superconscious" that the client can use.

Fit in advanced generalist practice. Psychodynamic work is useful and often essential when the client's next developmental step is to uncover the origins and mechanisms of his internal dynamics. Many clients seem to need to have a deep understanding of these origins and mechanisms before they can generalize and maintain behavioral changes. Clients need to be sufficiently intelligent and motivated to do deep psychodynamic work.

These interventions are not used with clients who are still operating primarily at the prepersonal level of development. Such clients have not yet developed the internal structure (intact id, ego, and superego) necessary to tolerate deep, uncovering work. These interventions are also not used with clients who have not yet been able to develop a safe helping relationship with the worker. Thus, in many cases, psychodynamic work may not be useful in the beginning stage of the case.

Despite these limitations, psychodynamic work is fundamental work. Every client has a history, and the child is in many ways the father of every man and the mother of every woman. Although psychodynamic interventions are often focused on the early childhood years, the work can also focus on other experiences across the life span.

Key Intervention Strategies With Case Examples

The overall goal is to uncover (make conscious) the unconscious conflicts and to work through (build upon) these insights to develop more functional behavior patterns. Five key intervention strategies can be described that move in descending order from most direct to most indirect. The worker selects intervention based in part on the extent to which the client is ready to hear direct or less direct information.

Interpretation. An interpretation is essentially a direct "you message" that the worker makes about the client. When an interpretation is made, the worker links various aspects of the client's past history and present dynamics and functioning. Sometimes, interpretations are hard and even painful to hear, and clients become more defensive rather than open. There is always the danger that a worker will make interpretive errors. Workers will have either under- or overidentifications with *every* client that can create blindspots in the assessment (see Part V).

An example of a simple interpretation follows. A worker is running a therapy group for delinquent adolescent boys. One of the boys frequently criticizes the other boys in the group and disrupts the group process. The worker tells the boy, "I have noticed that you have been quite critical and disruptive again today. I wonder if the way you act in group is similar to the way you have learned to act at home when you felt unsafe around your family. I also wonder if being critical and disruptive somehow makes you feel safer when you are around people."

Although interpretations are often hard to hear, they can be effective in certain situations. Indeed, quite confrontational interpretations may be used successfully at times with some clients, and the effective social worker chooses interpretations when she believes the client is likely to benefit from the experience. The worker realizes that there can also be countertransference issues that motivate his desire for confrontation. For example, some social workers may use confrontational interpretations with sex offenders not so much because they believe their clients need such interventions, but because the workers dislike their clients' crimes.

Empathic response. The empathic response is essentially a less direct and sensitive way of giving information to the client. The worker essentially walks in the client's shoes and demonstrates to the client that she cares for the client. Used in self-psychology, empathic responses can be effective because most people feel uncared for when they are simply analyzed.[10] In the language of the street, a social worker may be called a "shrink" because she seems to shrink the client down to a diagnosis rather than see the client as a whole person. In an empathic response, the worker conveys an empathic understanding of why the client has a certain characteristic.

For example, using the same case introduced above, the worker turns to the angry boy in the group and states, "Billy, I remember what you told us about your family last week, and I am starting to realize how hard it must have been for you to live with a cocaine-addicted mother and two abusive big brothers. It must have worked well for you to act angry and defiant at home. I don't blame you for being so angry with people now. It must be hard to change that."

Artistic techniques. The social worker can encourage the client to use a variety of artistic techniques to facilitate psychodynamic work. In *journaling,* the client can be asked to write about various past life experiences. The client can also tape-record her memories of past experiences. This journaling can be structured or unstructured; the worker can suggest that the client write about certain kinds of experiences (e.g., when a parent was abusive) or about particular periods of time in the client's life. Usually, the client and worker process the assignment together after it has been completed.

For example, a client tells his worker that he has had a pattern of falling in love with women who are rather distant and unfriendly. The worker suggests that the client go home and make a list of characteristics that he did not like in his own mother and that he felt were damaging to him. The next week, the client reads the list to the worker. The first item on the list reads, "My mother was never very warm." The client and worker process the obvious similarities between the mother and the girlfriends. The client can also use other nonverbal expressions to help her or him get back in touch with deeper issues about the past. Other nonverbal expressions might include forms of drawing, singing, and movement. For example, in a psychodynamic therapy group, clients can be asked to each draw a picture of their childhood. Then, clients can take turns describing what they see in each other's drawings. Finally, each client can share how accurate they thought the perceptions were.

Psychoeducation. The social worker may choose to use psychoeducation, particularly with those clients who are cognitively dominant. The worker essentially teaches the client a psychodynamic model of consciousness. A simple model to teach is the transactional analysis (TA) model.[11] Essentially, every person is seen as having three ego states that communicate with each other and sometimes struggle for power within the psyche. The parent ego state is our internal authority or conscience. The parent is an internalized version of the primary adult or adults who were our authorities when we were growing up. The child ego state is the part of us that is like a child. The child has emotions and needs, and wants to express the emotions and fulfill the needs. Finally, the adult ego state, or observing self, is essentially the observer and the referee who watches the interactions between the parent and child ego states and sometimes intervenes to help problem solve or resolve conflicts.

For example, a social worker may be working with a young gay couple who are experiencing a tremendous amount of verbal fighting in their first year of marriage. The social worker may first teach the TA model (using a blackboard) to both men and have them individually examine their internal ego states. To oversimplify the process, it turns out that John's parent usually overwhelms his child (he feels typically guilty and responsible for most things, including his partner Bill's welfare). and Bill's child seems to overwhelm his parent (in this case, he has a hard time taking responsibility for his own life and expects John to take care of him).

Storytelling. Many religious and spiritual traditions use stories to teach various beliefs and doctrines, because stories are often powerful teaching strategies. For clients, storytelling may be a useful way to learn about themselves. Many children, for example, will be able to listen to a story much easier than an interpretation or even an empathic response. The same may be true for many adults. The worker tells a story (real or fictitious) that conveys a message about the client's dynamics. The worker often adds a happy ending at the end of the story that suggests what the next, positive step in the client's process might be. Storytelling is playing, can be co-created by both worker and client, and can be facilitated through the use of various materials (such as toys or art materials).

For example, the worker is seeing a middle-aged couple who have been locked in "holy deadlock" for years, almost constantly involved in power struggles that seem to go nowhere. The worker tells them a story:

> Once upon a time a young person was walking a path in the forest when he suddenly noticed a madman [or madwoman] approaching with a knife. Naturally the young person tried to escape, but was soon confronted with a swift and dangerous mountain stream that was impossible to cross. An old log lay on the bank though, and the young person pushed it in the water and escaped by clinging to it until it came ashore downstream. The person was so grateful to the log that he hoisted it up on his shoulders and carried it around the rest of his life. Perhaps one day he realized that the log was a burden and made it impossible to relax enough to be close to anyone, so he finally put it down.[12]

One danger in storytelling is that the client may not consciously make the connection between the symbolic message and his own issues. (The argument could be made, however, that an unconscious connection may be enough for change and even superior to a conscious connection). The worker may need to use interpretations, empathic responses, or psychoeducation to help bridge that gap.

The psychodynamically oriented social worker might use a number of additional methods, including listening, asking questions, confronting, and clarifying. Through the process of helping, the client gains more insight but also needs genuine affect and real awareness before he can work through the insight, achieve synthesis, and make behavioral change.[13]

Work With Couples, Families, and Other Groups

First Force interventions can be used to help couples, families, and group members resolve obstacles to relationships that are rooted in the past. The worker can use any of the key intervention strategies outlined above, including interpretation, empathic response, artistic techniques, storytelling, and psychoeducation. When there is a history of maltreatment (e.g., physical or psychological abuse) perpetrated by a client with relatively more power (e.g., physical strength) on a client with less power, the worker does not use psychodynamic interventions until the abusive behavior can be controlled.

In *couple work,* when there is sufficient safety (equal power) in the relationship, the social worker can ask each client to essentially do individual work openly in front of the partner. The goal is to help the clients better understand each other's past issues and related inner conflicts, which may now be obstacles to intimacy and love in the relationship.

For example, a social worker is seeing a gay couple in which each person complains of frequent arguments and a loss of love. The worker may at some point in the sessions ask each man to describe in detail his own history of love, beginning with his family of origin.

Collective work can also be done, which is simultaneous work with both members of a couple. For example, using transactional analysis[14] techniques, the worker can show the couple how their parental and child ego states interact in the relationship. With one particular heterosexual couple, the worker was able to show them two interaction patterns. The man plays the role of the judgmental and distant father in response to his wife's role of the needy and obedient girl. The woman plays the role of the all-accepting mother in response to her husband's role of the naughty and rebellious boy. The worker helps the couple see how these patterns originated in the family of origin of each client. Many couples may benefit from psychodynamic work; such work may help them deal more effectively with the complex environmental etiologies of their marital dysfunction.[15] The worker can help clients see how they are attracted to others who have the same developmental failures they have. Most people are viewed as tending to reenact earlier relationships (usually with their own parents) through a process called "projective identification." This process may involve collusion, in which each partner supports the other's self-perceptions. As each partner matures, the "splitting" decreases; the client is better able to accept the good and bad qualities in self and partner.

Not all couples are ready and able to understand these theories and accept their own processes, but those who do are often able to further individuate (accept and express the differences between themselves and others). As each individual's ability to love (or "object relations") improves, the relationship becomes more mature. The social worker can ask couples to explore these processes with each other. While one partner is working on his or her issues, the other partner is helped to listen and support.

In *family work,* when there is sufficient safety in the relationship, the social worker asks parents and children to do their own selected individual work with each other. The goal is to help parents and children better understand each other's past issues and related inner conflicts, which may now be obstacles to effective parenting and family functioning. The worker will not ask the parents to describe every intimate detail about their own lives, but may find it useful to have the parents describe when they were the same age that their children are now.

For example, a mother and her 16-year-old son come to see a worker. The mother complains that the son is constantly acting out in ways that infuriate her. After a few sessions, the worker has the mother talk about what life was like for her when she was 16. It turns out that she was overcontrolled by her parents and was afraid to ever act out. The mother realizes that she was never allowed to express any normal rebellion (individuation) as an adolescent. The mother and son are able to better understand why the mother has such a hard time accepting her son's rather normal rebellion.

In *group work,* when there is sufficient safety in the group, the social worker will ask participants to review selected past experiences and events. Sometimes, the worker will involve other participants in the process by asking them to provide empathy, support, and their own sharing. The worker generally tries to discourage group members from interpreting each other too much (because such analysis tends to lead people away from their feelings and into their head, and can result in projections and defensiveness).

Experiential Exercises to Enhance Conscious Use of Self in Psychodynamic Paradigm

1. Using marker pens or crayon, on a plain sheet of paper, draw your life. Begin at birth (or before) and continue on to the present. Then share your drawing with a partner in dyads.

2. Write down a list of qualities for each of the one or two most important adult caretakers in your childhood (e.g., father, mother, teacher) in your

life. Include those qualities that you both liked and disliked. Then, discuss with a partner in dyads which of those characteristics you have taken on and which you have rejected.

3. In dyads, discuss to which client characteristics you would most likely have strong countertransference reactions (i.e., those with which you would under- and overidentify). Much of your answer may be based on your answer to Item 1.

4. In groups of four, discuss who were the most significant mentors in your life. Explain what it was about those people that most influenced you in a positive way in your life.

5. Because the work of a relationship could be seen as the clarification of where one person ends and the other begins, consider where you are in your current ability to establish such clear boundaries with another, perhaps significant, person in your life.

Impact on Individual, Family, Local Community, and Global Community

A psychodynamic social worker might say that if you want to understand who an individual really is, understand that person's love life. Psychodynamic work can help the individual understand how her lifelong personal experiences of loving and being loved have contributed to her current ability to get her needs met in relationships with others.

When an individual in the family increases his ability to love and be loved, marital-type relations and parent-child relations can improve. Family structures may or may not change (e.g., divorce, remarriage) as individuals in the family better understand what they need. In families where there has been an intergenerational history of dysfunctional relationships or maltreatment (including child abuse, marital abuse, abuse of vulnerable adults), psychodynamic work may reduce the chances that individuals will become future victims or perpetrators of family maltreatment.

A community of people becomes more effective at supporting each other's development as people within that community learn how to have more effective (more loving) relationships with one another. Such a community becomes less violent, because individuals are healing their past trauma and are learning to get their current needs met without having to resort to antisocial behaviors (less effective or distorted ways to seek love). Such a community is less likely to tolerate oppression of any group because individuals are becoming less likely to project unloved characteristics of themselves upon others.

A global community in which people do their own psychodynamic work is less likely to be warlike and destructive of the environment. This is because First Force work fosters whole object relations. People can only wage war on others or destroy the ecosystem if they split their object relations (e.g., view other people and the ecosystem in negative terms that justify their destruction). When people have whole object relationships, they are aware of all of the qualities in other people and themselves, and they are less likely to project unloved aspects of themselves on others.

CHAPTER 10

Cognitive/Behavioral/ Communications Paradigm

Key Elements

Focus. In general, these models focus on changing the way clients think and/or act. The focus is on reducing unwanted symptoms and replacing them with more desirable thoughts and actions.

Developmental dimensions. Emphasis is upon cognitive development (modifying thinking) and social development (developing new social skills).

View of health. The client uses realistic thinking and has functional behaviors.

View of pathology. The client learned dysfunctional (maladaptive) patterns of thinking and acting.

Goal. The goal is developing more functional cognitive and behavioral change in the here and now.

Art and science. There is a relatively well-established empirical base. Cognitive and behavioral methods have been studied frequently and have been shown to produce changes in thinking and behaving, respectively, although the relative long-term generalizability and maintenance of these changes remains uncertain. Although the research base is stronger than that of the other paradigms, the overall effectiveness of cognitive/behavioral interventions relative to interventions based upon other paradigms still remains uncertain. Practitioners can select Second Force interventions based on empirical research, theory, and worker and client intuition.

Relationship. Traditionally, there often was a rather vertical relationship. In such cases, the worker took the role of the expert, the educator, and the physician who treated the client. A more horizontal relationship is not only possible but may be particularly effective in many cases.

Strengths. Relatively quick results are often expected. These methods may especially fit into short-term treatment models. Many clients find it easier to change their thinking and behavior than to deal directly with their emotions or spirit.

Limitations. Results may not extend to all aspects of the client's life (generalize), nor may they last (be maintained).[16] Perhaps, at least in part because of the vertical nature of the relationship, cognitive/behavioral/communications approaches may be experienced by many clients as reductionistic and dehumanizing.

Some theoreticians have expressed fundamental concerns about the limitations of cognitive/behavioral/communications approaches. For example, Mahoney points out that "rational psychosocial workers (be they cognitive, behavioral, or otherwise) tend to operate from an authority-based (justificational) perspective" (p. 239).[17] He forwards evidence that such a perspective is much more limited and less useful than is a "teleonomic" approach, which has no one single, explicit goal.

Fit in Advanced Generalist Practice
With Four Forces of Social Work

Cognitive/behavioral/communications approaches can be used to help clients move from insight or awareness into action. Thus, these approaches can follow First, Third, or Fourth Force interventions.

Cognitive/behavioral/communications approaches can also be used to help clients who are not ready or able to do deeper uncovering work. Very young clients; very dysfunctional clients; and very unmotivated, defended, or hostile clients may respond to these approaches. These approaches may help provide the external structure that clients at the prepersonal level of consciousness may need.

Studies have shown that emotion is not an exclusively limbic process, and that knowing is not an exclusively neocortical process.[18] The human processes of feeling and knowing are complex and interrelated. Therefore, social workers should not work in an exclusively cognitive (or affective) manner with any client or population.

Social workers often find themselves using these interventions with nonvoluntary clients. Abusive and neglectful parents, for example, may be unwilling or unready to do the deeper work drawn from the First, Third, or Fourth Force psychologies. Second Force interventions are practical, tend to be simple, and can have immediate results (e.g., getting a child back from the protective custody of the state).

The insight generated in First Force interventions is usually not enough to foster development. Most people need to make behavioral changes. Second Force interventions can build upon the insight and other internal (intrapsychic) work of First Force interventions, helping to foster external (interpsychic and environmental) life changes in the lives of clients.

Key Intervention Strategies

In general, cognitive/behavioral/communications work is focused on the immediate factors associated with current human behavior. The goal is to modify and/or replace current undesirable behaviors. Behavioral psychology shifted the focus of assessment and intervention from internal (intrapsychic) issues to external (environmental) influences on human responsiveness.[19] The goal of cognitive therapy "is to help the client identify, examine, test, and correct cognition and schema that are the root of current emotional, behavioral, and coping difficulties" (p. 179).[20] The theories of communications therapy formed the basis of such family therapy approaches as the strategic and structural modes, which focus upon practical, short-term results and emphasize problem solving over insight and feelings.[21]

When working in the cognitive/behavioral/communications paradigm, the social worker replaces dysfunctional cognition with more functional cognition when necessary and works to alter the client's environment in order to encourage the desired behaviors. Several key interventions can be listed here in descending order of directness of style:

Replacing unhelpful thoughts with more helpful thoughts. The social worker suggests new ways of thinking that may help the client. Sometimes, the social worker first helps the client become aware of the nature, origins, and limitations of the existing, unhelpful thoughts that seem to be related to her life difficulties. Depending upon their own styles and the needs of the client, some social workers may prefer to move directly into modifying thoughts, and others prefer to build a foundation of insights before making those modifications. Cognitive techniques have been shown to be helpful in at least initially eliminating many common symptoms. For example, anxiety, which remains the most common symptom complaint, often responds to cognitive interventions that help clients relax and improve their functioning.[22]

Practice can be viewed in part as a struggle between the worker's view of the client and the client's view of the client. The most effective worker involves the client as much as possible in talking openly about this process, to the extent that the client is developmentally ready to do so. This cognitive work is most effective with clients who have the necessary intellectual ability. The worker and client work together to evaluate progress and modify the interventions as needed.

For example, a street social worker is working with homeless men in a downtown area. One of the men, a white male alcoholic, continues to complain that there is no use for him to try to get a job because "no one cares about white men anymore." The worker says, "I can see why you might think that way, because you have been let down so many times in your life. However, even though I respect your intelligence, I'm not sure that your thinking is completely correct this time. For one thing, *I* care about you, and I believe in you. For another thing, I don't see how your attitude helps you at all. Sure, there have been unfriendly people in your world, but they can't keep you down unless you let them."

Social workers will usually find that the core thinking errors underlying most dysfunctional thought are shame-based beliefs that the client is inferior or worthless. The worker strives to help the client continue to examine his beliefs to determine what core beliefs may be at the root of his difficulties.

For example, one client's presenting problem is that she feels that she cannot make everyone happy in her life. She is 39 years old, married with three children, and currently going to school to learn a new profession. Her husband is very angry with her because she no longer cooks his meals. Her children are also angry with her because she is no longer as available to transport them places, help them with homework, and so on. Her professors are upset because her assignments have sometimes come in late. The social worker labors with the client to help her review what she believes about herself and the world. They first realize that she thinks, "If I don't make everyone happy, then they will be mad at me." They next determine that underlying the first belief is the root belief, "If everyone is mad at me, then I am worthless." The social worker then helps the client reframe her root belief to, "I am much more than what I do, and I am worthwhile even if I accomplish nothing."

Replacing unhelpful behaviors with more helpful behaviors. The social worker also can help modify the client system to encourage desired behavioral changes. Research in behavioral science has shown convincingly that rewarding desired behaviors is a much more powerful strategy than punishing less desired behaviors.[23] The social worker looks for ways to reward the behaviors that are desired. The worker may encourage the client to create, practice, and plan for behavioral changes in the actual sessions; create mutual agreements within the client/system; and modify the client/system to reward desired behaviors.

The worker helps the client create, practice, and plan for behavioral change. Again, just like with the psychodynamic interventions, this intervention might be either direct or indirect. Depending upon the needs of the client, the worker might use interpretations, empathic responses, storytelling, or psychoeducation to communicate about behavioral objectives with the client. The worker encourages the client to participate in the creation of behavioral objectives, to the maximum extent that the client is developmentally ready to do so. The worker can then help the client practice the desired behaviors. Sometimes, the client needs the worker to model the desired behavior before he is ready to practice the behavior in role-plays with the worker. Finally, the client and worker can plan when, where, and how the new behavior can be first attempted in the client's life—usually in a relatively safe life situation.

The worker can sometimes help create mutual agreements within the client/system. These agreements involve provisions where individuals assent to modify specific behaviors in return for similar promises by others. For example, a social worker might help a single father and his 15-year-old daughter make a mutual agreement. In this agreement, the father agrees to let the daughter stay out for a later curfew in return for the daughter agreeing to keep her room clean.

Finally, the social worker can help modify the client/system to reward desired behaviors. For example, a social worker was called when a 90-year-old man had escaped out of the window of his nursing home, despite a fractured hip, and returned to his former apartment. The social worker realized that the man understandably wanted to live as independently as possible, but the worker also wanted to minimize any dangers to his client's health. The worker supported the client's independent living by asking some of the client's friends to help look after him and also by setting regular visits from a home health nurse and housekeeper. The worker and client continued to evaluate the case progress and modify the interventions as needed.

Conflict resolution and other problem-solving skills. These practical interventions are oriented around solving real-life problems and resolving conflicts in families or other groups. The social worker guides the client(s) through basic problem-solving steps. The social worker encourages the client(s) to participate in the problem-solving process as much as the client(s) is developmentally able.

The problem-solving process includes several steps:

1. *Increase problem awareness.* The worker and client strive to increase their awareness of the problem. The development and welfare of both the client and the client/system are considered. If there is a conflict, all different points of view are considered.

2. *Review alternative solutions.* The worker and client examine the choices that are available and consider the likely advantages and disadvantages of each choice for both client and client/system.

3. *Choose the best solution.* The worker and client select the solution that has the best combination of maximum advantage and minimum disadvantage for both the client and the client/system.

4. *Implement the best solution.* The best solution is implemented by the client and, when appropriate, also by all other parties in the client system.

5. *Evaluate results.* The worker and client evaluate the outcome. If the outcome is unsatisfactory, at least some of the steps in this problem-solving process may need to be reworked.

Therapeutic maneuvers. Whereas social workers usually encourage maximum (and developmentally appropriate) client participation in interventions, there are interventions that may be particularly effective when implemented with little or no client participation. The social worker takes responsibility for choosing and implementing techniques that are designed to help the client shift her way of thinking or acting.

One therapeutic maneuver is *reframing.* When the social worker reframes, he adapts a cognitive perspective that is different and, it is hoped, more helpful than the perspective the client currently has. Such a shift in perspective can sometimes have a profoundly helpful impact on the client and client/system. For example, a father may complain to the family therapist that his youngest son, a 13-year-old, is too much of a bookworm. The social worker assesses the boy and determines that he is very intelligent and high-functioning, but simply not as talented an athlete as his older brothers and father. The worker makes the reframe, "Mr. Smith, your son seems to be a very intelligent young man, a lot like his father. I imagine that you are proud of him."

Another is *humor.* When the social worker uses humor therapeutically, she may take a perspective that exaggerates the perspective that the client already has. For example, a social worker might notice that every time she gives her male client a compliment, he responds by mildly putting himself down. She might say to him, "Bill, I notice that I am feeling tempted to give you another compliment today. I just want to warn you ahead of time so that you can prepare yourself in case my compliment is too positive again."

Another maneuver is *paradoxical.* The most common paradoxical interventions use the strategy of "prescribing the symptom."[24] The social worker asks the client to recreate and/or exaggerate an unwanted cognitive or behavioral symptom. Thus, the client is put into a situation in which he cannot lose. If the client does recreate or exaggerate the symptom, she is in control of the symptom (rather than having the symptom in control of the client). If the client cannot recreate or exaggerate the symptom, the client is at least temporarily relieved of the symptom.

The social worker does not use paradoxical interventions with clients who show risk for suicidal, homicidal, abusive, or other dangerous behaviors. An example of a paradoxical intervention follows. A man who is divorcing his wife complains to his worker that he is feeling tremendous guilt about the situation. The social worker determines that the guilt is excessive, so the worker says, "Ralph, I want you to set aside a 'guilty hour' every night, starting tonight, in which you are to sit somewhere in your house and feel as guilty as possible."

Psychoeducation of knowledge and skills for living. With some clients, the most appropriate goal is to teach specific knowledge and skills for living. A wide range of knowledge and skills may need to be taught. Some clients need to learn how to be more assertive, and others need to learn how to tie their shoes and cook their own meals. The teaching of such material does not always have to be didactic; indeed, clients seem to learn most effectively when taught with examples and with opportunities for experiential learning. Workers can model new behaviors and then have clients practice these behaviors in the office.

Work With Couples, Families, and Other Groups

Second Force interventions can be used to help couples and families change the way they think and act so that they can develop more functional relationships with each other. The worker can use any of the key Second Force intervention strategies outlined earlier. Often, the worker arranges a reciprocal contract in which one client agrees to change certain well-defined behaviors in return for certain behavioral changes in the other. When there is a history of maltreatment, the worker may use Second Force interventions to help control the abusive behavior.

In *couple work,* the social worker can challenge each client to change his thinking and behaviors in the relationship. The worker may ask the clients to reframe the way they view themselves, their partners, and the relationship. The worker may also ask the clients to replace old dysfunctional behaviors with new, more functional behaviors. Often, the worker asks the clients to define which behavioral changes they would like to see in themselves and their partners.

For example, a social worker is with a lesbian couple who complain of frequent arguments and a loss of love. The worker may, at some point in the sessions, ask each woman to view her partner as a wounded person who does not mean to harm her (rather than someone who is intentionally trying to hurt her). After this reframing, the worker might also then have the couple form a reciprocal contract, in which each agrees to change one behavior. One woman asks her partner to stop yelling at her. In return, she agrees to stop nagging.

Often, reciprocal contracting techniques can be useful in making assessments and interventions with couples. Each week, each person agrees to change one specific behavior in return for a reciprocal change by the partner of one behavior. For example, John will come home earlier if Mary leaves him alone for an hour before they interact. If the couple is unable to agree upon a simple contract in the office, or if they are completely unable to have any mutual success at home with even a very simple contract, then the social worker considers the possibility of lack of commitment to the relationship or of more serious pathology in the relationship. A social worker might try to regularly leave couples with some kind of mutual agreement or other homework assignment at the end of each session. There is only 50 minutes of therapy time per week compared to more than 100 hours of waking time between sessions that can be used by the clients.

In *family work,* the worker also tries to help clients change the way they think or act. Often, there are specific complaints that parents make about their children's behaviors (and vice versa). The worker may try to help the parent change the child's behaviors, if the worker believes these changes would be in the child's best interests. Often, the worker strives to help the parent view the child more positively and to help the parent discipline the child more effectively.

For example, a mother and her 16-year-old daughter come to see a worker. The mother complains that the girl is constantly acting out in ways that infuriate her. The worker decides to focus first upon the poor communication between the mother and daughter. She has the two clients practice using "I" messages and empathic listening.

Structural interventions can sometimes be helpful with maltreating families that are unable to work with psychodynamic interventions. The overall goal of structural family therapy is to help the family make inflexible boundaries more flexible, resolve symptoms, and make structural changes in dysfunctional family patterns.[25] Techniques that may be helpful include (a) joining with and accommodating to family, (b) challenging family beliefs, and (c) altering boundaries through family sculpting. Sculpting interventions may be effective with families who are particularly uncomfortable in the office, dysfunctional, or referred nonvoluntarily. These techniques seem to work as both icebreakers and catalysts. For example, a family can be asked to stand up and assemble in the center of the room, and then choose a location to stand that reflects their comfort level with the rest of the family. Family members often end up standing in locations ranging from the center of the room to the most distant corners. Each member can be asked informally for observations and comments.

For example, the social worker can ask, "What do you think about where everybody is standing? Does it reflect reality?" This exercise can lead to a discussion that can easily last the rest of the hour. Additional follow-up exercises might include having members (a) exchange positions, (b) stand in a spot that represents where they would like to feel, and (c) take turns moving family members around to where they would like them to be. Social workers may benefit from learning more about such structural family therapy concepts as coalitions, patterns, and boundaries. These concepts may be helpful in the assessment and treatment of families. Most maltreating families that workers see do have difficulties with boundaries. Often, parents are either extremely enmeshed with or disengaged from their children to the extent that the development of the children has been damaged. Role reversals between children and parents are common. The mother-daughter relationship in a father-daughter incestuous family, for example, usually have reversed roles so that the child takes on the family role of the wife.

The examination of systemic family dynamics can help the social worker and client both see that the identified patient often is not the most disturbed family member, and that the presenting problem often is not the most serious family problem. For example, in a case where the father has repeatedly beaten his oldest son, the other children may be as damaged by the family dynamics as the abuse victim.

The diagramming of family genograms[26] is also a very useful strategy to help understand abusive family systems. All social workers who have not done so may want to take the time to diagram their own family of origin and process their reactions with a supportive person. This exercise is a good way to become acquainted with genogramming and also can assist the social worker in identifying possible countertransferences that they may encounter in working with maltreating families.

Strategic family therapy techniques[27] may also be used as cognitive/behavioral/communications with families. Simply said, people usually try Plan A to solve a problem. If Plan A does not work, they usually try Plan A twice as hard. If that does not work, then they try Plan A three times as hard, and so on. In strategic therapy, the social worker does not seek insight, but rather develops a strategy that is designed to produce behavioral changes (a Plan B).

For example, a family is referred that has a very patriarchal structure—the father is very controlling of his wife and three sons. The presenting problem is that the youngest son wants to try out for the poetry club in high school instead of the football team, like his older brothers. The father has repeatedly tried to change his son's vocational goal. The strategic social worker might reframe the situation by telling the parents, "What a wonderful job both of you have done in supporting your son to become such a talented boy!"

In *groups,* Second Force interventions have many applications. Often, social workers will use these interventions with populations that need external structuring, require specialized skills, or cannot tolerate the uncovering interventions used in the other forces. In some children's groups, workers may focus upon encouraging simple, appropriate social interactions between the children themselves. Some client populations may benefit from a psychoeducational approach in which certain knowledge (e.g., child developmental theory for parents) or skills (e.g., job interviewing skills) are taught and practiced. A group for anxious adults may focus on eliminating and replacing common thinking errors.

Experiential Exercises to Enhance Conscious Use of Self in Cognitive/Behavioral/Communications Paradigm

1. In groups of two (dyads), describe to your partner a current problem or challenge that you are now facing in your life. The person playing the role of the social worker is to help the person playing the role of the client to consider what thinking errors may be contributing to the problem or challenge. The social worker then helps the client replace the thinking errors with more helpful and realistic beliefs. Switch roles when you are finished.

2. In groups of three ("threedads"), first choose who will play the roles of a social worker, a parent, and a child. Then, the parent and child are to act out a parent-child conflict (e.g., the parent and adolescent disagree about what time curfew should be on school nights). The social worker is to help the two clients resolve their conflict in a way in which both feel they have won. Consider using problem-solving and conflict resolution skills.

3. Again in threedads, first choose who will play the role of a social worker and the roles of two people in a couple relationship. The couple is to make up a story of how they are upset with one another in the relationship. Then, the social worker is to assist the two clients in setting up a reciprocal contract, in which each person agrees to make one behavioral change in return for the other person also making one behavioral change. In the role-play, find out what happened during the week by having another meeting the next week.

Impact on Individual, Family, Local Community, and Global Community

A cognitive/behavioral/communications social worker might say that there are no human thinking or behavior patterns that cannot be modified. Most individuals can make at least some immediate behavioral changes that are often followed later by changes in thinking and, finally, in feeling.

When Second Force technologies are used in the family, communications in marital-type and parent-child relationships can become much more effective. Families can learn effective and nonviolent ways to resolve conflicts and solve problems.

When communities apply Second Force technologies to their local conflicts and problems, there are also opportunities for more effective and nonviolent conflict resolutions and problem solving. Communities can focus resources toward helping local populations at risk by working to modify thinking errors and dysfunctional behaviors both in those populations and in the community as a whole. Thus, communities can use public education strategies to combat oppression and improve social justice.

As our global community learns to apply Second Force technologies to international conflicts and problems, humanity becomes more effective at resolving such global survival threats as overpopulation, poverty and hunger, nuclear war and terrorism, and environmental deterioration. Humanity can no longer afford to use violent methods (e.g., war, threats of war) to resolve our international conflicts and problems.

CHAPTER 11

Experiential/Humanistic/ Existential Paradigm

Key Elements

Focus. The focus is upon the fostering of growth toward self-actualization through self-awareness, self-acceptance, and self-expression in the here and now.

Developmental dimensions. Affective development is emphasized, particularly the awareness, acceptance, and expression of feelings.

View of health. Healing is wholing; healing is having integrity (wholeness). The healthy individual is self-actualizing, or becoming herself. The client feels good about herself, is responsible for herself, and able to express who she is openly and honestly. The client can find meaning in her life.

View of pathology. The client is not actualizing, does not feel good about herself, suppresses and does not trust her personal experience, and cannot find meaning in her life.

Art and science. There is considerable evidence that such relational worker variables as genuineness, empathy, an ability to relate, and an ability to show caring to the client are more important than technique in predicting success. However, overall, the empirical base of Third Force methods remains limited. Practitioners can select Third Force interventions based upon empirical research, theory, and worker and client intuition.

Relationship. The worker develops a horizontal (equal) relationship with the client in which both people, it is hoped, co-create an authentic relationship with one another.

Strengths. These methods tend to bring energy into the helping relationship as issues and objectives are experienced in the here and now. The work is not only intellectual, but goes below the head into the rest of the body as well. The use of empathy, warmth, and genuineness tend to help build the helping relationship.

Limitations. The client may not yet be ready to take more responsibility for her own growth. The client may still be functioning primarily on the prepersonal level and thus not have enough internal structure yet to be unable to tolerate the work. Changes in awareness may or may not lead to changes in feeling, thinking, and behavior.

Fit in Advanced Generalist Practice With Four Forces of Social Work

The advanced generalist social worker does not want to be limited to interventions designed only to heal (First Force) or reduce symptoms (Second Force). When clients struggle with their symptoms, they can move beyond healing toward growth. Clients may want help in furthering their development, to self-actualize. Third Force interventions work best when they are included with First and Second Force interventions, because healing and growing processes are usually interrelated. Some clients may need to heal trauma before they make certain developmental progress. Other clients may be able to move relatively quickly through trauma into a process of growth and self-actualization. The reduction and replacement of symptoms may also either precede or follow particular developmental stages.

Third Force interventions often can be used to follow up on psychodynamic interventions. After initial insight into past and present dynamics is established, these interventions can be used to provide the client with here-and-now experiences that provide opportunities for increased awareness and growth. These interventions can also be used to enhance client motivation to make cognitive and behavioral changes.

The social worker using Third Force interventions has a horizontal relationship with the client; the client is recognized as being an expert about herself in the world. In the helping process, social workers may choose at times to be transparent about themselves with their clients, when such disclosure is appropriate and meets the needs of the client (rather than those of the therapist). Being genuine with the client is often helpful in all stages of the helping process and with all intervention paradigms of the therapeutic process. In particular, genuineness seems to enhance the building of a therapeutic relationship during the beginning stage of the work. Genuine feedback and personal disclosure often assist in the working or middle phase as well. In termination, the social worker's genuineness may be very meaningful and helpful to the client who is processing issues related to transition and loss.

When a client is ready to focus on the emotional and other experiential dimensions of personal growth, these interventions can assist the client in accelerating development. Research has demonstrated that emotional growth is vital to human development.[28] The consideration of the client's experiences has also been shown to be vital in the helping process: "the evidence is now substantial that person variables, human factors, self-referencing processes pervade all human experience" (p. 213).[29] Existential approaches emphasize the client's ability to take responsibility for his own life and to make decisions based upon this recognition of responsibility. The client needs to recognize that choices exist in his life and then creates the will to make decisions.[30]

Third Force interventions can thus help enliven First and Second Force interventions; they give clients the opportunity to reexperience the past, experience who they currently are, and encounter their possible futures.

Key Intervention Strategies With Case Examples

Several key interventions can be identified that range in descending order from a direct to more indirect style. The social worker selects interventions that match the needs to the client.

Confrontation. The social worker directly challenges the client to grow. Perls often used a confrontational style in which he would confront clients with his perceptions of what was going on in a session.[31] Often, he would ask the client to become aware of the apparent incongruence between the client's beliefs about self and reality. For example, the worker might tell a depressed man, "You are complaining a great deal today."

Experiments. The social worker asks the client to try a new behavior that is designed to promote the client's growth. These experiments often require the client to role-play different parts of her self, and then to process the experiment with the worker. The client may also play out old and new ways of being in situations, and then process these experiences with the worker. For example, the worker might ask a delinquent teenage girl who hates her mother to try acting like her mother in a session.

Self-esteem work. The social worker strives to help the client increase her self-esteem using a variety of strategies. The first strategy uses "unconditional positive regard."[32] This means that the worker consistently values the client as a human being. For example, a client says, "I really screwed up when I lost my temper and told my boss that she was too rigid." The social worker says, "It is understandable that you finally said what you had been thinking all these years. At least you did not become verbally abusive. I think you have been very self-controlled at work."

Another strategy uses "confirmation of otherness."[33] This means that the worker not only consistently values the client as a human being, but also values herself. The worker strives to establish a dialogue with the client in which the uniqueness of both individuals is valued and individual differences can be safely expressed. For example, during her initial interview, a mother says, "If that daughter of mine acts like a tramp, I will slap her again, I don't care what anybody says." The child protective services worker replies, "I think I can understand why you are worried about your daughter and why you think using physical punishment might help her. However, I think I need to let you know where I am coming from so you know who I am. I do not believe that physical punishment helps any child. I think you can find a more effective way to help your daughter than by slapping her."

A third strategy is to increase the client's awareness of his self-esteem through a variety of techniques, such as interpretations, empathic responses, storytelling, and experiments. For example, a social worker is seeing a 70-year-old woman who is depressed. The worker might say, "As you tell me your story, I can't help but notice how hard you have tried all of these years to take care of everybody's needs in your family. I imagine that it must be difficult to have your own daughter criticize you for being selfish. Indeed, it seems you have never had anyone tell you that you are a good person; it's no wonder that you are so critical of yourself."

Client self-direction is another strategy. The social worker creates the core conditions of growth and lets the client lead the way in the helping process. The worker lets the client take the lead in self-exploration and expression and is empathic, warm, and genuine. When the worker is transparent about her own feelings, she may offer empathic responses to the client, such as, "When I hear you tell your story, I feel very sad."

Evaluation. Evaluation is as important in Third Force intervention strategies as it is in any other social work practice paradigm. Maslow[34] found that self-actualizing people tend to become self-evaluating, and social workers often ask clients to evaluate their own progress when using Third Force intervention strategies. However, any form of evaluation can be used, and workers may select formal instruments, particularly if they can find ways to use them without compromising their horizontal and humanistic relationship with the client and client/system.

Work With Couples and Families

Third Force interventions can be used to help couples and families become more aware of their here-and-now emotional experience and develop greater emotional intimacy. Third Force interventions can be powerful means of helping clients directly experience their issues and can complement First and Second

Force family interventions. The worker can use any of the key intervention strategies outlined earlier. When there is a history of maltreatment, the worker does not use Third Force strategies until the abusive behavior can be controlled.

In *couple work,* when there is sufficient safety in the relationship, the social worker can have the clients do both their own individual and their collective work together. The worker strives to help clients become more aware of how they feel about themselves, their partners, and their relationships. There is much room for creativity. Often, the worker has the clients express these feelings directly with each other. The expressions may be verbal or nonverbal (e.g., drawings, sculpture, psychodrama).

For example, a social worker is seeing a heterosexual couple who complain of frequent arguments and a loss of love. The worker may at some point in the sessions ask each partner to exaggerate the way they suspect their partner really wants them to act. The woman gets down on her knees in mock drama and bows to her husband, saying, "Oh, my patriarchal master, please forgive me for wanting to have a self. I am your obedient servant." They both laugh. Then, the man takes out his wallet and says, "Honey, here's a blank check for you, I am going to start working 100 hours a week so you can have all that you want. And anytime you want to process feelings, please let me know and I will listen." The exercise breaks the ice for this couple and enables them to look at some deep issues in their marriage.

When couples first fall in love, they often experience an intense emotional intimacy. Often, that sense of intimacy will fade unless the couple works (strives to understand, accept, and communicate) the shadow aspects of the relationship. These include the vulnerabilities, limitations, and imperfections of each partner that inevitably become activated in any lover relationship. The worker uses Third Force interventions to help the couple understand and express the shadow emotional experience in the relationship. Many couples expect that emotional intimacy should continue but are unwilling or unable to do the necessary work to develop that intimacy. Some professionals try to help couples rebuild their affectionate bond by teaching them how to be more empathic with one another.

For example, a worker might have a young couple talk about their last fight and examine what feelings they felt (but had not yet directly expressed). The woman discovers that underneath her anger was fear of abandonment and a great deal of hurt about how her husband had ignored her since they were married. The man discovers that his anger is mostly about a fear of engulfment; he realizes that he has felt a loss of freedom since his marriage.

In *family work,* when there is sufficient safety in the relationship, the social worker asks parents and children to be more aware and expressive of their emotional experience. In order to do such work, clients often have to talk first about how and why they have not yet felt safe to share such deep feelings in the family.

For example, a mother and her 16-year-old son come to see a worker. The mother complains that the son is constantly acting out in ways that infuriate her. After a few sessions, the worker asks the boy to start talking with his mother about what he really has been feeling. Over several sessions, he gradually tells her that he resents her divorcing his father and marrying a new man who turned out to be an alcoholic. The mother feels a great deal of pain but is able to hear her son. They cry together.

With *groups,* the social worker may use Third Force techniques for a variety of reasons. Some groups may be support groups in which the worker simply strives to encourage and maintain (rather than radically alter) the clients' life patterns. A nondirective approach to such groups may be used, in which the worker helps create a safe, empathic, warm, and genuine group atmosphere.

Clients may also need to use Third Force techniques to encourage deeper sharing of emotions between group members. The social worker may become more active and ask the clients to address each other directly, make eye contact, and experiment with different words and other behaviors. For example, a worker may ask the members of a men's group to take turns giving each other positive feedback.

Experiential Exercises to Enhance Conscious Use of Self in Experiential/Humanistic/Existential Paradigm

1. Sit in dyads with a partner. Look in each other's eyes for 60 seconds without talking. Then share what the experience was like for each of you. How did it feel to look but not talk? Was it easier to look when talking was allowed again? What are the implications of all of this for doing "talk therapy" with clients? Does talking always help us be closer to each other or our clients?

2. Arrange the group in two concentric circles, one inside of the other. Have each person in the inner circle stand, facing one person in the outside circle. With your first partner, the person on the inside is to share the first impression they had of that person. Then, the outside circle rotates one person to the right and the exercise is repeated with a new partner. Repeat until everyone has a chance to give and receive first impressions from all of the others in the group.

3. Using the same two-circle format above, stand facing your partner. The person in the inner circle asks the person on the outside for feedback about a particular issue (e.g., "Tell me how you perceive my ability to communicate" or "Do you think people like me?"). The other person is to give any feedback that they think may be helpful. Repeat until everyone has a chance to give and receive feedback from all of the others in the group.

Impact on Individual, Family, Local Community, and Global Community

An experiential/humanistic/existential social worker might say that the emerging result of the human potential (or self-actualization) movement has not been a "me generation" but rather a "we generation." Studies show that self-actualization leads not only to individual fulfillment but to individual responsibility for collective well-being. Individuals who self-actualize therefore tend to become committed to enhancing the well-being of themselves and the families, communities, and globe in which they live.

When Third Force strategies are applied at the family level, the family becomes a safe and supportive arena for growth. In such families, there is a balance in emphasis between the well-being of the individual and the well-being of the family as a whole. As individuals in the family develop, they tend to cultivate healthy interpersonal boundaries; dialogue is valued, and violence is discouraged. Dialogue is only possible when there is safety in the family for individuals to be all of who they are, to be different. Violence is monologue because the victim is silenced. There is a high priority to protect the most vulnerable and least powerful family members from all forms of maltreatment (e.g., child abuse and neglect, couple abuse, abuse of vulnerable adults).

A community of self-actualizing people is a community of people who are healing, who are "wholing." Such people strive to become who they are meant to be, regardless of their gender, race, culture, sexual orientation, age, or any other particular human characteristic. Such people also do not tolerate intolerance or oppression of human development against any other individual or subpopulation.

A global community that values human development will not tolerate global processes that inhibit development, including preparations for wars of mass destruction, deterioration of the environment, and poverty and hunger. A global community that values dialogue will seek nonviolent, win-win solutions to international conflicts and problems.

CHAPTER 12

Transpersonal Paradigm

Key Elements

Focus. The focus is on spiritual growth that includes both stewardship of the highest levels of well-being and integration of the shadow parts of self that are underdeveloped or have been lost.

Developmental issues. Spiritual development is emphasized, although all of the other dimensions of development are considered interrelated with spirituality.

View of health. As the client develops her spirituality, she is developing greater connection with the innermost self (or soul) and the universe. The client may also develop greater peace of mind, freedom from excessive attachment to ego, and a sense of purpose and service in life. The goal is not escape from pain but rather to develop mindfulness (awareness and acceptance) of self and the world.

The client discovers that therapy does not so much remove symptoms as it puts them in the background so that they no longer distract the client's internal and external functioning. In other words, clients do not change so much as they become the person they were meant to be and learn to love that person more. Clients are seen not as people who are trying to learn to be spiritual but as spiritual beings who are trying to learn how to be the best people they can be.

The healthy client is able to not only tolerate the many diverse spiritual paths he may encounter in other people, but also assertively express his own spiritual beliefs when necessary. This ability to affirm the uniqueness of both self and others is an aspect of "confirmation of otherness."[35] The client who is on her spiritual path is likely to feel greater joy in life.

View of pathology. The client is having difficulty navigating successfully through a particular phase of his spiritual path, which may be at the prepersonal, personal, or transpersonal levels of development. For example, the client may have become "ego attached" to her wealth, power, or status or is perhaps going through a "dark night of soul," when her direction is especially unclear.

Although spiritual development can be viewed as a lifelong process of letting go of ego, people may gain new ego attachments during the developmental process. This seemingly paradoxical tendency, which may be called "spiritual materialism,"[36] is a form of "egoitis" in which a person becomes especially affixed for a time to a particular way of thinking or acting.

Art and science. Investigation into effectiveness is still in its beginning stages. However, there is substantial evidence of a body-mind-spirit connection, as well as increasing multidisciplinary evidence that suggests that a person's religiosity and spirituality tend to foster her biopsychosocial well-being.[37] Therefore, practitioners can select transpersonal interventions based on empirical research, theory, and worker and client intuition.

Relationship. The worker develops a horizontal relationship with the client. In this relationship, the worker and client are not only equals, but also both have access to wisdom about the world. Although the worker remains the only professional helper in the relationship, the worker views the client as another teacher in his own life.

Strengths. All dimensions of human development are considered, especially the spiritual (which is often ignored in social work practice). The diversity of clients (e.g., across age, culture, gender, etc.) is considered to have an essential spiritual dimension that can be related to. Transpersonal theory is inclusive; interventions from First, Second, and Third Force psychology are used.

Because most (if not all) problems encountered by social workers have a spiritual component, and because these components are often the most ignored, Fourth Force interventions provide a potentially vital helping method. In addition, more and more clients may be expected to be seeking spiritual development as the second millennium ends and the third begins.[38]

Transpersonal approaches may be particularly useful in helping some clients heal and grow through the practice of their own religious or cultural rituals. For example, some Native American clients have reported that their use of ancestral traditions such as the sweatlodge and the fast assisted significantly in their overall development.[39] Social workers should not, however, assume that all Native Americans would benefit from such experiences. In addition, social workers should always be sensitive to how any client may feel about the worker suggesting or using such interventions, particularly if the worker's culture and race is different from the client's.

Limitations. Transpersonal interventions may be inappropriate to use with certain clients. Clients who cannot tolerate First and Third Force interventions (such as clients who are working at the prepersonal level of development) may not be able to tolerate Fourth Force interventions either. There will also be many clients who have such negative associations with spirituality or religiosity that they cannot yet tolerate transpersonal interventions. In such cases, alternative language and/or interventions may be required.

Fit in Advanced Generalist Practice With Four Forces of Social Work

In the beginning phase of a case, clients who are comfortable in the spiritual dimension of development may relate particularly well to Fourth Force interventions. Social workers should consider the spiritual history of a client when considering if and when to discuss spiritual issues. In the middle phase, Fourth Force interventions can be used to build upon other interventions drawn from the other three forces of psychology, particularly when a client needs to heal spiritual traumas, when the spiritual component of a problem needs to be considered, or when the client wishes to foster his spiritual development.

The transpersonal, Fourth Force approach includes the cognitive, emotional, physical, and interpersonal dimensions. The spiritual dimension is especially emphasized, a process that was foreseen by Maslow[40] as a logical extension of the humanistic/experiential/phenomenological theories of self-actualization and growth. The spiritual dimension can be understood as the innate drive in all beings to perfect themselves[41] and to discover or create meaning in life.[42] The cognitive/behavioral/communications idea of replacing dysfunctional cognition with more functional cognition also logically extends to spiritual beliefs. Albert Einstein, one of the most highly developed cognitive beings of our century, noted that the most important thing to decide about the universe is whether it is friendly or not. That decision can be defined as a spiritual question. As Coles[43] has noted, many prominent theorists representing all of the forces of psychology have considered the importance of spirituality in psychotherapy.

The term "transpersonal" means literally "beyond the persona," or "in addition to the mask of our personality."[44] Transpersonal psychology refers to that which is beyond the personality that all people have, to that which connects all of us together. Most of Western psychology, represented in the first three Forces, deals with the personality, which functions to seek recognition and protect from pain.[45] Transpersonal psychology does not exclude the personality from consideration; rather, it adds to the study of the personality the study of the human desire for higher levels of consciousness that most of the major religious traditions of the world address.

The transpersonalist perspective is informed not only by knowledge acquired through logical positivist, scientific means, but also through such domains as literature, philosophy, art, and religion.[46] Transpersonal interventions are not just for the upper and middle class, but can have relevance to the diversity of client populations because most of today's social problems are related to spiritual factors.[47] Social workers have successfully used spiritual interventions with a variety of client populations.[48]

Key Intervention Strategies
With Case Examples

Several key Fourth Force interventions can be identified, including three that draw upon strategies developed in the first three Forces of psychology. Although the emphasis in transpersonal work is on the spiritual dimension of development, the worker always considers all of the dimensions of development in the work.

Selfwork. The hallmark intervention in transpersonal social work is the social worker's own "selfwork." Selfwork refers to the worker's ongoing effort to grow in all of the dimensions of development, especially in the spiritual dimension. The worker's selfwork is driven, at least in part, by the client and client/system. The social worker recognizes her countertransference reactions to the client and client/system, including the spiritual countertransferences, and considers each reaction a clue to the selfwork the social worker needs to do now. As the social worker does her own selfwork, this process facilitates the client's own multi-dimensional (including spiritual) development.

Although the worker never forgets that her primary responsibility is to help the client and client/system, the worker also realizes that one of the most powerful ways to help clients grow is to work on her own growth. The client is seen as a teacher or mirror for the worker, in the sense that the client is reflecting the worker's need to grow in some area(s) of personal development. The worker conceptualizes the client as being in the worker's life to challenge the worker to do a particular piece of selfwork. In the process of that selfwork, both worker and client grow.

For example, a client tells his social worker in their first meeting that he wants to learn how to have more joy in his life. The worker notices that her countertransference reaction seems to be fear, and that she seems to be doing an unusual amount of intellectualizing with the client. After consulting with her own therapist, the worker starts to realize that the client is really mirroring the worker's own need to have more joy in her own life. She realizes that the reason she is afraid and "in her head" is that she feels too incompetent to help the client. Her own therapist helps the worker remember that her client does not need her to be perfect as much as he needs her to be aware of and accepting of her own imperfections. In her selfwork, the worker lets go of her need to be an expert on joy and starts to take an honest look at why she is not as joyful as she should be.

She notices that her client seems to be involved in a similar process, and that she is now less fearful of and more compassionate about how hard it is for the client to learn joy. When she shares all this with her therapist, the worker's therapist smiles and says, "I guess it turns out that it really is good enough if you are only a week ahead of your client in this area of development, as long as you are aware and accepting of this process."

In another example, a social worker notices that he happens to now have several clients who are in the process of divorcing their spouses. Each of these clients has the normal internal conflict between their guilt and their desire for growth and joy. The worker notices that he seems to have an unusual lack of enthusiasm for the growth of his clients and seems to be wanting to point out the hazards and pitfalls of divorce. The worker suspects that he is having some kind of countertransference with all of his divorcing clients and does some selfwork with his own therapist.

What he discovers is that his clients are mirroring an extremely uncomfortable issue in his own life regarding his denial about the unhappiness in his own marriage. He realizes that this discovery does not mean that he needs to run out immediately and get a divorce himself, but it does mean he needs to look deeply at where his life is at and where he wants it to go. As he does this selfwork, he notices that he is better able to accept and have compassion for the processes of his clients.

As social workers do selfwork, they may begin to think that they are not so much social workers learning to become more spiritual, but spiritual beings learning to be the best social workers they can be. The social worker involved in selfwork may be more likely to have what Maslow called "plateau experiences."[49] The peak experience (developed as part of Maslow's Third Force theory) is a relatively intense, emotional, and brief episode of awe that tends to follow periods of growth. In contrast, the plateau experience is a calmer and longer lasting event (often stimulated by the awareness of mortality) in which spiritual development and a shift in consciousness are likely. The worker may find that clients are more likely to have plateau experiences in response to the worker's and/or their own selfwork.

Perhaps the most common recurring obstacle that social workers may have in doing selfwork is what Trungpa calls "spiritual materialism."[50] Spiritual materialism is a distortion of awareness in which a person mistakes the strengthening of egocentricity for spiritual development. Although spiritual development may be defined as a gradual process of letting go of ego attachments, workers may become attached to a particular practice, belief, knowledge base, or ritual that may service some ego need (to be smart, spiritual, trendy, etc.). Spiritual materialism need not be viewed as a pathological process; it can be used as a symptom of the very human, lifelong tendency toward egocentricity, as well as a reminder of to what the worker is currently still attached. The worker strives to be continually aware of how spiritual materialism may subtly sneak into his developmental process, and then gradually strives to let go of the latest attachments that have appeared.

Mindfulness and meditation. The concept of mindfulness, as developed in some Eastern spiritual traditions, involves the development of self-observation, usually through meditation. The usefulness of such techniques may be limited unless the client also has the benefit of a social worker who can function as an objective, but imperfect observer.[51] If the social worker tries to act too perfect (if she takes on the role of a spiritual guru who has completed all possible spiritual development), then the client is unlikely to feel that his own imperfections are acceptable.

Interventions Drawn From the Psychodynamic (First) Force

The social worker can help the client uncover and heal spiritual traumas that have occurred in the client's past. Such traumas are often associated with the way spirituality and religiosity were dealt with in the client's family, church, and/or culture. The social worker can also help the client process positive spiritual experiences that the client has been unable to understand and accept.

The worker remembers that clients may reject (repress or deny) aspects of self that are viewed by the client as undesirable, as well as aspects of self that are viewed as very positive. In other words, clients often feel as uncomfortable about their highest (or most spiritually developed) aspects as they do about their least developed (shadow) aspects. Thus, the worker strives to help the client uncover, reclaim, and accept all aspects of self.

The worker can use interpretations, empathic responses, storytelling, and psychoeducational interventions to assist the client in this process. The worker often helps the client see that the client's symptoms are not so much a sign that something is broken and needs to be fixed, but more a sign that the soul is still working correctly and is trying to tell the client that spiritual growth is required.

An example of an interpretation is a case involving a 60-year-old male alcoholic client. The man tells the worker that he has been depressed since he was a young man. The worker replies, "Bill, you have been depressed for many years. I wonder if your depression is linked at least in part to the fact that you have forgotten who you really are. It sounds like you used to dream about making a difference in the world, and then you gave that up after you entered the service. That part of you does not like being ignored, so you get depressed."

An example of an empathic response can be given using the same case example. In this example, the worker might tell the depressed client, "Bill, while you were talking, I was imagining what it would be like to have lived your life. It must have been hard all these years to feel like you had to go it alone. You never had anyone who was particularly encouraging or helpful to you. I can see why it is hard now for you to be coming here and letting me help you a little. I don't blame you for being depressed; it would be depressing to believe that there is no opportunity for you to give or receive love in this world."

A storytelling intervention might look a little different. The worker tells this client, "Bill, let me tell you a story. There was this young man who was born on the South Side of Chicago. One of the gifts he was born with was a connection with his innermost soul and the outer world, particularly with nature. Unfortunately, his father discouraged these connections in his son because the father believed that spiritual development was unmasculine. The young man learned to hide his spirituality, not only from others, but from himself. He gradually became more and more depressed, and he used alcohol to reduce the pain of his life. However, when he was about 60 years old, he began rediscovering his soul. He started to realize that his father was wrong, and that his spirituality was an essential part of his self."

The worker could also use psychoeducation with Bill. The worker could tell him, "Bill, a lot of people think that if the depression can be reduced, then the person is cured. However, another way to view depression is that it is the soul's way of telling a person that something needs to be attended to." In that sense, depression is a sign that something is working right (transpersonal model), not that something is broken (medical or pathological model). Often, depression is suggesting that a person has forgotten about his highest self. Depression can also suggest that the person needs to reclaim some of her shadow material.

The social worker can also use the transactional analysis (TA)[52] model to help clients understand any inner conflict they may have about spirituality and religion. Often, clients have an imbalance between the parent and child ego states regarding their spirituality. The worker strives to help the client become more aware of these internal dynamics and rebalance the internal power struggle. Either the parent or the child can have too much power in the psyche.

When the internal parent has too much power, the client is paralyzed by toxic shame and excessive guilt about his spirituality. Usually, this shame and guilt has its origins in early experiences of spiritual maltreatment, when the client was shamed or punished for his own spiritual experiences or expressions.[53] For example, a 20-year-old female sees a social worker at the college counseling center. She feels toxic shame and excessive guilt about her sexuality, to the point that she has become depressed and quite anxious (symptoms that used to be called neurotic). She was taught in her church as a child that it is a sin to masturbate or be sexual in any other way until one is married. She tells the worker she would like to feel less guilty. The worker shows her how her internal parent has too much power and helps her see how her shame and guilt originated in her past. The worker suggests several books for her to read and refers her to a women's support group.

When the chid has too much power, the client is unable to regulate, contain, or delay gratification of her own needs and may use spiritual development as a rationale for her behavior. There is insufficient guilt (internal parent) to control the internal child's impulses. The client usually has what psychologists now call characterological disorders, such as borderline or narcissistic traits. For example, a 50-year-old minister is court-ordered into counseling after an adolescent in his congregation complains that he has tried repeatedly to kiss her. The minister tells the worker that he was trying to help the girl in her religious training. The worker uses the TA model to illustrate how the man's internal child has too much power in his psyche. The worker also refers the client to an empathy training program for male sex offenders.

Interventions Drawn From the Cognitive/Behavioral/ Communications (Second) Force

The social worker often strives to help the client change the way he thinks or acts. A variety of intervention techniques can be used.

The social worker can use modeling and rehearsal techniques to help the client change behaviors. For example, a 39-year-old man states that, although he has achieved his career and financial goals, his life seems empty and meaningless. The social worker finds out in the assessment that the man was once quite poor himself and is interested in the welfare of the homeless. The worker takes the client downtown to a soup kitchen and models talking with the homeless people in the soup line. The worker has the client rehearse simple helping interventions in the office. Later, the client joins the worker in volunteering at the soup kitchen.

The social worker can reframe the way the client views the universe. If the client views the universe as an unfriendly place, the client's behaviors will tend to be oriented toward self-protection rather than self-development. The worker tries to help the client view the world more realistically (positively). For example, a teenage girl is depressed. Her boyfriend started going out with another girl, and she started feeling despair that she would ever find another relationship. In the assessment, the girl explains how she has grown up in a family system that was very negative about the world. She remembers how her mother made such comments as, "All men want is one thing" and "If a girl doesn't have a man, she doesn't have nothing." The worker helps the girl become aware of where her negative views of the world came from and how unrealistic they are. The worker suggests new ways of viewing the world and encourages the girl to view herself as valuable whether or not she is in a relationship.

The worker can ask the client to use various visualization techniques to help the client change her thoughts and behaviors. Visualization techniques are used by sports psychologists to help athletes prepare for competitive games or events. Ahsen[54] has shown how clients may be able to use visual imagery to heal and grow. The client's spiritual development may be fostered through the use of such techniques. For example, a middle-aged housewife states that she would like to have more peace of mind in her life. The worker teaches her a visualization technique in which the woman first relaxes her body and then imagines being in a safe outdoor place where she can consult with her own higher self.

Interventions Drawn From the Experiential/ Humanistic/Existential (Third) Force

A variety of techniques can be used to help clients.

Self-acceptance work[55] may be quite helpful in the process of furthering spiritual development. The social worker believes that the best way to help the client develop spiritually is paradoxically to help the client accept exactly where she is spiritually in the here and now. For example, if the client says, "I am so judgmental of others; I wish I could be a more loving soul," the worker might respond with, "I am impressed with how much you already love and how much you want to learn to love more. Since someone cannot love parts of a person that they are unaware of, I also think that your willingness to look at your own imperfections (in this case, your judgmentalness) enables you to love yourself and others more."

Various forms of psychodrama can also be used to help clients develop their spirituality. The Gestalt technique of empty chairs[56] can be used to increase client self-awareness and self-acceptance. For example, a 25-year-old client tells her worker that she feels guilty that she is angry at her parents. The worker determines that this woman grew up in a very strict religious environment that included serious physical and emotional abuse. With the client's permission, the worker has the client do a role-play with God in the room. The client sits in a chair, acts as if she is God, and talks to an empty chair that represents herself. As she plays God, the client, with help from the worker, is able to tell herself that it is OK to get in touch with her anger toward her parents.

The worker can also be nondirective[57] with the client. The worker allows and even encourages the client to state not only the objectives but the interventions used in the sessions. The worker goes with the first statements made by the client at the beginning of the session. These statements may become the basis of the theme of the work each week. For example, a client comes in to see a worker at a counseling center. The client's first statement is, "Sorry I am late, I had to rush across town from the office. I had to get this report done before I could leave for my lunch hour." The worker says, "It sounds like you are really busy again" (reflective listening). The client begins talking about how busy she is. The worker may then ask, "What would be most helpful for us to do today?"

Spiritual transferences and countertransferences. The social worker strives to work with spiritual transference and countertransference reactions. These reactions are responses that the client or worker has to the other's spirituality.

Spiritual transferences are reactions that the client has to the spirituality of the worker. There are two common transferences, which are opposites: spiritual idealization and spiritual disapproval.

Idealization is a necessary developmental stage in which the client idealizes the worker and sees the worker as being all good and as the perfect spiritual teacher. When the client idealizes the worker, the client usually needs to have an ideal spiritual teacher in his life at the time whom he can model. The client needs to incorporate some of the characteristics of the worker in order to develop spiritually. The client needs the worker to accept his process. The worker understands that the client needs to idealize the worker so that the client can further develop his own spirituality. The worker does not try to help the client see the worker's limitations until the client is ready. For example, one client began working with an older social worker who had a local reputation as being spiritually developed. The client, a young man in his early 20s, at first saw his social worker as a perfect being. The worker saw the young man's idealization clearly, but waited 3 months until the client disagreed for the first time with the worker. The worker said, "I am glad you can disagree with me. They say that in the first half of the therapeutic process, the worker tries to get the client to trust the worker, and in the second half, the worker tries to let the client down easy. Perhaps you are now ready to begin seeing my imperfections."

Disapproval occurs when the client is very critical of the worker and sees the worker as all bad or even as being evil. The worker does not try to get the client to change her view of the worker but, rather, strives to understand and accept the client's experience. For example, a young female client is a devout member of a church that preaches the doctrine that wives should remain faithfully married to their husbands regardless of any circumstances. She happens to be assigned to a female social worker who has strong feminist views that women have the right to live free of abuse and to strive for happiness. The client tells the worker that her husband told her to go to counseling because she "needs to learn to be a better wife." The worker determines that the client has been emotionally, sexually, and physically abused by her husband, and she encourages the woman to protect herself from more abuse. The client tells the worker, "I am afraid that you are being influenced by the devil to corrupt me." The worker replies, "It must be difficult to come here for help and to then experience me as being so unfriendly." The client begins to cry, and the women continue to talk. The worker realizes that the client's fears have a long history, and that the client has been frightened about the devil for a long time in her life.

Spiritual countertransferences are reactions that the worker has in response to the client's spirituality. Workers will have either overidentification or underidentification countertransference reactions.

Overidentification reactions occur when the worker views the client's spiritual path as identical to his own. The worker makes the mistake of assuming that the client needs to take the same steps as the worker. The worker strives to become aware of this reaction and to be open to becoming aware and accepting of the unique path that the client needs to take. For example, a social worker who had belonged to a particular church since her childhood starts to work with an adolescent girl who happens to go to a church of the same denomination as the worker's. The worker notices that she feels the impulse to give the girl advice, even before the assessment had been completed. After consulting with a supervisor, the worker does some selfwork, gets in touch with the countertransference, and resists the impulse to give any advice to the client. Instead, the worker asks the client to talk about what she wants.

Underidentification reactions occur when the worker so dislikes what he sees in the client that the worker cannot feel empathy for the client or accept the client's spiritual path. Often, this reaction is associated with spiritual and religious trauma in the worker's own past. There are many social workers who are quite angry at adults in their family or church who were spiritually abusive or neglectful. These adults may have used religion to rationalize physical or sexual abuse, they may have tried to stop their children from developing their own spiritual beliefs, or they may have taught their children to feel toxic shame about themselves or unnecessary fear of the world. For example, a social worker is seeing a family for therapy that belongs to a patriarchal church in the community. The worker notices that she has a very strong dislike for the father, who is, in the name of God, very controlling and harsh with his wife and children. The worker processes her reaction in her selfwork and realizes that the father is like her own father and the male church leaders with whom she grew up. She realizes that she does not need to condone the father's abusive behavior, but she eventually becomes able to empathize with him and to accept his spiritual path. He responds to her acceptance with a positive shift in behavior.

Evaluation. Evaluation is also important in Fourth Force intervention strategies. Although formal strategies of measuring spiritual development are still underdeveloped, social workers can use informal measures in their practice. Such measures may likely include client participation in the definition and consideration of spiritual development. Wilber's[58] model of spiritual development can be used to help inform the evaluation process.

Work With Couples and Families

Fourth Force interventions can be used to help couples and families develop individual spirituality and collective spiritual intimacy. When there is a history of maltreatment, the worker does not use Third Force strategies until the abusive behavior can be controlled.

In *couple work,* when there is sufficient safety in the relationship, the social worker can have clients do both individual and collective transpersonal work. The worker may, at times, work with one client individually while the partner watches. The worker may also try to help the couple develop spiritual intimacy. Spiritual intimacy may be defined as the "sharing of souls," in which both partners experience a connectedness with their own soul, with the world, and with each other.

> If we understand marriage as only the commitment of two individuals to each other, then we overlook its soul, but if we see that it also has to do with family, neighborhood, and the greater community, and with our own work and personal cultivation, then we begin to glimpse the mystery that is marriage. (p. 48)[59]

Thus, the social worker realizes that, no matter how well a couple communicates and handles conflicts, reads manuals on human sexuality, and follows the cognitive/behavioral tasks given to them by their psychotherapist, without spiritual intimacy, there may be an emptiness that remains unfilled.

> It is the primary task of the marriage partners not to create a life together, but to evoke the *soul's* lover, to stir up this magical fantasy of marriage and to sustain it, thus serving the particular all-important myth that lies deep in the lover's heart and that supplies a profound need for meaning, fulfillment, and relatedness. . . . In order to fulfill its need for divine coupling, the soul needs something less tangible than a happy home. . . . It requires in the people involved a vivid sense of its own mystery and an awareness that purely human efforts to keep it alive and thriving always prove insufficient. (pp. 51-52)[60]

The worker strives to help clients become aware of their hunger for spiritual intimacy and of ways they might seek more of that kind of intimacy. For example, a social worker is seeing a gay couple who complain of sexual dysfunction in their relationship. The couple has purchased self-help books, but all of their knowledge and techniques do not seem to help. The worker asks the partners to shift their view of the sexual dysfunction from a problem to a soul expression. After some dialogue and searching, the clients start to realize that they both feel alienated from each other. After they acknowledge the disconnection, they begin to develop a more soulful connection between them.

In *family work,* when there is sufficient safety in the relationship, the social worker asks parents and children to be more aware and expressive of their spiritual development. The social worker helps the parent understand the spiritual component of parenting that deepens the parent-child relationship as spiritual intimacy deepens the relationship between two lovers. The spiritual aspect of parenting is not so much about mastery of methods of discipline, child development theory, or empathic listening. The spiritual aspect of parenting is about the sharing of souls between a parent and a child. The worker helps the parent remember that his child has needs for spiritual connection with the parent.

The most common error that parents make today is to overemphasize the importance of telling their children what their own spiritual beliefs are and to underemphasize the importance of listening to their children talk about their own spiritual experiences with their parents. Children need *both* kinds of loving assistance, to know where their parents are coming from spiritually as well as to be able to explore their own spirituality safely (without judgment) with their parents.

Often, there are religious-based parent-child conflicts, such as rules about sexuality that are given to a child by his parent and church. The social worker's job is not to change the family's religion (without their permission) but to help the parent understand and foster the spiritual development of herself and her child.

For example, a mother and her 16-year-old son come to see a worker. The mother complains that the son is constantly acting out in ways that infuriate her. After a few sessions, the worker starts to help the client trace back her own spiritual history. As the mother gains more empathy for her own spiritual path and the trials she had encountered, she becomes more empathic toward her son's own path.

The worker might also strive to help parents and children further develop the spiritual dimension of their relationships. That spiritual dimension of family life may be thought of as the process of caring for soul, both of self and other family members:

> Care of the soul is not about understanding, figuring out, and making better; rather, it resuscitates images of family life as an enrichment of identity. . . . To care for the soul of the family, it is necessary to shift from causal thinking to an appreciation for story and character, to allow grandparents and uncles to be transformed into figures of myth and to watch certain familiar family stories become canonical through repeated tellings. (p. 29)[61]

For example, a family is referred to a social worker after the 14-year-old daughter becomes pregnant by her boyfriend. At some point in the work, the worker might ask the family to sit in a circle and share stories about how other family members, living and dead, dealt with pregnancy and childbirth.

In *group work,* the social worker can lead children, adolescents, or adults in a variety of collective experiences. Often, clients can benefit from a guided visualization, during which a piece of transpersonal work can be done. One simply begins by having clients close their eyes, get comfortable, and then do whatever they need to do to relax. If they need help, clients can be taught one of a number of relaxation exercises. Following this, the worker can ask them to select a safe place where no one can bother them and where they have complete control of the surroundings. This place can be real or imagined. They are asked to describe and experience this place after they find it. Then, they are asked to imagine a television set (widescreen and color, of course) and a VCR and a remote control unit in their hands. At their feet is a box of videotapes from which they can select various videos of scenes on which they want to work.

Disidentification/Reacceptance Game

Layer 6: POSSESSIONS

Layer 5: BEHAVIORS: social roles, games, gestures, interaction patterns

Layer 4: MIND: roles, opinions, biases, beliefs

Layer 3: BODY: tensions, imbalances, pains

Layer 2: PSEUDO-FEELINGS: guilt, boredom, nervousness, frustration, depression

Layer 1: FEELINGS: sad, mad, glad, scared

Layer 0: CORE or SOUL

Figure 12.1. Disidentification/Reacceptance Game

Clients can be allowed to continue talking with the worker if they wish during the visualization. Clients can be told that they can come back and open their eyes at any time for any reason. When they want to come back, they can turn off the TV and VCR and can return to their safe place any time they would like. They may also select a loving force or wise being to enter their safe place and assist them in some work they are doing. These forces or beings may be people, figures, animals, plants, voices, or anything else the client creates.

In a group, clients can be asked to do a meditation in which they let their loving force love them totally and unconditionally, either in the present or in some particular past scene. They can be asked to allow themselves to experience a sense of self-acceptance to the extent that they are ready.

In a group, clients can also be asked to do a meditation in which they experience a gradual disidentification and reaccepting of their various layers of self. For this exercise, clients can use an adaptation of a diagram developed by Hendricks and Weinhold[62] and illustrated in Figure 12.1.

In this exercise, the client is introduced to the illustration before the visualization begins. Then, after she is relaxed, the client is asked to recognize each layer in turn, beginning with Layer 6 and working toward the core. For example, the client is asked to notice which typical behaviors he usually "wears" each day in his current life. Then, he is asked to imagine for a moment what it would be like to give up all of these behaviors. If they were gone, what would be left? If support is needed with the loss, the client can have his loving force available to help. After all the layers are identified and given up, the client is asked to experience the core and to imagine how he would be different today and this week if he knew his core better in daily life. Then, each layer is reaccepted into the self. For example, the client is asked to bring back the feeling layer: "Hello feelings, welcome back to my personality. I can see and accept your purpose and place in my life."

Experiential Exercises to Enhance Conscious Use of Self in Transpersonal Paradigm

1. With a partner in dyads, interview each other about your spiritual and religious histories. Discuss such issues as how religion and spirituality were dealt with at home, in church, and in the culture in which you grew up. If you were taught a religion, discuss how that religion either fostered or hindered your spiritual development.

2. Using crayons or markers, on a white sheet of paper, draw your own spiritual path. You may want to draw where you have been, where you are now, and where you think you are headed. Share what you drew with a partner in dyads.

3. Have everyone in the group do the disidentification exercise described above in this section. Each person is introduced to the illustration before the visualization begins. Then, everyone is asked to recognize each layer in turn, beginning with Layer 6 and working toward the core. Next, each person is asked to imagine for a moment what it would be like to give up all of these behaviors. If they were gone, what would be left? If support is needed with the loss, the person can have her loving force available to help. After all of the layers are identified and given up, each person is asked to experience the core and to imagine how she would be different today and this week if she knew her core better in daily life. Then, each layer is reaccepted into the self.

Impact on Individual, Family, Local Community, and Global Community

The transpersonalist social worker might say that not only most clients, but also humanity as a whole, is hungry for spiritual development. She might go on to talk about the evidence of a worldwide interest in spiritual development in the Middle East, South and North America, the Pacific Rim, the Soviet Union, China, Europe, and so on. The social worker might conclude by saying that this interest in spirituality reflects, at least in part, a growing collective awareness that the spiritual dimension of development is now necessary not only for human evolution of consciousness, but also for the very survival of our species.

When family members prioritize spiritual development, individuals in the family strive to be connected not only with their innermost cores or souls, but also with the outer world. They may also seek to develop peace of mind, meaning in their lives, and a path of service to others. In such families, connectiveness between people is not based so much upon duty or commitment, but upon the joy of sharing souls (having a spiritual connection). Marital-type relationships that have strong soul-sharing connections may tend to be more fulfilling and meaningful for both partners. When parents strive to develop a spiritual connection with their children, they support the development of each child's unique spiritual path. Each child would be helped to own and love both highest self and shadow self. When families strive to support the spiritual development of all members, each individual is more likely to develop his ability to experience love in life.

A community of people that focuses upon spiritual development is, first of all, tolerant of all spiritual paths; from earliest childhood, people are encouraged to discover and express their own spirituality. Although there is a value that all people should have equal access to basic services, resources, and opportunities, such a community does not tend to worship materialism because there is a recognition that there is much more to life than how much wealth, power, and fame a person can accumulate in a lifetime. Healthy models of adult maturity (spiritually developing individuals) would receive more attention in the media than would those who are only rich, famous, or powerful. In such a community, vocation is seen as one's calling rather than as merely a way to make money. The local natural environment would be valued and protected. Finally, such a community does not tolerate social policies that are intolerant of freedom of the diversity of spiritual experience and expression.

Social workers will find that spiritual work with the aging population may enhance not only the lives of the aging, but also the lives of the entire community and culture. Social workers who work with aging clients often find that they are hungry to discuss their spirituality. As Jung[63] and others have pointed out, in the later years of life, spiritual development becomes an increasing priority for most people because as people age, they usually begin to have more and more difficulty ignoring the fact that they are mortal. Thus, as the aging segment of the population of the United States increases in size, the number of people who prioritize spirituality is also likely to increase. The impact of this increase of spiritual development on our culture is likely to be consequential, timely, and beneficial for all of us living today and in future generations.[64]

A global community that fosters individual spiritual development would share fundamental social work values. The welfare of both the individual and the collective whole would be valued in each family, community, and nation. The well-being of the planetary source of human life (our global ecosystem) would also be valued highly. Although the choices and voices of all people would be equally respected, nonviolent means of international conflict resolution and problem solving would be valued. Resources would be diverted from preparations for war to preparations for individual and collective well-being. Resources would be diverted from private accumulation of wealth and power to models of shared wealth and power and policies that prioritize the unique spiritual development of every individual.

Notes

Part III Introduction

1. Maslow, A. H. (1971). *The further reaches of human nature*. New York: Viking.

2. Sperry, L., & Carlson, J. (1991). *Marital therapy: Integrating theory and technique*. Denver: Love; Corey, G. (1990). *Theory and practice of group counseling*. Pacific Grove, CA: Brooks/Cole; Fenell, D., & Weinhold, B. (1989). *Counseling families: An introduction to marriage and family therapy*. Denver: Love.

3. Bronfenbrenner, U. (1979). *The ecology of human development: Experiments by nature and design*. Cambridge, MA: Harvard University Press.

4. Zastro, C., & Kirst-Ashman, K. K. (1994). *Understanding human behavior and the social environment*. Chicago: Nelson-Hall.

Chapter 9

5. Ursano, R. J., Sonnenberg, S. M., & Lazar, S. G. (1991). *Concise guide to psychodynamic psychotherapy*. Washington, DC: American Psychiatric Press.

6. Bellow, G. (1992). Structurally based theories and self psychology: Questions of compatibility and integration of theory. *Clinical Social Work, 29,* 431-444.

7. Wilber, K. (1986). Treatment modalities. In K. Wilber, J. Engler, & D. P. Brown (Eds.), *Transformations of consciousness* (pp. 127-160). Boston and London: New Science Library/Shambhala.

8. Jung, C. G. (1954). *The collected works of Carl Jung* (Vol. 17). Princeton, NJ: Princeton University Press.

9. Hayek, F. A. (1978). *New studies in philosophy, politics, economics, and the history of ideas*. Chicago: University of Chicago.

10. White, M. T., & Weiner, M. B. (1986). *The theory and practice of self-psychology*. New York: Brunner/Mazel.

11. Berne, E. (1961). *Transactional analysis in psychotherapy*. New York: Grove.

12. N. Silverstone, personal communication, September 1993.

13. Strean, H. S. (1979). The psychoanalytic theory of therapeutic intervention. In *Psychoanalytic theory and social work practice* (pp. 85-110). New York: The Free Press.

14. Berne (1961).

15. Sperry and Carlson (1991).

Chapter 10

16. Freeman, A., & Dattilio, F. M. (Eds.). (1992). *Comprehensive casebook of cognitive therapy*. New York: Plenum.

17. Mahoney, M. J. (1991). *Human change processes: The scientific foundations of psychotherapy.* New York: Basic Books.

18. Mahoney (1991).

19. Bandura, A. (1969). *Principles of behavior modification.* New York: Holt, Rinehart & Winston.

20. Wright, F. D. (1988). Cognitive therapy. In R. A. Dorfman (Ed.), *Paradigms of clinical social work* (pp. 179-195). New York: Brunner/Mazel.

21. Fenell and Weinhold (1989).

22. Bowers, W. (1985). Cognitive therapy for anxiety disorders. *Journal of Clinical and Consulting Psychology, 53,* 45-55.

23. Bandura (1969); Bandura, A. (1977). *Social learning theory.* Englewood Cliffs, NJ: Prentice Hall.

24. Weeks, G. R., & L'Abate, L. (1982). *Paradoxical psychotherapy: Theory and practice with individuals, couples, and families.* New York: Brunner/Mazel.

25. Minuchin, S. (1974). *Families and family therapy.* Cambridge, MA: Harvard University Press.

26. McGoldrick, M., & Gerson, R. (1985). *Genograms in family assessment.* New York: Norton.

27. Nichols, M. (1984). *Family therapy: Concepts and methods.* Boston: Allyn & Bacon.

Chapter 11

28. Frank, J. D. (1973). *Persuasion and healing* (2nd ed.). Baltimore, MD: Johns Hopkins University Press.

29. Mahoney (1991).

30. Yalom, I. (1980). *Existential psychotherapy.* New York: Basic Books.

31. Perls, F. S. (1969). *Gestalt therapy verbatim.* Moab, UT: Real People.

32. Rogers, C. R. (1965). *Client-centered therapy.* Boston: Houghton Mifflin.

33. Friedman, M. (1983). *The confirmation of otherness: In family, community, and society.* New York: Pilgrim.

34. Maslow (1971).

Chapter 12

35. Friedman (1983).

36. Trungpa, C. (1987). *Cutting through spiritual materialism.* Boston: Shambhala.

37. Worthington, E. L., Kurusu, T. A., McCullough, M. E., & Sandage, S. J. (1996). Empirical research on religion and psychotherapeutic processes and outcomes: A 10-year review and research prospectus. *Psychological Bulletin, 119,* 448-487.

38. Wilber, K. (1987). The spectrum model. In D. Anthony, B. Ecker, & K. Wilber (Eds.), *Spiritual choices: The problem of recognizing authentic paths to inner transformation* (pp. 237-265). New York: Paragon House; Wilber (1986); Wilber, K. (1977). *The spectrum of consciousness.* Wheaton, IL: Theosophical.

39. Diaz, S., & Sawatzky, D. D. (1995). Rediscovering native ritual: Coming home to my self. *Journal of Transpersonal Psychology, 27,* 69-85.

40. Maslow (1971).

41. Szent-Györgyi, A. (1975). Drive in living matter to perfect itself. *Synthesis, 1,* 14-26.

42. Frankl, V. E. (1975). *The unconscious god: Psychotherapy and theology.* New York: Simon & Schuster; Frankl, V. E. (1978). *The unheard cry for meaning: Psychotherapy and humanism.* New York: Simon & Schuster.

43. Coles, R. (1990). *The spiritual life of children.* Boston: Houghton Mifflin.

44. C. Berney, personal communication, 1986.

45. Hendricks, G., & Weinhold, B. (1982). *Transpersonal approaches to counseling and psychotherapy.* Denver: Love.

46. Wilber, K. (1989). Let's nuke the transpersonalists: A response to Albert Ellis. *Journal of Counseling and Development, 67,* 332-335.

47. Hendricks and Weinhold (1982).

48. Sermabeikian, P. (1994). Our clients, ourselves: The spiritual perspective and social work practice. *Social Work, 39,* 178-183.

49. Cleary, T., & Shapiro, S. I. (1995). The plateau experience and the post mortem life: Abraham H. Maslow's unfinished theory. *Journal of Transpersonal Psychology, 27,* 1-23.

50. Trungpa (1987).

51. Tart, C. T. (1991). Mindfulness, spiritual seeking, and psychotherapy. *Journal of Transpersonal Psychology, 23,* 29-52.

52. Berne (1961).

53. Bradshaw, J. (1988). *Bradshaw on: The family.* Deerfield Beach, FL: Health Communications.

54. Ahsen, A. (1977). *Psyche self analytic consciousness: A basic introduction to the natural self analytic images of consciousness eidetics.* New York: Brandon House.

55. Olny, R. (1991, July). *Self acceptance training.* Paper presented at the Summer Institute, Graduate School of Social Work, University of Utah, Salt Lake City.

56. Perls (1969).

57. Rogers (1965).

58. Wilber (1986).

59. Moore, T. (1994). *Soul mates: Honoring the mysteries of love and relationship.* New York: HarperCollins.

60. Moore (1994).

61. Moore, T. (1992). *Care of the soul: A guide for cultivating depth and sacredness in everyday life.* New York: HarperCollins.

62. Hendricks and Weinhold (1982).

63. Jung (1954).

64. Henderson, R. (1954). The gifts of age. *Common Boundary, 13*(5), 24-31.

Intervention Paradigms: Paradigms of Integration

As described in Parts I and II, advanced generalist social work practice is inclusive inasmuch as the universe of available interventions is used. These interventions can be organized into seven paradigms. In this section, three additional paradigms are described: (a) case management, (b) biopsychosocial, and (c) local and global community level.

Interventions drawn from the Four Forces tend to focus upon psychosocial factors in the client/system and are designed to foster human welfare and development through the use of primarily "talk therapy" interventions with individuals, couples, families, and small groups. Interventions in this section are paradigms of integration that foster human welfare and development through the establishment of community linkages (case management), body/mind/spirit connection (biopsychosocial), and community- and global-level connection.

The *case management* paradigm deals with formal and informal support systems in the client's community. These support systems may be viewed as part of both "microsystem"[1] and "mezzosystem."[2]

The *biopsychosocial* paradigm deals with the client's body and its relationship with the mind and spirit and natural ecosystem.

The *community*- and *global-level* paradigms deal with the client's relationship with systems larger than small groups.

Because advanced generalist practice is eclectic, interventions drawn from all seven paradigms introduced in Parts III and IV can be used in practice. The advanced generalist worker recognizes that the most effective strategies use a blend of interventions. Therefore, many of the case examples in this section are additive in that they demonstrate ways to include interventions drawn from many paradigms for use in a single case.

CHAPTER 13

Case Management Paradigm

Key Elements

Focus. The focus is on improving the quality and accessibility of resources and opportunities that support individual client development and the collective welfare of all diverse populations.

Developmental dimensions. Although there may be a focus on the furthering of all dimensions of human development, social development is particularly emphasized (e.g., social skills that empower client to develop and use resources in equitable and sustainable ways).

View of health. There is a focus on the ability of the client/system to provide the diversity of individuals, families, and communities with equal access to resources, political power, and opportunities for individual development. Self-sufficiency is maximized, and there is a focus on strategies that support sustainable resources.

View of pathology. The unhealthy client/system does not provide the diversity of individuals with equal access to resources, political power, and opportunities for individual development. Human and natural resources are depleted rather than kept sustainable, and maximum self-sufficiency is not encouraged.

Art and science. Although social science has tested the efficacy of some case management strategies, we still do not know enough about how the availability and use of resources and opportunities in the environment influence biopsychosociospiritual well-being and multidimensional human development. Practitioners can thus select case management interventions based on empirical research, theory, and worker and client intuition.

Relationship. Although some traditional case management forms have taken approaches that appeared quite vertical to clients, the social worker can take a horizontal or vertical relationship with the client and client/system, depending on the developmental ability of the client(s) to share in responsibility for creating and implementing intervention strategies.

Strengths. Case management interventions should be considered in every case because the effective social worker always views the individual in the context of her client system (which includes both the human and natural environment). The worker strives to both modify that environment to maximize the client's welfare, and encourage the client to share in responsibility for the collective welfare of the client/system. Because many of the factors contributing to human problems are related to institutional or community characteristics, case management thus expands the repertoire of the worker's intervention toolkit to include strategies of help that are not included in the Four Forces of psychology. Case management services are often especially useful with clients who are vulnerable because of chronic mental or physical disabilities or challenges.

Limitations. When case management interventions focus primarily on improving the quality and accessibility of resources and opportunities that support individual development and collective welfare, some clients may experience case management interventions as being rather mechanical, or even impersonal. This may especially occur when the provision of such basic services as housing, food, and employment takes exclusive priority over the client's personal development. The provision of services that fulfill basic needs is, of course, important, but often not enough. Many clients who desperately need such resources as money, food, shelter, legal assistance, or medical care may often also need assistance in dealing with the emotional, cognitive, social, physical, and spiritual dimensions of their lives as well. Regardless of their needs, of course, all clients certainly need to be treated with dignity, respect, and caring.

The case management literature still largely ignores the importance of limiting the use of resources to that which can be sustained by the local or global community. There is also insufficient concern given to encouraging all people (rich and poor) to not just take from the community but to also give back as they are developmentally capable.

Fit in Advanced Generalist Practice

Although there is still limited consensus, two main functions of case management have been identified in the literature: (a) providing individualized advice, counseling, and therapy to clients in the community; and (b) linking clients to needed services and supports in community agencies and informal helping networks.[3]

The first function mentioned can be considered a subset of the many individual, couple, family, and group interventions drawn from the Four Forces as described in Part III. The effective social worker uses first function interventions to facilitate second function interventions. Such second function interventions are emphasized in the case management paradigm in this book.

Thus, the focus of (second function) case management is on the linkage of the client to services and supports and the resolution of what will be defined as first-level obstacles to such linkage. First-level obstacles are obstacles that can be resolved through microlevel (individual and small group) changes in thinking and acting (as opposed to second-level obstacles that require macrolevel, system changes).

Case management services are often the first interventions provided to clients in the beginning phase of treatment. This is because many clients have immediate need for basic resources (e.g., child protective services, food stamps, housing, job counseling, a battered women's program). Protection of client safety (e.g., risks of suicide, maltreatment, homicide) and fulfillment of other basic needs should always be the initial priorities in a case. Social workers find that many clients will have difficulty responding to interventions drawn from other paradigms of practice until such safety issues and other basic needs are dealt with.

Case management interventions are also likely to be used during the termination phase of treatment. The success of new linkages between the client and the environment can be evaluated, and modifications made as appropriate. Often, clients may need referrals to other resources following the ending of the relationship with their social worker (and often with an agency as well). Such referrals may be particularly helpful to clients when their cases are ended because of external pressure for short-term treatments.

The worker does not assume that poor or vulnerable clients always need case management services, or that the rich and powerful do not. There is still insufficient evidence to support Maslow's[4] theory that "deficiency" needs (e.g., for food, clothing, and shelter) always must be met before the client can seek to meet "growth" needs (e.g., for freedom, goodness, unity, justice, beauty, wholeness, and self-fulfillment). The effective worker takes an inclusive position and strives to help each client identify and meet his own unique set of needs in each life-moment.

Key Intervention Strategies With Case Examples

Of all helping professionals, social workers are especially prepared to perform case management interventions because the management of a case requires appreciation of the ecological, person-in-environment perspective. Case management (or "managed care") is a paradigm of practice that is especially useful with clients who need long-term care. Many dependent clients may require case management services, particularly in this conservative era of accountability characterized by limited, uncoordinated, and selective service systems.

One way to conceptualize case management interventions is to describe when they would be used in relationship to the three phases of a case.

Beginning Phase

Safety/protective issues. Screening begins for safety/protective issues that may exist in the client/system. Appropriate case management responses to any safety/protective issues may include those legal/formal responses required by state statute (such as reporting laws) and/or legal precedence (such as the Terisoff ruling). For example, if the worker determines that the elderly grandmother in a family is being economically exploited, the worker phones the adult protective services and makes a report under the guidelines of the state statutes. The effective and wise social worker keeps informed of reporting laws and other legal requirements.

Crisis intervention. Initial case management interventions include crisis interventions, which may be necessary because clients may be in crisis at the beginning of treatment. Case management interventions may be used in any of three crisis intervention stages.

In Stage 1, the tasks have traditionally included the relief of distress, completion of initial assessment, planning of intervention strategy, and contracting. However, the most effective social workers do not assume that the client necessarily needs to have pain taken away. A focus on symptom reduction may also reduce the opportunities for growth for which the client's psyche or soul, through the language of symptoms, is asking.

The emotional pain in which many clients find themselves may eventually lead them to higher levels of development. When appropriate, the worker helps the client reframe the distress (chronic stress reaction) as a sign that something (e.g., the soul) is *working,* rather than broken. The worker also realizes that contracting is not always appropriate for every client.

For example, a social worker serving as an intake worker in a community mental health center sees a woman in her mid-30s who presents with symptoms of major depression. The woman's father had just died that morning. It turns out that the woman has lost her husband, her own mother, and her job, all in the last 6 months. The worker gives an empathic response, "I am not surprised that you are depressed. If I had gone through what you have gone through recently, I'd be depressed too." The worker goes on to discuss with the woman what immediate tasks she has to deal with (e.g., contacting other family members, selecting a burial site, contacting life insurance company and family lawyer).

In Stage 2, social workers traditionally have used a Second Force, problem-solving approach to case management. One Second Force intervention is the "task implementation sequence," which includes enhancing commitment, planning task details, analyzing and resolving obstacles, rehearsing behaviors, and summarizing. Although Second Force interventions may help clients quickly make rapid cognitive and behavioral changes, the effective social worker also targets affective, spiritual, and psychosocial changes, and therefore uses relatively brief interventions drawn from all Four Forces of social work practice. A social worker might, for example, be working with a man who has just learned that he has HIV. The worker determines that the client is very interested in spiritual development, spends a few minutes asking the man to explain more about his personal spiritual path (the client is a Catholic), and may then refer the man to Catholic Community Services and a local church.

Stage 3 includes anticipatory guidance and the provision of referrals and follow-up as required. The traditional goal of crisis intervention was to help the client return to the level of functioning that she was at before the crisis. From a transpersonalist perspective, however, the social worker should also strive to help the client use the opportunity provided by the crisis to go *beyond* the developmental level at which the client was functioning before the crisis began. For example, a social worker saw a woman briefly whose lover had suddenly left her. The woman had been dysthymic for 6 months prior to the crisis. The worker encourages the woman to think about beginning to move beyond her depression and refers her to a women's growth and support group that specializes in issues of relationship.

Ecological assessment. As described in earlier chapters, the client/system is assessed on all ecological levels in an ongoing process. Time limitations may restrict how much attention can be given to assessment.

Establishment of psychotherapeutic relationships/support system. In managing a case, the social worker strives to not only establish and develop her own therapeutic relationship with the client, but also to establish and develop other formal and informal relationships and services for the client. Thus, for example, the client may refer a child abuse victim and her family to a specialized support group, seek individual psychotherapy for the nonoffending parent, and help a child victim get into an existing counseling group at his school. Responsibility does not end with the referral, however. Progress may need to be continually monitored, because clients sometimes are not well-served and may need new referrals. Thus, in addition to leaving the client with a business card, the worker may also follow up a referral with a phone call a month later to determine how successful the new referral has been.

Intervention Phase

Psychotherapy services. In the intervention phase, the social worker continues to develop the helping relationship with the client, establishing objectives, goals, tasks, and contracts as required. The worker may use conscious use of self, as described in Part I. The worker may use interventions drawn from any of the Four Forces of social work.

Problem solving. Clients can be taught to apply the problem-solving method. To review, Hepworth and Larsen[5] suggest six steps in the problem-solving process: (a) acknowledge problem, (b) analyze problem and identify needs, (c) brainstorm potential solutions, (d) evaluate options, (e) select and implement option, and (f) evaluate. Although these steps may seem self-evident to the worker, many clients may need to have the social worker not only teach and model this process, but then rehearse and support specific steps as needed.

Client/system linkage roles. A variety of needs may become apparent as the case progresses. In addition to the therapeutic needs described earlier, clients often have other intrapsychic and interpersonal needs (e.g., recreation, church support, intellectual stimulation, better diet, and health care). Overall, the worker strives to ensure that the client receives appropriate levels of support and structure, flexibility and firmness, and continuity of care. In times of crisis, clients may also seek assistance with such specific issues as income, housing, medical care, employment, and child care. The social worker keeps an updated list of community resources (because phone numbers and guidelines for resources constantly change), which he always carries when seeing clients. The development of client strengths is emphasized. For example, a social worker is helping a 20-year-old man who has multiple diagnoses of manic depressive disorder and mental retardation. The worker determines that the young man needs an organized and predictable environment (he is placed successfully in a halfway house) and ongoing services (including case monitoring by the worker, medication evaluations by his psychiatrist, and supportive counseling in a group run at the halfway house). The young man wants to have some kind of meaningful vocation, has developmental strengths in the physical dimension, and eventually decides to train in carpentry.

The social worker may provide consultation, collaboration, advocacy, monitoring, mediation, and brokerage, and educational services as appropriate.

Consultation generally means case contacts with other professionals or family members. The worker may provide and/or ask for information and advice in these contacts. The effective worker discusses such contacts with the client before making them. The worker usually asks the other professional for his opinion first.

Collaboration means that the worker cooperates with other professionals who are helping the client. The social worker may serve as a coordinator of all of the services that the client receives from various professionals. Many service systems have developed team approaches to case management, and the social worker may be an important member of that team.

Advocacy happens when the worker acts to promote the client's welfare by contacting other professionals or significant people in the client/system.

When the worker *monitors,* she oversees and evaluates the client's functioning. The worker strives to ensure that the client's basic needs are met and that the client's opportunities for independence and autonomy are developmentally appropriate. The worker also strives to ensure appropriate continuity of care.

Mediating involves assisting clients in the peaceful negotiation and resolution of conflicts. For example, an older client may be in danger of eviction from his apartment by his landlord because of several late rent checks. The worker may be able to mediate a new lease by suggesting a new agreement that protects both parties.

When the social worker acts as a *broker,* he is an intermediary who helps provide or link resources and services to the client. For example, a social worker learns that her client has suddenly lost his job again and is living on the street. The worker calls up the director of the local shelter and arranges to have the young man get his old job and room back at the shelter.

Educational services include the provision of information to the client that will help the client meet basic needs and function more effectively. For example, a veteran asks his worker about social security benefits for the disabled. The worker collects some information for the veteran and helps him fill out application forms.

These case management interventions often can be blended together. For example, when clients are experiencing distress related to the legal system and/or other formal institutions, social workers can be of significant assistance to clients by (a) educating clients about how the system works (e.g., the typical functions of the protective service system involved in maltreatment cases); (b) as appropriate, facilitating communication and information exchange between the client and other professionals; and (c) working as appropriate with other professionals to develop plans, documents, and reports that serve to protect and enhance the well-being of clients.

In another, more specific example, the social worker is serving a family who has recently immigrated to a small Great Basin town from Southeast Asia. The worker determines that the family needs a variety of services, some of which are available in the county in which they live. These services include education in the English language and job retraining for the adults, and special education testing and recreational programs for the children. The worker consults with the school psychologist around testing services and collaborates with the school social worker and teacher to design a special education program for two of the children. Although the children want to play in local team sports, they have little knowledge or skills in baseball or football, so the worker advocates for them with the team coach, who agrees to give them extra help. The worker also monitors the job retraining program into which the mother enters. The mother was having difficulty learning word processing and finally needed to be reassigned to another program in which she could be more successful. The father was assaulted at his job site (on a ranch), apparently by several young men with racist motivations, and the worker had to mediate some changes with the ranch supervisor that reduced tensions and increased cooperation. The worker had to act as a broker for the family during the Christmas holidays by arranging for the family to receive emergency food when their income dropped. Finally, the worker set up educational services for both parents at the local community college, where they could study English as a second language.

Client/system modification roles. The social worker sometimes needs to intervene to reduce first-level obstacles that interfere with the client's ability to access resources in the client/system. There may be intrapsychic and/or environmental obstacles.

Internal obstacles are barriers within the client, such as fear, lack of social skills, and lack of knowledge. The social worker's interventions may include encouragement, assertiveness training, and psychoeducation. The worker may refer the client for additional psychotherapy. For example, a battered wife is referred by her worker to the YWCA battered women's program, but the woman does not make the phone call and is beaten up by her husband again. At the next session, the worker determines that the client still feels that she is in love with her husband, and is also scared that she cannot make it on her own (and that he will kill her if she tries to leave). The worker does not criticize the woman for not leaving her husband, but strives to build a helping relationship with her over the next weeks. They go mall walking together, and the worker volunteers to go with her for the first time to the YWCA group.

Environmental obstacles are barriers external to the client and in the client/ system, such as the prejudice of a client's neighbor, the lack of knowledge that a client's teacher has about the client's learning disability, or poor communication skills between members of the church that the client attends. The social worker's interventions may include psychoeducation and advocacy. For example, a worker refers a young couple to their local HMO for medical services when they suspect that they are pregnant. Unfortunately, although they state that they prefer to have as natural a birth as possible (and there are no medical reasons found to prohibit their choice), the HMO insists that the couple have their child in a standard hospital room setting. The worker, at the couple's request, calls the HMO and finds out that the receptionist has not informed the couple that they do have other options under their insurance coverage plan.

Termination Phase

Social workers have the responsibility to consider a number of issues in termination. The client may need to emotionally process the termination of the primary therapeutic relationship. Evaluation of the case on all ecological levels is an ongoing progress, and evaluation at the termination stage may indicate that clients need additional referrals or follow-up services. In some cases, ongoing supervision may be required to help protect dependent and vulnerable clients (e.g., a visiting nurse might continue to visit a family regularly to make sure the newest baby does not also develop failure-to-thrive symptoms).

Case Management in Short-Term Treatment

Case management interventions may be selected when the social worker is faced with external pressures to shorten the length of treatment. Case management interventions may be used to connect clients quickly with available services in the community. However, effective social workers prioritize the welfare of the client and client/system, and they realize that short-term treatment may not, in some cases, be appropriate or even ethical. Some basic elements in short-term intervention can be outlined that are similar to the stages of crisis intervention outlined above.

Beginning phase. The social worker's first task is to help the client deal with and learn from her stress and distress. Whereas stress is an unavoidable part of everyday living, distress is an unhealthy and chronic state of stress that can be relieved through a variety of interventions, including meditation, exercise, cognitive work, and social contact.[6] When assessing, the social worker strives to determine which (if any) problems and challenges of the case can actually be resolved in a short-term time span. The worker then plans intervention strategies and makes contracts with the client for the resolution of those short-term problems and challenges. The worker also informs the client about those problems and challenges that may well be long-term, and discusses options that may be available to the client. The worker acts to connect the client with services that can assist her in achieving goals.

Middle phase. Interventions drawn from all of the Four Forces of social work practice may be used to help the client with short-term problems and challenges as well as to help the client begin to also deal with those problems and challenges that are likely to be long-term. As these interventions are implemented, the worker continues to assess which problems and challenges can be effectively dealt with before termination. Again, a variety of case management interventions may be useful; the worker continues to connect the client with services that can assist him in achieving goals.

Ending phase. In this phase, the worker helps the client become more aware of which problems and challenges have and have not been resolved. The worker again uses case management interventions to help the client connect with resources in the client/system that can help the client continue to develop after termination. The case is evaluated, and appropriate referrals and follow-up interventions are made.

For example, a social worker sees a new client, referred by the court system, at a suburban community mental health center. The client is a 60-year-old man who was caught soliciting prostitution in a police sting operation at a local shopping mall. The man is a successful businessman, is married, and has five children and three grandchildren. The worker assesses that the man is not only very depressed, but also at risk for suicide. The worker also determines that the man has felt trapped in an unhappy marriage for 35 years because of religious and social pressures. In the beginning phase, the worker reframes the crime that the man committed as an understandable self-expression of a need for love; helps the man feel and express his emotions (sadness, fear, anger); and refers him to an aerobic exercise program. In the middle phase, the worker discusses therapy options with the man and helps him deal with such practical matters as legal fees, how to tell his employer, and how to deal with his family and people in his church congregation. In the ending phase, the worker refers the client to a therapist in town and meets together with the client and therapist for the first session.

Work With Couples, Families, and Other Groups

Social workers may often use any of the key case management interventions described above to link couples and families and other groups with services and opportunities in the community. The purpose of such linkages is not only to provide such basic services as housing, employment, and food, but also to reconnect people in their communities. Such reconnections often help people normalize their experiences and behaviors and provide the basis for new development of self-awareness, self-acceptance, and practical life skills.

Many couples may be relatively disconnected from other couples in their community and are likely to feel that their problems are unique and therefore particularly pathological. Social workers may help such couples link with other couples through informal support networks (e.g., new friendships through church, club, or various recreation groups) or more formal networks (e.g., a psychotherapy group for couples, a seminar on couple communication). The worker should monitor such referrals in order to help couples either continue to reach out to others when needed, or to try another support network if one turns out to be unsatisfactory. There may also be a need to make individual linkages for one or both members of a couple. For example, a battered woman may well wish for the support of other women (e.g., at the YWCA battered women's support group). Her husband may wish to attend a men's group, at a local agency, that focuses on anger management.

In families, parents may also be quite isolated from other parents in their community, and they can develop feelings of frustration and even despair in their isolation. The worker may also want to refer these parents to various informal support networks (e.g., other parents who may attend the local parent-teacher organization or the local church) and more formal networks (e.g., a parenting class at the local community college, a workshop on parenting taught by a social worker in the school district). The worker should monitor such referrals in order to help the client either continue to reach out to others when needed or to try another support network if one turns out to be unsatisfactory. Individual family members may require personal referrals. For example, an alcoholic mother may need to be linked to an Alcoholics Anonymous group. Her 16-year-old daughter may need a referral to an Alanon Group.

When leading groups, the social worker may refer clients to resources that will help support individual and group goals. Such referrals may or may not be appropriate for all members of a given group. For example, a social worker who is leading a men's group may refer several of the men to an organization that advocates for the legal rights of fathers. Another social worker who is leading a parenting class may want to provide the group parents with a short handout that lists resources in the community for parents (e.g., day care programs, baby-sitters).

Experiential Exercises to Enhance Conscious Use of Self in Case Management

1. Go to an agency or institution to which you have referred clients and sit in the waiting room for an hour. If ethically possible, actually apply for services or resources. Notice which emotions, thoughts, and behaviors you experience. What does this suggest about how social workers need to handle referrals of clients?

2. In dyads, discuss the experiences each of you has had when you have sought some kind of services or resources. Discuss what it was like to be referred or self-referred. Were your first contacts by telephone or in person? What were they like?

3. Many social workers say that their most challenging work is not with clients but with other professionals. Discuss in dyads what kinds of challenges each of you has had when working with other professionals (e.g., physicians, teachers, other social workers, supervisors, colleagues). What do you think are the root causes of the kinds of challenges you have faced (e.g., turf battles, competition and envy, lack of cooperation)? What kind of mistakes have you made when working with other professionals, and what mistakes have other professionals made with you? What do these experiences suggest about how social workers need to deal with other professionals?

Impact on Individual, Family, Local Community, and Global Community

A social worker who does case management might say that the most unique and important contribution that social work has made to the helping professions is the concept of person in environment and the need for both individual- and environmental-level interventions. Sometimes, case management interventions can help establish a working relationship more effectively than any other intervention. This is because some clients in need will begin to trust a worker only when the worker helps provide the client with basic services or resources (rather than provide talk therapy). Some individuals who have meaningful work, adequate housing, and sufficient food may often be more likely to heal and grow in all of their developmental dimensions.

Similarly, when the worker helps provide services to vulnerable members of the client's family, such case management interventions can help form the foundation of a helping relationship. Families that have their basic needs met are less likely to be in distress (chronic stress) and thus less likely to experience maltreatment of vulnerable members (because there is a relationship between stress and maltreatment).

When the social worker helps provide services to members of the local community, the worker models responsible behaviors for members of that community. Because such motivations as poverty and powerlessness are reduced, such a community is also less likely to experience violence. Individuals who receive case management services do not become lazy because of those services; rather, they have opportunities to heal and grow again.

A global community that receives case management services is also less likely to be violent. The growing disparity between the have and have-not societies is replaced with a global community that cares for all of its members. In such a community, war and terrorism are less likely because many of the motivations for violence have been reduced. In such a community, poverty and mass disease are less likely because cooperation between peoples is possible. Opportunities for international cooperation are improved when the basic needs of populations are met.

CHAPTER 14

Biopsychosocial Paradigm

Key Elements

Focus. The focus is on fostering the client's physical development and body-mind-spirit-environment interconnection (the paradigm could be renamed bio-psychosocioenvironmental).

Developmental dimensions. The client's physical development is emphasized, although the client's multidimensional (i.e., affective, spiritual, psychosocial, and cognitive) development is also fostered through physical interventions.

View of health. The healthy client is aware of her body-mind-spirit-environment interconnection. The client accepts and can enjoy his body and is aware of and responds to the body's needs for regular exercise, rest, nutrition, and self-care.

View of pathology. The client is not aware of the body-mind-spirit-environment interconnection. The client does not accept or enjoy her body, and is not aware of or does not respond to the body's needs for regular exercise, rest, nutrition, and self-care.

Art and science. There is considerable evidence of a body-mind-spirit-environment connection. There is less evidence of the efficacy of various physical interventions in fostering multidimensional development. Practitioners can select biopsychosocial interventions based upon empirical research, theory, and worker and client intuition.

Relationship. Although the traditional Western medical approach tends to be associated with a vertical physician-patient relationship, the social worker can take a horizontal or vertical relationship with the client and client/system, depending on the developmental ability of the client(s) to share in responsibility for creating and implementing biopsychosocial interventions.

Strengths. Biopsychosocial interventions provide ways to work directly with the client's body (physical dimension). Most clients can benefit from simple physical interventions, such as modifications in diet and exercise. Sometimes, physical interventions are the best or even the only ways to help particular clients heal or grow. These interventions also allow the client to verbally explore his own body experiences and related values and beliefs (e.g., about his sexuality).

Although most social workers realize that their primary means of intervention is verbal (i.e., talk therapy), the limitations of such approaches are seldom discussed. Most social work interventions ignore the client's body (or at least those parts of the body below the brain). However, most problems and challenges that clients face are associated with physical factors (e.g., biogenetic factors, lack of exercise) or a poor mind-body-spirit-environment connection (e.g., the client is unaware of her body's need for rest, change in diet, and outdoor activity). Biopsychosocial interventions enable the social worker to deal with these factors directly.

Clients usually feel safer when they can talk with their social worker. Many people experience discomfort and even anxiety when they engage in more than a few seconds of nonverbal eye contact with another person. However, as soon as they begin to speak with the other person, the discomfort and anxiety is usually relieved. Often, clients will say that they feel that people can see more about themselves in their eyes than they want them to see, and they may have also learned to avoid eye contact in their families and cultures. The effective social worker is aware of not only how the client may use words to defend herself (through intellectualization), but also how the worker herself may also use words more to protect herself than to help the client. The worker may use his own body awareness (use of intuition to understand where the client is at physically) as a guide in this process.

Most biopsychosocial interventions do not involve any direct touching of the client by the social worker. These interventions can be used with individuals, couples, families, and groups.

Limitations. Some biopsychosocial interventions may be too threatening or uncomfortable for some clients. Many people in our culture, of course, are very disconnected with and even hostile toward their bodies. Some clients may be particularly uncomfortable, perhaps because of a history of sexual or physical abuse or because of their cultural traditions. Such clients may not be ready yet to work directly with their physical dimension.

Many social workers are uncomfortable working with the physical dimension of clients. Many social workers express concern that they make themselves vulnerable to lawsuits if they touch a client. Certainly, the sexual abuse of clients by social workers is always inappropriate. However, current concerns about boundaries with clients may make clients more vulnerable to the same kind of isolation and alienation with which they live all the time in their lives. There is considerable evidence that human touch can assist the helping process.

The worker can discuss touch with clients and help them learn how to develop their own boundaries. For example, a social worker is working with a boy who recently lost his father in a hunting accident. The social worker asks, "May I hold your hand?" When the boy says, "I guess so," the worker holds the boy's hand, and the boy finally lets himself cry.

In addition, most biopsychosocial interventions do not require direct touch. As with any other dimension of development, the social worker who wishes to effectively help foster clients' physical development starts by working on her own physical development. Such work is likely to help the social worker desensitize and familiarize herself with biopsychosocial interventions.

Fit in Advanced Generalist Practice

Biopsychosocial interventions can be made throughout the beginning, middle, and ending phases of a case. As is true in working with any other developmental dimension, the most effective social worker uses physical interventions initially with clients who are most comfortable in the physical dimension, thereby building on the developmental strengths of those clients. Similarly, the effective worker delays physical interventions with clients who are not as dominant in the physical dimension.

Biopsychosocial interventions can be linked to assessments or to interventions drawn from any of the other paradigms of advanced generalist social work practice. The social worker can begin by using biopsychosocial interventions to help the client and worker assess the client's development and identify goals. Then, other interventions can be used to follow up. The social worker can also use biopsychosocial interventions to follow up on other assessment or intervention procedures.

Key Intervention Strategies With Case Examples

The biopsychosocial issues include all biological factors that are interrelated with other intrapsychic, interpersonal, and environmental factors in a case. These biological factors include all of the physical processes and structures of the body, which may include human physical development, sexuality, genetic factors, psychopharmacology, substance abuse processes, the aging process, and health care.[7] Because professional helpers often consider that such biological factors are the sole domain of the medical profession, they are often uninformed and limited in their ability to make complete assessments and interventions and effectively manage cases.[8]

Although the term *biopsychosocial* has usually been used as an inclusive term to describe the interconnectedness between the body, the psyche, and the social dimension, in this book, the term is used specifically to describe physical interventions that can be used to foster multidimensional development.

Thus, the social worker considers biological factors when involved in the assessment, intervention, and termination phases of a case. In work with child maltreatment cases, for example, a knowledge of the physical symptoms of failure to thrive, physical abuse, and sexual abuse is often necessary.[9] Social workers also need to be aware of biogenetic factors that may be associated with the symptoms that are associated with child maltreatment cases. Many aspects of temperament in children and adolescents are genetically determined and tend to persist across the full life span.[10]

Psychotherapy is usually also required when children and adolescents are given pharmacologic interventions, and social workers need to be informed about the common medications that may be used to treat the various symptoms.[11] In work with middle-aged or aging adults, biological factors are also often very important in assessment and intervention.[12]

There is considerable theoretical and empirical support for the interrelationship between physical health and mental/spiritual health.[13] Thus, in making assessments in maltreatment cases, social workers should also consider such factors as diet, aerobic exercise, sleep, and physical health history. In making referrals and interventions, social workers should consider traditional as well as alternative, holistic techniques. These holistic techniques may include therapeutic massage, biogenetics, and other bodywork forms.

The tenets of holistic medicine are consistent with such social work principles as client self-determination and the ecological perspective. A growing literature supports the efficacy of using such physical interventions to help a client heal and develop. A variety of resources are available to clients who wish to do their own reading on empirically supported holistic or natural medicine and thus take more control over their own self-care.[14]

A variety of key biopsychosocial interventions can be presented here. The social worker should be aware that there may be ethical and/or legal restrictions on their ability to use the names of particular models in their practice unless they have been certified as trained in that model. For example, there are Biogenetics, Rolfing, and Trager training programs in which social workers can enroll. Different cities or states may also have licensing regulations regarding the use of techniques such as therapeutic massage or acupuncture.

Aerobic exercise. A growing literature supports the efficacy of physical exercise in fostering the multidimensional healing and development of clients when such exercise creates no additional physical risk.[15] Aerobic exercise involves the use of regular, brisk workouts in which the client achieves a target heart rate over an extended period of time (e.g., running, walking, swimming, biking, dancing, and rowing). The social worker should refer the client to a medical professional for evaluation and consultation before recommending any specific aerobic program.

Direct bodywork. Social workers who are appropriately trained and licensed may incorporate direct bodywork techniques in their practice with clients. Direct techniques require that the worker physically touch the client's body. Social workers should inform themselves of the legal requirements for such practice. In most states, a license is required for direct bodywork. There are many bodywork techniques available[16] that may be grouped into five broad categories:[17]

- *Traditional Western massage:* The most common form is Swedish massage, which is usually relaxing, uses gentle strokes, and is relatively nonintrusive.

- *Structural/functional/movement integration/somatic education:* These forms of bodywork attempt to help the client become more aware of and heal old patterns of muscular tension, movement, and trauma in the body. Models include Rolfing, Aston-Patterning, Guild for Structural Integration, Hellerwork, the Alexander technique, and the Feldenkrais Method.

- *Other contemporary Western bodywork practices:* These bodywork forms use a variety of methods and include myofacial release, Trager, Rubenfeld, and Rosen Method.

- *Eastern practices:* Traditional methods from the Eastern hemisphere are incorporated into these forms, which include shiatsu, reflexology, and aromatherapy.

- *Energetic bodywork:* These forms use methods designed to help clients become more aware of and use energy patterns in their bodies. They include therapeutic touch, craniosacral therapy, reiki, holotropic breathwork, and polarity therapy.

When a social worker incorporates such techniques, he can provide interventions that help clients improve their body-mind-spirit-environment connection. The social worker always informs the client about the potential benefits and risks of the particular bodywork intervention being used and gives the client the choice of whether she wants to proceed. As a social worker does direct bodywork, clients may experience cognitive or emotional responses that the worker can help the client process.

For example, one client tells the worker that he has had an unusual tension and pain in his back, behind the diaphragm muscle. The worker has the client lie face down on the massage table and applies some pressure to that area. As the social worker does the bodywork, the client is soon aware of feelings of anger and then sadness. The worker has the client talk about these feelings, and they explore together the possible connections of those feelings to the tenderness in the back and the client's life. The client realizes that his back started to become tighter when his wife told him that she was thinking about leaving her job. He realizes that he is angry with her because he has felt that he has had to take on an unfair share of the financial burden in the marriage. The man decides to talk with his wife about his feelings.

Increasing numbers of clients are seeking professional help that blends bodywork with talk therapy. Such clients tend to already be familiar with and relatively comfortable with such techniques as therapeutic massage and movement. The social worker's effectiveness in assessment and intervention can be enhanced in such approaches because the body can provide many additional opportunities for assessing and intervening. It is hoped that increasing numbers of social workers will respond to this growing recognition of the body-mind-spirit-environment connection.

Sex therapy. A variety of sex therapies now exist[18] that include strategies drawn from all Four Forces of psychology. Social workers can refer clients to a sex therapist or use these techniques themselves with their clients. Many clients may first require basic information on human sexuality, and excellent materials are available for clients of all ages and walks of life.[19] A growing literature describes the problem of sexual addiction,[20] in which the client has lost the ability to achieve deep sexual satisfaction and, as a result, tends to become compulsive in his sexual expressions. Many approaches used to treat sexual addictions draw upon Second Force, cognitive-behavioral strategies designed to help clients give up their addictive behavior and related thought patterns and replace them with healthier patterns.

Physical disciplines. The social worker can directly teach (or refer the client to) a variety of physical disciplines that may help the client heal and develop. For example, Zen yoga therapy considers illness (including anxiety and other mental disorders) to be a natural attempt by the body to achieve health, and it uses interventions with posture and diet.[21] Therapeutic breathing exercises teach clients how to posture and breathe to assist in the healing of common diseases.[22] The many various forms of martial arts provide clients with other means of developing personality and character through long-term study of a movement discipline.[23] Martial art traditions come from not only China and Japan, but also India, the Philippines, Korea, and Indonesia. Contrary to what many clients may believe, these traditions generally do not teach violence, but rather self-discipline, self-control, and even love for an opponent.[24] Because there are a variety of teaching philosophies, when making a referral, the social worker may want to link the client with a teacher who stresses self-discipline and self-control rather than only competitive success.

For example, a social worker is seeing a young man who was incarcerated after participating in several gang-related activities. The worker encourages the young man to study martial arts with an instructor whom the social worker knows well. At first, the young man thinks he will become even tougher and enthusiastically competes to be the best fighter in his class. After several weeks, however, the instructor has wisely started to teach the young man much deeper lessons about life through the movement discipline. The instructor becomes a model for the young man, and eventually, the client becomes an instructor himself.

Dance movement. Dance movement interventions are designed to help clients embody, and thus own and accept, emotions, thoughts, and experiences. Studies show that there is a neurological basis for the mind-body connection often observed in dance movement interventions.[25] Social workers may use dance movement therapy techniques to help clients heal and develop.[26] Dance movement therapy is the use of expressive movement and dance as a vehicle through which an individual can engage in the process of personal integration and growth. It is founded on the principle that there is a relationship between motion and emotion, and that by exploring a more varied vocabulary of movement, people experience the possibility of becoming more securely balanced yet increasingly spontaneous and adaptable. Through movement and dance, each person's inner world becomes tangible, individuals share much of their personal symbolism, and in dancing together, relationships become visible. The dance movement therapist creates a holding environment in which such feelings can be safely expressed, acknowledged, and communicated.[27]

For example, a social worker is working with hospitalized children. She decides to use dance movement therapy with a group of children. She first plays games of hide-and-go-seek, and then animal charades, with the children to help them develop trust. Then, in a later session, she strives to enhance body awareness by having the children do charades of their illness, using props such as scarfs, magic wands, colorful fabrics, and flags. One child who has leukemia acts out the disease by laying on the floor wrapped up in a piece of cloth and rolling back and forth. The social worker has the child then show through movement what might help her in her healing. The girl takes a magic wand and waves it above her head as she runs in a circle around the worker.

Social workers may combine music with movement to increase the effectiveness of the interventions. For example, a social worker might have a group of adolescents prepare costumes that represent themselves. Then, he gives the group a selection of drums and has them walk around in a circle outside. The worker starts drumming, and soon, all of the young people have joined in. Later, each boy and girl has an opportunity to do their own individual movement or chanting in the center of the circle. These experiences are later processed verbally.

Psychopharmacology. When appropriate, clients should be referred to appropriate medical professionals for consultations involving the need for medications and other medical interventions. Social workers often pay most of their attention to psychological, social, and other nonphysical factors, perhaps because they are focused upon emotional pain and social dysfunction and because they are usually taught that only physicians may deal with the body. However, when biological factors are neglected, the potential effectiveness of the social worker and the healing process itself can be severely limited.

Although only licensed medical professionals can prescribe psychotropic medications, there are many reasons why social workers should be at least familiar with major medication issues. Most, if not all, problems seen in social work practice are associated with at least some physical factors, such as genetics, diet, exercise, the aging process, and physical health. When physical factors are particularly important (e.g., with bipolar disorders), clients will probably not respond well to just talk therapy and may need to be referred by the social worker to a physical health care specialist. Some social workers, particularly in medical model settings, will work with clients who are already taking psychotropic (psychologically active) medications. Social workers can consult various publications to help inform themselves about traditional psychopharmacology.[28]

Clients can be informed that alternatives to psychopharmacology also exist. For example, Acu-Yoga uses body awareness, breathing, meditation, relaxation, and acupressure to relieve stress and tension.[29] The worker can educate the client (or client's caretakers) about the choices available in the local community and help the client find information about the various advantages and disadvantages of different treatment approaches.

Biopsychosocial Interventions Based Upon the Four Forces of Social Work

The social worker can select existing models and interventions drawn from the Four Forces and modify them for use as biopsychosocial interventions.

First Force. Psychodynamic models may help the social worker work with the body to help the client gain insight into and heal from past trauma. The worker uses interpretations, empathic responses, psychoeducation, and storytelling to help the client gain these insights. For example, a worker notices that his client's foot is constantly wiggling whenever she is talking about her past lovers. The worker says, "Please don't stop what you are doing, but just notice what your leg is doing now. . . . Now what I would like you to do is exaggerate that motion. . . . Good. What does your leg seem to be trying to do? What is it telling you? [Client says she feels like running away.] Yes. Does that relate to how you feel about these past relationships?"

Bioenergetics[30] is a First Force model that can provide a social worker with theoretically based interventions that link the body with deep psychology and uncovering work. Bioenergetics provides a system of classification of body types that correspond to psychosexual development. The worker helps clients become aware of their body type, as well as of their body's own unique ways of protecting itself from pain. The goal is to help the client work through such body insights so that he can more fully experience body pleasure, particularly in intimate relationships. As with any other approach, social workers who do not accept the theoretical framework of bioenergetics may still wish to use similar kinds of techniques. Specialized bioenergetics training programs are also available to workers.

In an example of a bioenergetic intervention, a social worker sees a 30-year-old female client who complains about a pattern of unhappy relationships with men. The worker determines that the client has an "oral" body type, suggesting that she has experienced trauma in the oral psychosexual stage of development and therefore tends to be a caretaker (rather than someone who can both give and receive love) in her intimate relationships. The worker has the client stand with her knees bent and breathe deeply until she begins to feel and express emotion.

Second Force. Second Force models give the worker methods to help the client change the way she thinks about the body and uses the body in daily living. The client may have beliefs about his body that are thinking errors quite unhelpful to development. For example, a young female client might believe that she is gaining too much weight, when in fact, she is anorexic. A young male client might believe that he is too thin, when in fact, his body weight is normal for his size and age. The worker can also give homework assignments that require the client to change the way he uses his body during the week. For example, the worker can ask that the client try to get 8 hours of sleep 5 days a week, or that the client begin a simple aerobic exercise program.

The worker can help educate the client about health issues and help the client reframe unhelpful thinking errors that she may have about her body. The worker can, for example, show the client that there are a number of alternative and equally legitimate ways of viewing disease and health:

> Doctors focus upon physical disease process . . . acupuncturists study the energies of health . . . shamans address the bigger questions of why this person got sick and not another. . . . Of course many doctors would readily dismiss the works of an acupuncturist or shaman as ignorant superstitious quackery, but that unwillingness to consider the evidence simply reflects their immersion in the scientific world view of their training, which . . . we share as patients and members of the modern world, that is, the last 800 years of White, Euro-American civilization. (p. 40)[31]

Third Force. These interventions focus on helping the client improve here-and-now body awareness and authentic body expression, and they include various techniques used in humanistic, Gestalt, and psychodrama models.

Hendricks and Hendricks[32] offer Third Force techniques that may be particularly appealing to social workers because they target deeper feelings and experiences yet do not require any direct physical contact. These techniques (or what the authors call "principles") are presenting, magnification, breathing, moving, grounding, and manifesting:

Presenting means that the worker helps the client simply put attention on the body (or a body part) without trying to do anything else. For example, if a client has a headache, the social worker asks the client to be aware of that headache and gently focus on the pain. Often, the client reports that she has been avoiding such awareness and notices a reduction in pain when presenting. Another client is asked to pay attention to his posture. When he does this, he realizes that he leans forward when he walks, and he links this to the pressures he feels in his life.

Magnification means that the client is asked to exaggerate some body language that the worker is observing. A client throws up her hands when she talks about her husband. When asked to magnify this gesture, the client realizes she is trying to throw him away from her. Another client whose lover recently left him sits with his hands gripped together in his lap. As he magnifies this grip, the social worker asks him to make a noise. The man starts to groan and says, "I can't let go!"

Breathing means that the client is asked to try various breathing techniques (such as breathing deeply and fully with intent and awareness), especially when the client is having powerful emotions or other experiences. One client was repeatedly molested by his uncle when he was a child. However, the client has been unable to let out any emotion about these molestations. The social worker asks him to do some breathing exercises, and the man starts to sob.

Moving means that the client lets the body express an emotion or other experience and then observes any other spontaneous body movements. One client complains about her job at a financial center. The worker asks her to act out physically what it feels like to be at work. The client collapses into a little ball on the floor and says, "I have to be very small and controlled here." Then, the worker asks her to express physically how she would like to be at work. The client immediately jumps up and starts to dance dramatically across the floor, saying, "I am finally being creative and expressive . . . and it feels wonderful!"

Grounding means that the client is asked to experience her feet on the ground and feel connected with the earth. A client complains to the worker how anxious and worried he feels in his new relationship. The worker has him stand in the middle of the office, bend his knees slightly, and breathe deeply and slowly. The client starts to get in touch with feelings of sadness that he feels about the loss of his last relationship and reports, "The anxiety has gone away, and although I feel this pain of sadness, it is a pain that does not seem to scatter me the way the anxiety did."

Manifesting means that the client begins to realize the internal work she has done in her outside world, and she harvests the results. For example, after striving for months to become more aware of how he feels in his body when he is out on a date with a woman, a young man reports that he has finally found a person with whom he seems compatible. The changes he has made have generalized to his real life.

Fourth Force. Fourth Force interventions focus upon the interconnection between spiritual development and the body. The client is encouraged to discover and develop his own spiritual perspective on various biopsychosocial experiences and processes.

There are, of course, many diverse ways of experiencing and conceptualizing the body-mind-spirit-environmental connection. One way is to view all matter (including the matter that makes up the human body) as interconnected energy systems. When clients are comfortable with such terminology, the social worker can help them experience the energy of their own bodies and the energy of the world. For example, in a group he is running, the worker can ask his clients to pair off in twos and sit silently facing each other, making only eye contact. Each client can take turns "opening" and then "closing" the movement of energy through the eyes. (Each person may need to conceptualize this differently, but the idea is to first open the eyes to the transfer of energy or love with the other, and then to close down the eyes and protect them from any such transfer of energy or love.) The worker's clients may discover that they do, in fact, have control over the extent to which they can let energy move between them and another person.

Clients may also be asked to consider what meanings they make out of their physical experiences. In many tribal societies, the shaman might suggest what the meaning of a client's illness is. "Human development may be fostered by disease: illness can transform an individual's life and society's assumptions about sickness and health" (p. 40).[33]

The social worker operates like a postmodern shaman, assisting the client in making his own meaning out of illness. For example, a social worker has been seeing a client who has chronic diabetes. The client regularly attends Alcoholics Anonymous meetings and believes in a higher power in her life. The worker asks the client to talk about why she believes that her higher power "gave" her diabetes.

Work With Couples, Families, and Groups

Any of the key biopsychosocial interventions described above may be useful when working with couples, families, and groups. Biopsychosocial interventions may help people not only improve the physical intimacy in their lives, but also progress in all of the other dimensions of human development.

Many couples will report dissatisfaction in their physical intimacy together. The social worker may want to help the clients assess the topology and origins of these problems. Most sexual difficulties fall into one or more of three categories: disorders of desire, disorders of excitement, and disorders of orgasm.[34] The most effective social worker uses an inclusive approach to sex therapy that draws upon all of the paradigms of advanced generalist practice.

From the biopsychosocial perspective, the social worker may encourage couples to try new ways of physical relating that are likely to help remove obstacles in a particular category. For example, John and Mary have noticed a mutual decline in desire after 10 years of marriage (a disorder of desire). The worker may ask them to schedule engagements for lovemaking, in which they take turns setting up ahead of time in which physical interactions they will participate (e.g., in the first week, Mary sets up a date for Friday night and asks that John touch her only in nonsexual ways). In another case, Bill reports that he often loses his erection when making love with Mark (a disorder of excitement). The worker may teach Bill some relaxation exercises and suggest that he not try to have intercourse with Mark but concentrate on his own feelings of pleasure. Finally, Sally reports that she has never been able to have an orgasm with her lover (a disorder of orgasm). The worker might have Sally learn how to give herself orgasms through masturbation as a first step.

Couples may also benefit from strategies that encourage other, nonsexual physical interventions. Couples who are primarily "in their heads" (relate primarily on the cognitive dimension) may benefit from such activities as simple massage, taking walks together, and doing dance therapy movement. For example, a worker asks one couple who has been arguing to sit down on the rug during the middle of a session and give each other a neck rub.

The social worker may use biopsychosocial interventions in family work as well. The social worker might teach expecting parents how to use loving touch to help their new baby develop. The worker might have all of the members of a family stand in a circle and do a simple dance to music. A medical social worker might have the members of a family take turns going in to the hospital bed of their dying mother and grandmother and simply holding her hand.

Social workers may find that biopsychosocial interventions are often particularly useful in facilitating the group process and helping to further other group goals. For example, a social worker is leading a group for grade school-age children of unhappily married parents. The worker realizes that talk therapy techniques are not working very well and asks the children to do movement games at the beginning of each group. In their favorite activity, the children take turns acting out silently in front of the group how their week was. The worker discovers that the movement games seem to help further group cohesion. In another example, a social worker is working with a group of aging clients in an adult day health program. Every morning, the worker has the group do some yoga and meditation before the psychoeducational program begins. Adult clients may also enjoy movement exercises. For example, one social worker has the clients in her women's spirituality group move to music from the "Dances of Universal Peace."[35]

Experiential Exercises to Enhance Conscious Use of Self in Biopsychosocial Work

1. Sit quietly with your eyes closed and take inventory of your body. Consider which areas of your body seem to be tense or painful. Consider which

kinds of messages those discomforts might have for you (e.g., you need to relax, you ate too much). Now meet in dyads and share your experience. Do we have much to learn from our own bodies? If so, what obstacles might there be to our being more in touch with our bodies?

2. Sit with a partner and silently draw a picture (with colored crayons, pencils, pens) of your partner's energy. There are no right or wrong ways to do this. Some may draw a body shape, whereas others may choose to experiment with various colors and patterns. Then, share these pictures with each other. Discuss what each of you sees in the drawings and what they seem to show about both the artist and the subject.

   Next, take turns trying to work with each other's energy. The partner playing the social worker role should consider where the energy in the client seems to be blocked. The social worker might modify the picture that he first drew. The worker might use some of the interventions described above. For example, she might ask the client to be more aware of some aspect of his energy, amplify (or exaggerate) the aspect, and perhaps try a healing movement.

3. Ask half of the class to leave the room. Ask the half remaining to make the following intervention. When the class reassembles, people meet again in dyads. Then, the partner playing the social worker does an interview of the partner playing the client. The social worker first tries to assume a body posture that is as opposite as possible from the one the client has. Then, slowly, the worker is to assume the posture of the client and mirror that posture. After a few minutes, each small group stops the interview and discusses what changed, if anything, when the posture changed.

Impact on Individual, Family, Local Community, and Global Community

A social worker who works from the biopsychosocial perspective might say that the body is more likely than the mind to tell the truth. Perhaps this is especially true in the present era. Today, the most common dominant dimension of development in most clients is cognitive, and many clients are at least as knowledgeable as their social worker about the many self-help philosophies available for mass consumption in bookstores and on talk shows. At the same time, many clients have become less knowledgeable about their bodies. Although clients may exercise and diet rigorously, they may be out of touch with their body's needs for rest, movement, and expression. Biopsychosocial interventions may serve to help the client heal and grow without interference from intellectualizations that have become habitual and problematic.

Individuals who are more aware of their body-mind-spirit-environment connection are less likely to become perpetrators or victims of violence in the family. This is largely because such individuals are more likely to get their needs met and more likely to be aware of and willing to defend their personal physical boundaries. When parents are aware of their bodies, they model such awareness for their children. Couples that are in touch with their bodies are more likely to be aware of their sexual needs and are able to ask for what they want in intimate relationships.

A community that values the physical dimension of development would strive to help young people mature in that dimension from an early age. Physical education would move away from its current focus on competitive sports, where only a few can be successful stars, to programs that help everyone develop body/mind/spirit/environment connections. Adults would be less likely to focus on maintaining a youthful physical facade and more likely to focus on maintaining physical health across the life span.

A global community that is more in touch with the physical dimension is more likely to stay connected with the environment. People who value their physical development are less likely to ignore the condition of their natural physical environment because they are in touch with how the two are intimately interrelated.

CHAPTER 15

Local and Global Community Paradigm

Key Elements

Focus. The focus is on the co-creation by clients and social workers of local and global communities of diversity that support the welfare and development of all members, as well as the welfare of the natural local ecosystem. Clients are encouraged to be more response-able stewards of their communities, which means that they participate in the improvement (or creation) of their local community and ecosystem and, by doing so, enhance their own welfare and development. Clients also become more connected with their environment, which, of course, includes the entire universe.

Thus, all community-level interventions have the twin interrelated goals of individual and collective good: Clients who reconnect with and foster their communities directly benefit from their commitment to a larger cause, and their communities hopefully benefit from each client's connection and commitment.

Developmental dimensions. The client's multidimensional (i.e., affective, spiritual, social, physical, and cognitive) development is fostered. Social development is particularly emphasized because the use of advanced social skills is required to effectively foster community change. Spiritual development is also particularly emphasized because it involves the fostering of the client connectedness with both soul and the outside world.

View of health. A healthy local or global community values nonviolence, social justice, and confirmation of otherness on the individual, community, and international levels; provides all individuals, communities, and nations with equal access to opportunities, resources, services, and power; and facilitates dialogue and cooperation between diverse populations. A healthy local or global community also values the welfare of the natural ecosystem, which includes all living things and the natural environment. A healthy global community encourages members to be response-able stewards of the community, and it is sustainable, in that the natural ecosystem can support the above healthy characteristics over time.

The healthy client is aware and accepting of her interconnection with the human race and the rest of the universe, and she is a responsible steward of the local and global community and natural ecosystem. The healthy client's developmental process is free from the unhealthy socialization patterns of current culture (e.g., worship of wealth, power, status; use of violence to solve problems and resolve conflicts; destructive consumption of the remaining natural resources). Thus, the healthy client also supports human diversity and social justice.

View of pathology. An unhealthy local or global community values or condones individual-, community-, and international-level violence, oppression, and intolerance of diversity; provides individuals, communities, and nations with unequal access to opportunities, resources, services, and power; and tolerates or encourages oppression and competition between its diverse populations. An unhealthy local or global community also devalues the welfare of the global ecosystem, does not encourage response-able stewardship of the community, and does not support a sustainable relationship between its economy and the natural ecosystem.

The unhealthy client is unaware and nonaccepting of his interconnection with the human race and the rest of the universe, and he is not a response-able steward of the local and global community and natural ecosystem. The unhealthy client's developmental process is significantly controlled by the unhealthy socialization patterns of current global culture (e.g., worship of wealth, power, status; use of violence to solve problems and resolve conflicts; destructive consumption of the remaining natural resources). Thus, the unhealthy client cannot support human diversity and social justice.

Art and science. Although there is a literature that suggests that community-level interventions and responsible community stewardship can ultimately foster human development, there is still insufficient evidence of the efficacy of these interventions. Much more research is still required to demonstrate the likely relationships between the state of the natural ecosystem and the biopsychosociospiritual well-being of people within that system. Practitioners can select local community-level interventions based on empirical research, theory, and worker and client intuition.

Relationship. The social worker can take a horizontal or vertical relationship with the client and client/system, depending on the developmental ability of the client(s) to share in responsibility for creating and implementing community-level interventions.

Strengths. These interventions provide ways to work indirectly with larger systems by fostering the healing and development of individuals, couples, families, and small groups. For most clients, it is easier to "think global but act local" than to both think and act on a global level. There are also biopsychosocio-spiritual problems that seem to respond best to community-level interventions (e.g., poverty, hunger, gangs, threats of war, overpopulation, and environmental pollution and deterioration).

Every social work problem is interrelated with local and global community issues; there is always a community context for every problem. In an era when most people experience a crisis of decline of quality of life in their local communities, there is also an opportunity for radical change. Part of the decline of community can be traced to the attempt to retreat from the urban challenges of human diversity and environmental deterioration. Unfortunately, typically homogeneous suburban communities may not be as creative in solving human problems as communities of diversity have historically been.[36]

Limitations. One of the traditional limitations of community-level interventions has been that the social workers who make these interventions have often been trained to be exclusively "macro-minded." Many of these social workers do not receive adequate training in microlevel interventions drawn from the Four Forces of psychology, case management, and biopsychosocial theory.

There is growing evidence that microlevel interventions can be very helpful in achieving macrolevel change, because people skills are basic skills in the process of organizing communities.[37] The most effective advanced generalist social worker thus uses interventions drawn from all of the paradigms of social work practice, whether her practice is micro and/or macro.

Fit in Advanced Generalist Practice

Community-level interventions can be made throughout the beginning, middle, or ending phases of a case.

In the beginning phase, the worker can help the client assess his problems from a local or global community level (in addition to the micro or global levels). In the middle phase, the worker can help the client take some steps to improve community welfare. In the ending phase of a case, the worker can encourage the client to set some long-term goals.

Community-level interventions provide a means of helping the client deal with some of the macrolevel factors (e.g., social oppression, ecological decay) that contribute to his microlevel problems. As Freire[38] noted, social oppression and common microlevel problems are interrelated:

> The peasant is dependent. He can't say what he wants. Before he discovers his dependence, he suffers. He lets off steam at home, where he shouts at his children, beats them, and despairs. . . . He doesn't let off steam with the boss because he thinks the boss is a superior being. . . . He gives vent to his sorrows by drinking. (p. 51)

Key Intervention Strategies
With Case Examples

In this book, community-level work will focus on direct practice methods with individuals, couples, families, and small groups that directly benefit the client as well as facilitate the building of healthy communities of diversity and client connectedness with the larger environment.

Community building with small groups. One way the social worker can help clients build community is to work with them in the community development process. Peck's[39] theory of community building suggests four intervention stages in social work practice with small groups:

- *Pseudocommunity:* In this first stage, members try to be amiable with one another, and conflict is generally avoided. Individual differences have not yet emerged. When a community is in this stage, the worker may try to help members become more aware of which issues they are *not* discussing. As a result, the members might develop enough inter-personal safety to facilitate greater intimacy.

- *Chaos:* In the second stage, members show their diversity overtly. Members try to change each other's thoughts and behaviors. There is a power struggle. In this stage, the worker may help members become more aware of their emotional reactions to each other, and practice ways to communicate assertively and with kindness (rather than passively or aggressively).

- *Emptiness:* In this stage, members ask what they each need to let go of in order to become a more responsible steward of this community. The answer to that question may vary from individual to individual, but essentially, each person strives to let go of the power struggle. Now, the worker may help clients do their own inner work (through interventions drawn from the Four Forces), learn to listen and support each other more effectively, and then share their inner processes with each other as they are ready.

- *Community:* People begin to talk with each other from the deepest parts of themselves. There is safety and support for diversity, as well as a confirmation of otherness. The worker reminds members to be vigilant about any tendencies that the group may have to regress to earlier levels of development.

An example of small group community building can be forwarded here. A social worker is teaching as an adjunct in a school of social work in a research-intensive university. The dean of that school has begun an initiative to create better relationships between the local community and the school.

The social worker suggests to the dean that the school itself needs to create a healthier community of scholars before it can model healthy community building for others. The dean agrees, and the two of them use Peck's model to assess and intervene. They determine that the school faculty is still stuck in the pseudocommunity, and they help the faculty co-create a safer environment by modeling assertive behaviors in faculty meetings and beginning a faculty writer's group that models cooperation rather than competition. Gradually, they help shepherd the faculty through the stages of community building.

Psychosocial therapy. Another advanced generalist community-level strategy might be called "psychosocial therapy." The effective social worker realizes that the individual development of the client is not only related to the welfare of the local and global community and ecosystem, but also to that client's ability to *improve* her environment. Thus, in every microlevel intervention, the effective social worker strives to connect individual, couple, family, or small group issues with relevant local community and ecosystem issues. Thus, there are two equally important and interrelated parts in a psychosocial-therapeutic intervention: enhancing connectiveness and social response-ability.

The worker strives to help the client *enhance his connectiveness* with the community and ecosystem. Connectiveness is an aspect of spiritual development in which the individual becomes more aware of her interdependence and relationship with both soul and outer world. The worker may assist the client in relating immediate and personal issues to community-level issues with the hope that the new perspective will help foster the client's development.

For example, a couple comes into the office complaining that their marriage is dead. The couple says that between their demanding jobs and the needs of their children, they have little time left to spend together (and that time is usually spent in fighting). The worker helps them see that their problems are, in fact, quite common, and that most adults in their community are also working so much that they have little time left for recreation (or re-create-ing). The community's emphasis on materialism (material gain has become the priority goal of adult development) has led to the overdevelopment of the local forests and wetlands, which has led to a decline in recreational opportunities and overall quality of life. The problem is thus reframed as being both micro (individual and marital) and macro (collective worship of material gain over emotional and spiritual development).

As described in Part II, the worker strives to help clients become more *responsible stewards* for the community-level issues that are connected to their microlevel issues. Stewardship means that a person is a trustee or caretaker for other people or other parts of the world. Stewardship does not imply ownership of, but rather commitment to, the community. The social worker may view all people as stewards of each other and the world.

Global social work. In what might be called "global social work," the advanced generalist social worker strives to help the client develop his global consciousness, which involves the client's connection with the global human community and ecosystem. The worker may assist the client in relating immediate and personal issues to global issues with the hope that the new perspective will help foster the client's development. When the client takes a broader (global) view of her problem, the new perspective may help the client heal and develop. The worker can help the client relate to any global issues, including the following six interrelated concerns:

1. Social justice on the global scale. The argument might be made that the greatest social issue of our times is the wide and still widening gap between have and have-not populations on the planet. This issue is a factor in every person's life because we all belong to one of the two groups, and we all share an increasingly smaller planet together.

For example, a social worker is doing family therapy with an upper-class family. The presenting problem is that their only son has been acting out, using and dealing cocaine, and skipping school. The father is a lawyer, and the mother is a school teacher. The social worker tells the family, "It appears that your family has been blessed with prosperity. But despite that prosperity, the family has suffered tremendously. Johnny's problems have served to remind you all that something is still missing in your lives. We know that the crime and dropout rates for the children of other affluent families in this country are increasing. Perhaps we can explore together what the shadow side of prosperity is, and then make whatever changes need to be made to help Johnny get his life back together."

2. Global survival threats and the need for peaceful international conflict resolution. The current crisis of global survival threats requires that people learn how to dialogue, cooperate, and resolve conflicts and solve problems nonviolently. Such global threats as overpopulation, weapons of mass destruction, environmental pollution, and the waste of natural resources can be reduced only through global cooperation. The worker can link the client's issues to such global issues.

For example, the worker is seeing an abusive family. The parents were referred to counseling by the court after the mother beat her 8-year-old son and his grade school teacher reported the bruises. The social worker relates the need for change to what is happening on the planet: "I think that what your family is trying to learn is similar to what people across the planet are trying to learn today. That is, we are all recognizing the need to find ways to resolve our conflicts without violence, because we recognize that our very survival now depends on this."

3. The cost of "winning" the cold war. In past decades, a gigantic proportion of human and natural resources was spent in preparing for war. When the end of the cold war was announced, there was little cheering, perhaps because nothing really changed in terms of the collective welfare of the global community. Preparations for war still continue on a vast scale. The "silent war" that had not ended is the ongoing assault on the welfare of the global have-not populations and on the global natural ecosystem. When people are unaware of such oppression, they are unlikely to take action steps to change but are likely to have symptoms such as depression, anxiety, and even despair.[40]

For example, the worker is seeing a young gang member who was arrested for stealing food from a restaurant (he ran without paying the bill). The man is a recent immigrant to the United States. The worker tells the man, "It is remarkable that you have done as well as you have in your life, given how little you had as a child growing up where you did. I can also understand why you have become angry. There is so much food available to those of us who live on this side of the border, and with all of our country's wealth, there should be enough food for everyone. It makes me angry too. You don't need to be locked up, you need to be out in the world contributing your energy toward resolving these big problems. Let's talk about ways to use your anger that would be more likely to help yourself and other people."

In another example, the worker is seeing a depressed single mother. "You know, I can see why you would be depressed. Our culture is so wealthy, yet we do so little to support those who are raising our next generation by themselves. I get angry when I hear politicians attack mothers like you. The problem is not so much the fact that young women are getting pregnant, but that we do not share more in the responsibility of raising children. There are few societies in which women have been expected to raise children by themselves, as you and many other mothers have been doing. Let's think about your depression as a signal from your deep inside, a recognition from your soul, that you need to belong to a community of people who can support one another, that you are too alone."

4. *The cost of being productive.* The worship of wealth, of economic growth in the West, has led to a situation where the average adult in the overdeveloped nations has less recreational time than the average adult in the underdeveloped countries.

For example, the worker is seeing a couple who is having marital difficulties. The wife tells the worker, "I work all day long, and by the time I get home, I have little energy or patience left for Ralph or the kids." The worker replies, "I am glad you are starting to talk about your feelings in these sessions. You may not realize this, but your experiences are not a reflection of some personal problem you have. You are not lazy, like you seem to think you are. Your difficulties are being shared by many other women and men in our community who are finding that they are working long hours and seem to have less life satisfaction than they had when they worked less hard. It is a problem that is, in fact, shared by people all across our country."

5. *The need for a sustainable global community.* The social worker is aware that a healthy society must be sustainable, inasmuch as it must be able to

support a particular way of life, social order, and higher values over time. We are not currently living in a sustainable society because "unlimited technological innovation and economic growth is unreliable . . . and the modern way of life works against psychic needs of parents and children. . . . [It] is spiritually and psychologically risky. . . . The current order is unjust and undermines social welfare systems" (p. 2).[41]

The social worker is particularly concerned about such interrelated global survival threats as overpopulation and the worship of materialism, both of which overload the ability of the earth to sustain the global human community.

For example, in an upper-middle-class suburban town, a social worker is working with a group of depressed adolescents. They have been talking about various topics each week. One week, the discussion partly involves the decline of the quality of life. One boy talks about how his favorite fishing area on a bay in Lake Michigan no longer seems to have any fish. In the next session, with parental permission, the worker takes the group out on a field trip in the agency van. They visit an industrial area, which is situated on the shore of Lake Michigan. The worker and the adolescents explore the area together and locate where untreated waste is being pumped into the lake. They decide to write letters to the company and to state and federal elected representatives.

6. The universe is expanding. In the days of Copernicus, people were suddenly confronted with a new cosmology, which was that the earth was, in fact, not the center of the universe, but only a planet in orbit around the sun. People were challenged to think differently about the human race, that we were not, in fact, the center of the universe. Today, we are also confronted with a new cosmology, which is that the universe is expanding from a tiny seed of mysterious primal matter that exploded in the Big Bang. Such a cosmology suggests that everything in our universe came from the same common matter and is thus physically interconnected. Another implication of this cosmology is that the human race is also expanding, evolving, and developing.[42] In an expanding universe, humanity is dynamic and inclusive; creativity and diversity is valued.

For example, a social worker is seeing a family. The parents are concerned that their son (who is 20 and still lives at home) is homosexual. The parents want the social worker to help the son become heterosexual again. The son admits that he has had sexual relationships with other men, but he states that he does not want to try to change his sexual orientation. He tells his mother, "I feel bad that you are so worried about me." The mother says, "I worry that Steve will suffer because of his sexual orientation, but all he seems to hear is that I disapprove of him." The worker replies, "I believe that you care about your son. I am impressed with how you and your husband are willing to expand beyond your own fears and discuss this topic with a therapist. I think many people in our generation are learning to think of humanity as expanding just like the rest of the universe. They are learning that there are many diverse ways to be human."

In another example, a worker is seeing a young woman who is very unhappy in her marriage but feels quite guilty about leaving her husband. The worker notes, "I think that your struggle is, in many ways, quite typical of the struggles of your generation. I think that we are learning that, despite what some politicians say, the high divorce rate actually suggests a growing recognition that people can be joyful in their lifetimes. Whereas in the past, duty and obligation dictated life decisions, today we can say that it is not only good for you, but it is good for your husband, your children, and ultimately the planet, for you to have more joy in your life. The planet needs more happy people in it."

Ecosystem social work. In what might be called "ecosystem social work," the worker strives to help the client develop his "environmental consciousness," or make connections between his own welfare and the welfare of the global ecosystem.

The effective social worker realizes that most clients are disconnected from their local natural ecosystem, and that this disconnection is a factor in the origin of many (if not all) biopsychosociospiritual problems. The social worker strives to teach all client populations that the protection and enhancement of the local natural environment and all of its living things must always be considered in any local development project. Clients need to know that communities can be overdeveloped (unnecessarily destructive of the environment) as well as underdeveloped. Social workers can no longer operate as if there are unlimited natural resources in the community.

Interventions drawn from deep ecology theory[43] can help clients reconnect with their local natural ecosystem. Some interventions focus on building awareness. Clients can be encouraged to rediscover their local natural ecosystem. Other interventions build upon new awareness and ask clients to take action steps to help protect and enhance the natural ecosystem.

In urban communities, clients are often particularly out of touch with nature. Although most of the urban environment is now manmade (or "womanmade"), clients can be helped to become more aware of the relationship between the condition of their streets, buildings, and parks and their individual and collective welfare. In addition, many city people probably need to regularly get outdoors in more natural environments in order to reconnect with the sources of their air, food, and water. Another, often overlooked aspect of the urban environment is the barriers that the city often creates to interconnections between people. Cities are seldom designed to facilitate integration of the diversity of its peoples. Social workers can take leadership roles in building awareness of how structures and machines can isolate people (e.g., automobiles, freeways, televisions, security systems) and in taking active steps to make the city friendlier.

In suburban communities, clients often still operate under the illusion that people can best connect with nature and themselves by subdividing the most beautiful land adjacent to the city into residential units. The effective social worker strives to help clients become aware of the cost of suburban sprawl on the human psyche (e.g., alienation, isolation, environmental destruction). The worker strives to help suburban populations reconnect with both the natural environment and the richly diverse populations of the nearby city. Alternatives to suburban sprawl are planned, which maximize the protection of the natural environment and the interactions between diverse peoples. The social worker also strives to help the affluent suburban populations appreciate the environmental costs of suburban living and to take active steps to reduce environmental destruction.

In rural communities, more emphasis may be placed on owning and profiting from nature than in protecting and connecting with nature. The expansion of recreational communities into wilderness areas reduces the quality of the natural ecosystem for all people. Although the need to use vast areas of nature for agriculture are obvious in a hungry and overpopulated world, the worker also strives to protect and encourage enlightened public use of the remaining less developed and wilderness lands. The welfare of ranching and farming populations is, of course, as important as the welfare of those urban and suburban populations who consume their agricultural products. The social worker realizes that regardless of their political or personal biases, all rural populations share a common interest in the protection of the natural environment. The effective social worker thus encourages public dialogue about land use and the selection of win-win solutions to land use conflicts. The worker recognizes that a factor in many common symptoms (e.g., depression, anxiety, antisocial behavior) may well be the deteriorating natural environment. As John Muir often said, a world without wilderness is not worth living in. Although, of course, every client does not need to backpack through the Himalayas to be happy, human beings are responsive to the environment in which they live. The social worker strives to help the client find interconnections between his own personal issues and the dynamic ecosystem in which he lives. The worker also tries to help the client become more responsible for the well-being of the global ecosystem.

The social worker can draw upon emerging deep ecology theory when planning ecosystem interventions. The essence of ecopsychology, or the "greening of psychology," is to

> identify those issues that are psychological in character and to turn to the people who might be able to help us most with those. . . . We have a bond with the planet that is basic. . . . In the long run, the goal of ecopsychology is to redefine sanity, in a public way. (pp. 42-43)[44]

The advanced generalist social worker may well be the professional most able to help clients with the psychosocial factors related to the current crisis in our global ecosystem. This is because the social worker always considers the person in the context of the environment. From the social work perspective, the redefinition of a sane society (or individual) would be one that realizes that it is interconnected with the natural ecosystem and therefore needs to be sustainable. From the social work perspective, the definition of patriotism in any land might include a sensitivity to the health of the global ecosystem.

For example, a social worker is leading a women's growth group. The women in the group express an interest in learning more about women's spirituality. The social worker refers them to some of the literature on deep ecology[45] and earth-based religions,[46] and at the next group, she leads the women in some related interventions. The women take turns choosing an aspect of the environment that they love (e.g., the sun, the wind, the mountains, the forest). Then, they role-play that environmental aspect, and talk about their life problems and challenges from that perspective.

One woman, who is going through a traumatic divorce, chooses the moon. She sits in a chair and pretends to be the moon, and she says, "I am the moon, and I am wise and in touch with the deepest emotions and spirits of the world. I am always in motion, always changing, and I honor this divorce as an opportunity for new growth. I have room for the pain, and I have room for new joy that will come."

Three key interventions in ecosystem social work can be outlined.

1. Focus on reconnecting with nature. There are many ways to foster connectedness with nature. The worker can help clients notice the "wounds" of the earth (e.g., scars on mountains for ski resorts, air pollution, clear cutting of forests). The social worker can encourage clients to sit in silence in a natural setting. The social worker can teach clients traditions of earth-based cultures that provide stories about the linkages between people and nature. Clients can be taught to shift from a belief in the duality of nature and humanity to a sense that people are as much nature as the sky and earth. Outdoor adventure counseling programs have been used by social workers across the country to help adolescents and adults with a variety of problems.[47]

For example, a Midwestern worker takes a group of grade school boys with ADHD out to the town park, which is on a small river. The worker lets the boys play in the water for 30 minutes. Then, he has the boys sit in a circle and cook hot dogs (vegetarian, of course) on a grill while he tells them an old story about that river. (The river is the Missouri, and the story was told by earth-based tribes who originally lived in the land of "slow-moving-water.")

2. Communication with nature. Current public interest and even fascination with the possibility of contact with alien life forms may, in part, reflect a desire to reconnect with nature and our natural source of being. If a client wants such a connection, the social worker can suggest that the client begin by trying to connect with animals or plants and nonliving things in his natural ecosystem. For example, the social worker might go outside with a client and spend time with the client on the shore of a pond, watching fish swim by. The worker could also use guided imagery to assist the client in making such a connection. At some point in the intervention, the worker has the client discuss her experience. Some clients may report that they felt a special closeness with not only the animal or plant, but also with their soul and the divine.

These interventions may be helpful to clients who are not avid environmentalists. The effective social worker considers incorporating elements of psychoenvironmental therapy in his work with every client. For example, although people in the United States still have more pets per person than people in any other culture, many clients can still benefit from opportunities to interact with animals. The social worker may encourage clients to purchase pets, visit pet stores or the zoo, or observe and photograph wild animals.

3. Simplicity in means. The social worker can help the client practice "deep ecology," which means that the client learns to make a lifestyle shift. The client is encouraged to become more mindful of her need for a lifestyle of high consumption. The worker and client try to discover together if higher consumption really leads to the highest levels of well-being (to spiritual development). "A lifestyle based upon voluntary simplicity, rather than ever increasing consumption, is consistent with a deep ecology philosophical position" (p. 82).[48]

For example, a social worker is seeing an urban professional man in his private practice. The man complains about depression and anxiety in his life. The worker forms a therapeutic relationship with the client and then begins to help the man examine his priorities. The worker reframes the man's symptoms as healthy expressions of soul, as expressions of spiritual hunger, of the need to connect again with the source of life. The client eventually decides to redefine what wealth means for him. He moves into a smaller house, cuts his workweek by 1/3 (to "only" 40 hours a week), and spends more time with his lover and children.

Subversive social work in the community paradigm. As Ann Hartmann[49] said, a good social worker is always subversive, in the sense that the goal of individual and collective welfare requires revolutionary changes, psychosocial movement, at the micro and macro levels. The effective social worker is also always radical, in the sense that the worker must see the roots of micro- and macrolevel problems before he can plan and implement change. Subversive and radical change does not necessarily require violent or destructive strategies, but can use more gentle interventions, such as the following 5 methods:

1. Mutual maintenance between community and support systems. The social worker strives to help clients build a community that supports supportive networks for people. As Garbarino has pointed out, "As the mother and father are parents to the child, so the community is parent to the family" (p. 11).[50]

We could also say that the community is also parent to other networks of support, including the church, the hospital, social service agencies, parent groups, and so on. Continuing the analogy, parents tend to be most successful when they have the developmentally appropriate support of their children.

Thus, the social worker also strives to help build support for the community as a whole from such networks.

2. The creation of new rituals. The most important work of our present generation may well be to create new rituals.[51] Rituals help the community validate transitions and other shared life experiences (e.g., birth, graduation, divorce, spiritual awakening, death). Many rituals of the postmodernist community no longer help people value such experiences. The effective social worker helps clients co-create rituals that are meaningful (and enjoyable) to them.

3. Work with the rich and the poor. The effective social worker realizes that community-level work in advanced generalist practice is not only directed toward the poor and disadvantaged, but also to the middle classes, and to the most affluent and powerful as well. The most effective strategies may be those directed at the most powerful members of the community. When the worker can help change the beliefs and behaviors of the rich and powerful, the potential gains to all populations may be dramatic. A communitywide change of values may be required:

> Since abusing the environment . . . has gradually come to be perceived as shameful behavior, is it too wildly unrealistic to expect that harmful hoarding might come to be regarding as a rending of communion? Only in a culture desperately estranged from its own depth of being could maximizing one's income be regarded by so many people as the major goal in life. (p. 170)[52]

4. Prevention as an intervention. The social worker will find many opportunities to develop prevention programs in the community. Although all intervention can ultimately be considered preventive, primary prevention is an intervention in which the worker's priority goal is to preclude the future occurrence of a problem. Any community-level intervention strategy can be used as a method of primary prevention.

5. Social worker as social visionary. More often, however, there is limited awareness of community issues, and no preexisting local groups for the worker to join. There may, in fact, be considerable local denial about critical community needs. The social worker then may act in a visionary role, which means that she uses all ways of knowing (artistic and scientific) to identify key community needs. The worker strives to help clients be more aware of the connections between their individual and collective welfare. For example, a social worker may become aware that there are few services and no coordination of efforts for children who have witnessed domestic violence in their homes. The worker encourages clients to see how this lack of services affects their individual and collective welfare.

Community-level interventions drawn from other social work paradigms. These interventions are drawn from all of the paradigms of advanced generalist social worker practice.

1. First Force interventions. The worker helps clients resolve any internal conflicts that may obstruct collective action. Often, clients have internalized the oppression to which they have been subjected. For example, a racial minority in a community may have gradually learned to act passively in the face of discrimination because it was not safe to speak out. Thus, this internalized voice of the oppressor could be conceptualized as an "oppressor introject" that continues to suppress the client's hurt and anger about issues of oppression in the community. The worker helps clients gain insight into the origins and nature of their oppressor introject.

The worker also helps clients review the ways that community (or lack of community) has either helped damage or foster their development. Such insight may help clients become more motivated to work for change. For example, a worker is trying to organize women in a rural community. The worker helps the women see how much the dominant local culture has limited their development. In this community, females are taught from childhood that their social roles should be limited to domestic work.

Awareness of the global ecosystem may best be fostered by outdoor experiences. For example, a social worker takes a group of women out on a river rafting trip. The women stop the first night out at a pretty side canyon. After an early dinner, the worker has her clients sit and watch the sun set. No one is to speak until the first stars become visible. Then, the group processes the experience. They talk about how long it has been since any of them has simply spent time like this out in nature watching the sun go down, and how unusual it is to spend quiet time with others. Clients do not have to take river trips out into the Utah wilderness, however, to get in touch with nature. The social worker can drive a group of children to an inner-city park and encourage them to interact with nature.

2. Second Force interventions. Clients function best as responsible community stewards when they have developed a variety of community-building skills, including effective communication, ability to self-disclose about one's private self, assertiveness to ask for equal consideration, ability to give unconditional support to those in need, ability to give everyone an opportunity to participate, and conflict resolution skills.[53] The worker strives to model such skills, help clients rehearse them, and help reward the use of such skills in community.

The worker often helps create small task groups in which clients identify and solve problems. The social worker may provide structure to help clients complete group tasks. For example, a social worker meets with a group of clients concerned about mounting gang violence in their neighborhood. The worker explains the problem-solving method to them and guides them through this process. The clients identify a number of possible responses to the problem and choose three strategies: regular neighborhood meetings, a midnight basketball league, and improved relations with the local police.

The worker helps clients work individually and collectively to change the way they think and act about community-level issues. The worker may challenge collective thinking errors that have obstructed social change. For example, in working with men in a suburban location, the worker realizes that most of these men think that their patriarchal institutions (including their churches, businesses, and local governments) provide them with more advantages than disadvantages. The worker helps the men see that patriarchal institutions can actually severely limit the multidimensional development of men.

Other cognitive interventions may be helpful. Social workers can teach clients how commitment to and responsibility for collective community welfare tends to bring about increased individual self-development and happiness. The worker can teach that the word "community" literally means "what is held in common or shared by many," and then help the client discover what he would like to (or does) share with others.

There may be many opportunities for straightforward behavioral interventions. The worker can give clients (or support them to give themselves) a variety of community homework assignments. Before clients go out in the community to do these assignments, they may need to have the worker model new behaviors and then rehearse those behaviors themselves. For example, a worker may be organizing delinquent youth in a rural area. The worker discovers that these young people want to work but do not have interviewing skills. The worker models how to interview for jobs and has them practice interviewing in role-plays. Finally, the worker encourages them to go out and interview at least once a week.

The social worker challenges the client's thinking errors about the global community and ecosystem. Such common thinking errors may include (a) "The welfare of people in other countries is not my problem," (b) "The welfare of the ecosystem has nothing to do with me," and (c) "The extinction of some animal or plant species is not going to affect me."

The social worker strives to help the client reframe various microlevel issues so that he can envision the issues as having an interrelationship with global-level issues. Any microlevel challenge or problem can be reframed from a global perspective. For example,

> many people go shopping when they're depressed. It's not that they want to buy more things. The core problem is the depression, and to get them to focus on why they're depressed is a way of dealing with an environmental issue: overconsumption. (p. 42)[54]

3. Third Force interventions. The worker catalyzes client awareness and collective action by encouraging client empowerment and self-esteem. Clients often need to become angry before they are motivated to take action. For example, the worker is meeting with a group of aging clients who are being forced out of their long-term downtown apartments. The worker realizes that this population cohort has been socialized to avoid conflicts or react passive-aggressively. The worker has the group of aging clients break into dyads and talk about their feelings.

Sometimes, psychodrama can help clients develop both their own awareness and the awareness of others. Psychodrama can also be empowering and enhance self-esteem. Boal[55] has developed methods to facilitate a "theater of the oppressed" in which people have opportunities to take on roles and wrestle with a variety of social problems. A first principle was that "emotion took precedence over all else and should be given a free rein to shape the final form of the actor's interpretation of a role" (p. 40). In preparation for acting, clients are encouraged to become aware of and relax their muscles; become more aware of their senses of taste, touch, and hearing; and to practice concentration, imagination, and emotional expression. Although no one is forced to do something she does not want to do, clients are given games in which they try to feel what they touch, listen to what they hear, use all of their senses, and see what they look at.

For example, a social worker encourages gang members who are playing in a midnight basketball league to become involved in an "urban theater." She has the young men develop expressions of the experiences in their lives. The men are able to develop dramatic scenes of racism, oppression, love, and struggle. They ultimately decide to perform their theater for children at local schools.

Another example is a worker who is serving homeless men in a downtown urban area. The worker helps the men develop a musical play that tells the story of how a middle-class man loses his job and family and ends up on the street. The men enthusiastically audition for parts in the play and practice their lines. Eventually, they begin performing the play at schools, churches, and the local urban college campus. The audiences learn that their stereotypes about the homeless (e.g., that they are lazy, antisocial) may be incorrect.

The social worker helps the client become more aware of her feelings, particularly in relation to the global community and ecosystem. Often, the client is unaware of how unaware she is. In such cases, the effective social worker first helps the client become aware of his defenses, which protect the client from feeling such emotions as sadness, fear, and anger.

Awareness of the global community may be fostered through interactions with people from other countries. One social worker has the clients in her adult day health care center communicate through the Internet system with aging people from England and Australia. After the electronic conversations, the group of clients meets and processes its experiences.

4. Fourth Force interventions. The effective social worker realizes that the spiritual dimension is as critical in working with community as it is in working with individuals, couples, families, and small groups. Spirituality or religion is probably the most common inspiration for launching a new community.[56]

As described earlier in this book, spiritual development can be conceptualized as a movement toward connectedness with both soul and world, and it often includes a commitment of service to others. The path of service tends to foster a sense of connectedness and spiritual development. As every social worker knows, when a person helps others, she helps herself, too. Service to others is thus, at its deepest level, an expression of spiritual development. As appropriate, the social worker strives to foster a path of service in the client. As Ram Dass stated, service is the "soul of community" that helps move members from a place of separateness to a place of unity: "Separateness and unity. How interesting that these root causes, revealed in the experience of helping, turn out to be what most spiritual traditions define as the fundamental issues of life itself" (pp. 89-90).[57]

The worker helps clients to identify and co-create spiritual beliefs that support or structure community goals. Sometimes, there is nothing quite as practical as a good theory; clients often need to develop a theory of the world that gives meaning and structure to their desire for community-level change. For example, a worker is helping a group of urban gay men organize. The men decide that they want to create a church to which gay men can go safely and freely. The worker has each man draw a picture of his own spiritual path and then share it with a partner. Then, the group discusses together what it would need to foster spiritual development in the new community. The group decides that the most important quality would be celebration of diversity.

For many adults, their key community is their workplace. Although many clients today may not think of their work as having a spiritual dimension, the word "vocation" originally referred to one's "calling by God." In our postmodern, postindustrial society, the workplace has lost that connection with personal meaning: "Modern corporations and the promise of the 'good life' have separated us from traditional ties to the land, to our families, to the community, and perhaps most importantly, from the connection to our own spirit" (p. 137).[58]

The social worker may strive to help people in corporate communities individually and collectively reconnect with land, family, community, and spirit. For example, a worker contracts with a large corporation to do team building with middle management-level employees. Following a brief presentation in which the worker introduces ideas about spirituality, the worker asks the managers to share in small groups what each of them is most connected with in his or her life now. In a large group discussion that follows, most of the managers state that they do not have that sense of connectedness that they would like.

Social workers can help clients co-create communities of spiritual renewal, which may be necessary for the highest human development:

> We can make people happy. One person has the capacity to be an infinite
> resource of happiness for others. The more we practice the art of mindful

living, the more we become a source of happiness and joy. This is possible.
. . . But we need a place . . . where we can go to renew ourselves.
(p. 101)[59]

Thus, social workers can help people create communities of true re-creation, in which people do the spiritual work they have needed to do but have been unable to do on the "outside." For example, following a needs assessment she completed for the mayor's office, a social worker realizes that a medium-sized city needs a place where adults in midlife transition (e.g., divorce, vocational change) can go to renew themselves.

When spiritual issues are discussed and spiritual rituals are shared, issues of spiritual diversity will surface and demand attention. All people have a spiritual dimension, of course, and all communities have a diversity of spiritual beliefs and practices. The effective social worker encourages communities to be inclusive, to allow each person her unique spiritual expression. When there are conflicts around spiritual diversity, the worker encourages dialogue.

For example, in one community group, a few people from the mainstream culture begin practicing rituals from an earth-based spiritual tradition of a minority culture. One of the people from the minority culture was offended by this practice, stating that he felt it was inappropriate for people from a different culture to borrow rituals from his culture without permission and training. Others in the group, however, thought that earth-based rituals belonged to everyone, that the intent was good, and that the borrowing of the ritual was a positive and healing experience. The social worker brought up the subject with the large group and asked members to dialogue about the general issue. After much discussion, the group agreed that, although no belief or ritual actually belongs to anyone in the community, it is also important for people to be sensitive to the cultural context of different beliefs and rituals. The group agreed that in the future, when people want to perform a borrowed ritual in front of the community, they will inform the group of their intent and include someone who knows the ritual in their preparation and performance.

When the social worker believes that it may be helpful to introduce new ideas about spirituality to a community, the worker offers them as suggestions, rather than as ultimate truths. For example, a worker is serving a population of immigrants who all identify with the Catholic Church. The worker determines that this population's greatest unmet need is for educational and vocational opportunities. The worker asks the clients to talk about what their religion teaches about social justice. During the discussion, some clients bring up the ideas of Martin Luther King, Mahatma Gandhi, and Matt Fox. The worker prepares a reading list of books about or by these men and circulates it at the next meeting.

The worker uses a variety of techniques at times to stimulate further exploration by community members. For example, the worker is trying to organize parents of severely mentally ill children. The worker determines that this population of parents has a very diverse collection of religious beliefs, from atheists to Mormons to New Age spiritualists. In a meeting, the worker asks clients to draw a picture of the spirituality of their children in relation to the school system and local culture. Then, the worker had the parents break out into small groups and share and discuss their drawings. What emerges is that many of the parents drew pictures that illustrated both the beauty of their children's spirituality and the oppressiveness of their environments. This exercise seemed to release many feelings and mobilized the parents to move toward some social actions.

The social worker can also help the client see that the overdevelopment of our planet and the overconsumption of our resources are "more of an addiction than a moral problem" (p. 42).[60] In other words, there may be a collective, shared process of addiction in which people try to achieve connectiveness (spiritual development) through materialistic gain or consumerism.

The social worker can help the client identify and gain wisdom, strength, and support from a sacred natural place. A sacred place may be one of the most important resources in the client's life:

> What imbues a site with the sacred is its ability to bring one closer to one's truest nature and to truths about the world; the context facilitates the journey inward. Hence, to be conscious of—and in—such a place is to be in contact with that which we call spirit. . . . Sacred space is not chosen, it chooses. (p. 25)[61]

For example, a client comes to a social worker and reports a spiritual crisis or "dark night of the soul." The issue is that the client left his job and an unhappy marriage 6 months ago and spent about half of the time since then living alone in his downtown apartment. The client started to become anxious as he noticed that he was detaching from his identification with his roles, beliefs, and possessions. In assessing the client's past, the worker realizes that the client strongly identifies with nature but has not had a good connection with it for some time. The social worker does a guided imagery intervention and asks the client to remember the most sacred place he had ever visited. It turns out that that place was a particular mountain in the Pacific Coast Range. The client imagines being there and then has a dialogue with the sacred place. The client realizes that he loves his sacred place because that place is very much in the here and now, in constant change, alive and vibrant. He decides that the wisdom of the place is that all that exists is the here and now and that he has been trying to go back to old attachments that are already gone for him.

The Fourth Force intervention of disidentification may help clients build connection with the global community and ecosystem. Identification with such elements as material possessions, roles, status, and power may be an obstacle to building this connection. Thus, the worker strives to help clients become aware of their identifications and to disidentify from them as they are developmentally ready.

5. Case management interventions. The worker strives to create an environment that is supportive of the client's work. For example, a worker is organizing a group of farmers that is in chronic financial trouble. The worker advocates with local banks to provide them with low-interest loans.

The worker also helps the clients get their immediate, basic needs met while they organize to ensure that their long-term needs are also realized. The worker provides the farmers with a list of services and resources in the county area. This rural area is quite limited in some of its services and resources, and the worker uses this information to help motivate the farmers to become social activists.

The effective social worker strives to educate clients, other professionals, and the general public on how the adequacy of social welfare systems depends on at least three key elements: (a) the nature and quality of the economy, (b) politics, and (c) knowledge.[62]

The worker also strives to create informal and formal networks of support for the client that will help the client become more aware of and responsible for the global community and ecosystem. Most clients need support because the mainstream culture tends to discourage such awareness and responsibility.

For example, a school social worker helps create a global awareness day at the local junior high school. She encourages students to work with a sponsoring teacher and parent team to coordinate the event. In another example, a social worker refers a man to a men's group in a nearby city, where he can interact with other men who have similar interests.

6. Biopsychosocial interventions. The biopsychosocial aspects of community may not be immediately obvious to the client, but according to science, they are profound:

> Biologically, man is a social creature. His throat and mouth are formed for delicately modulated speech, and that speech is a trait of social and not solitary animals. A man is not a normal organism by himself, but only in relation with others. . . . In mental constitution, men are more than social creatures. They are community animals. . . . Men live best in integrated groups of limited size. They crave community life, not simply social life. (p. 16)[63]

The worker uses physical interventions to provide community-building experiences. Often, the helping process can become obstructed as some clients engage in intellectualizing. The problem is that when clients stay only "in their heads," they often also remain defended and isolated. Meetings thus become "play pens for power struggles" instead of communities of diversity.

One intervention that may help clients move beyond intellectualizations and have an immediate experience of community is the use of ritualized dance. A growing number of social workers are using various forms of ritual circle dances to help participants make community connections.[64] For example, a social worker is helping a group of men make changes in custody law so that loving fathers may participate more fully in the parenting of their children. The worker has a group of men stand in a circle and then has every other man start to weave slowly around the circle, offering each man he meets with a handshake and a greeting.

The worker also uses physical interventions to help clients confirm their values in their bodies. For example, a social worker is organizing adolescents to help them work to save a local wooded area from development. The worker has the adolescents take a walk in the woods. They partner up and take turns leading each other on blind walks through the forest, in which the blindfolded adolescent is encouraged to touch and smell.

The worker realizes that one of the best ways to help clients organize may be through body awareness and expression. The worker strives to help clients become more aware of how their bodies feel. When clients listen to their bodies, they may hear important messages about what is going on in their local community. For example, the community may have created a cultural "trance" in which

> we have lost the ability to come to terms with pain and suffering, to be changed, informed, and even illumed by their presence in our lives. . . . When problems are quickly solved and we return to our old selves, the questions illnesses inevitably raise—and the insights and opportunities they offer—are erased and nullified. . . . Illness is the shadow of western civilization, the antithesis of the rampant extraversion and productivity it so values. As we attempt to exile disease from our world, it persists to haunt us with an ever-menacing guise, and we need it all the more to be whole, to save us from the curse of perfectionism. (pp. 42-45)[65]

Thus, the best intervention may be to become more mindful through body awareness. For example, a social worker is organizing in a working-class neighborhood that is highly industrialized. The worker leads his clients in a body awareness exercise that includes a guided imagery exercise in which members examine their own health with a "CAT scan." In the discussion that follows, most of the clients report that they experienced dis-ease in their bodies that was a direct result of the pollution of their urban environment. A decision was made to work for cleaner air and water.

The social worker encourages clients to become more aware of their bodies, because body awareness is linked to spiritual awareness and can lead to greater awareness of the global ecosystem.[66]

For example, one social worker begins all of his therapy groups at his inpatient mental health center with yoga exercises. He has his clients do "centering" and "grounding" exercises in which they feel the support of the earth beneath their feet. He also has them notice the weather outside and watch their reaction to the changing climatic conditions.

Another social worker also has her clients notice the weather outside and watch their reaction to the changing climatic conditions. Then, she has her clients in a growth group all dance their reaction to the daily weather at the beginning of each session.

Work With Couples, Families, and Groups

When working with couples, families, and groups, the advanced generalist social worker always considers the possible value of including local community interventions. The purpose of such interventions is often to empower couples, families, and other groups to participate in the improvement of their own environment. When couples and families become more involved in co-creating their local community, they become less alienated from themselves and from other people. Some couples, families, or groups (of course) may be in such a state of distress that they are unable to participate in efforts to help others.

Often, the problems that couples face are interrelated with conditions in the local environment. For example, many couples today simply work too hard; they cannot find time to get together, and when they do, they are unable to relax and be present with each other. The worker might encourage a couple to become involved in activities that modify the local community work ethic. For example, in one suburban setting, the worker encourages the couples with whom he works to join a group at a local church. The worker co-leads this group, which is called "Couples Against Time-Poverty." The group is engaged in a number of activities, including consciousness-raising work in the community; sharing of responsibilities (like child care, yard work, cooking); and mutual support.

Families may also benefit from their participation in improving the collective welfare of their community. One social worker, employed by the state Department of Juvenile Justice, encouraged several of her families to join a neighborhood pro-community task force. The task force met monthly and looked at ways to reduce gang violence in the local community. They were instrumental in helping to establish the city's first midnight basketball gang diversion program (which was fully funded by local businesswomen and businessmen).

There may be many opportunities for the group worker to involve clients in community-level interventions. Such interventions can help clients further their own goals through service to others. For example, one social worker is employed by a social service agency affiliated with a particular church in the community. The worker leads a support group for single adults. Several members of the group have recently commented on how dissatisfied they are with the limited opportunities available locally to go and meet other single adults. The worker helps the group decide to organize their own monthly singles spirituality group, in which single adults can come and participate in various activities planned by the steering committee (which anyone can join). In the first meeting, participants decide to bring their favorite form of divination (e.g., Tarot, Runes, I Ching, etc.) and then do playful readings with each other (with a focus upon self-exploration rather than prediction). Each group is to end with spontaneous drumming and dance, in which all are invited to participate.

Experiential Exercises to Enhance Conscious Use of Self in Community-Level Work

1. Discuss with a partner what your own personal history of communities has been. Consider, for example, if communities have fostered or inhibited your personal development. Discuss how this past history has affected the way you relate with communities today. Consider whether you now belong to a healthy or unhealthy community.

2. In dyads, take turns discussing what your ideal community would be like. Then, try to develop a model of a community that would work for both people in the dyad, developed out of the dialogue of different visions. Next, each dyad is to pair up with another dyad. The two groups should compare notes and try to negotiate a community model that works with all four people. Then, each group of four pairs up with another group of four. The process is repeated until the entire class has an opportunity to dialogue about models of ideal community. The group as a whole then discusses the process. Finally, people go back into their original dyads and compare their experiences.

3. Many, if not most, people today have experienced a decline in the quality of life in their communities. Discuss this issue in small groups. Consider why so many people have this perception, as well as which factors are related to the decline (e.g., damage to natural ecosystem, crime, loss of connection to community). Discuss what changes seem most necessary in your own community today.

4. Share in small groups what impact global-level events have had on your life. Most people living today have experienced the reality of global survival threats (deterioration of the environment, preparations for nuclear war, international terrorism). Often, the reaction to such threats is despair and depression. Consider your own cognitive, emotional, and behavioral reactions. Discuss and compare the possible alternatives that people have today.

5. Meet with a partner and take turns being a social worker and client. The client is to share first with which natural element in the global ecosystem he identifies most (e.g., the forest, a mountain, the sea, migrating water fowl). The client describes a current life problem or change. Then, the

worker helps the client role-play that favorite natural element. The client talks as if she is that element and gives advice about the life problem or challenge. Each dyad then processes how well this technique worked.

6. Discuss as a class the ways in which people can individually or collectively help contribute to global welfare. Consider the relationship between such service and individual mental health. Discuss the obstacles that inhibit people from becoming more responsible for the welfare of the global community.

Impact on Individual, Family, Local Community, and Global Community

A social worker who works on the community level might say that all social work practitioners need to be both micro-focused (on individual welfare) and macro-focused (on collective welfare). The social worker might use the analogy of treating a soldier with battle fatigue. No matter how effective the individual treatment is, if only individual soldiers are treated and the war itself is ignored, there will continue to be a steady stream of new soldiers needing treatment. The best solution is to both help the soldiers and stop the war.

Individuals who are more responsible for the welfare of their local and global community and natural ecosystem are more likely to have a well-developed body/mind/spirit/environment connection and are thus less likely to become perpetrators or victims of violence in their family or community. This is largely because such individuals are more likely to get their needs met and more likely to be aware of and willing to defend their personal physical boundaries.

Healthy communities act as retreats in which people can renew their mindfulness and love for themselves and others. In healthy communities, individuals, couples, families, and groups are thus more likely to be caring, aware, and joyful.

A global community that contains local communities of diversity is more likely to value nonviolent international cooperation.

Notes

Part IV Introduction

1. Bronfenbrenner, U. (1979). *The ecology of human development: Experiments by nature and design.* Cambridge, MA: Harvard University Press.

2. Zastro, C., & Kirst-Ashman, K. K. (1994). *Understanding human behavior and the social environment.* Chicago: Nelson-Hall.

Chapter 13

3. Rothman, J. (1991). A model of case management: Toward empirically based practice. *Social Work, 36,* 520-529.

4. Maslow, A. H. (1968). *Toward a psychology of being.* Princeton, NJ: Van Nostrand Reinhold; Maslow, A. H. (1970). *Motivation and personality* (2nd ed.). New York: Harper & Row.

5. Hepworth, D. H., & Larsen, J. A. (1990). *Direct social work practice: Theory and skills.* Belmont, CA: Wadsworth.

6. Selye, H. (1974). *Stress without distress.* New York: New American Library.

Chapter 14

7. Johnson, H. C., Atkins, S. P., Battle, S. F., Hernandez-Arata, L., Hesselbrock, M., Libassi, M. F., & Parish, M. S. (1990). Strengthening the "Bio" in the biopsychosocial paradigm. *Journal of Social Work Education, 26*(2), 109-123.

8. Cohen, D. (1988). Social work and psychotropic drug treatments. *Social Service Review, 62,* 576-599.

9. Johnson et al. (1990).

10. Chess, S., & Thomas, A. (1986). *Temperament in clinical practice.* New York: Guilford.

11. Hoberman, H. M., & Peterson, C. B. (1990). Multidimensional psychotherapy for children and adolescents. In B. D. Garfinkle, G. A. Carlson, & E. B. Weller (Eds.), *Psychiatric disorders in children and adolescents* (pp. 503-536). Philadelphia: W. B. Saunders.

12. Nemiroff, R. A., & Colarusso, C. A. (Eds.). (1990). *New dimensions in adult development.* New York: Basic Books.

13. Bloom, M. (1985). *Life span development: Bases for preventive and interventive helping.* New York: Macmillan; Cassius, J. (1980). *Horizons in biogenetics: New dimensions in mind/body psychotherapy.* Memphis, TN: Promethean; Krueger, D. W. (1989). *Body self and psychological self.* New York: Brunner/Mazel; Mindell, A. (1982). *Dreambody: The body's role in revealing the self.* Santa Monica, CA: Sig; Wender, P. H., & Klein, D. F. (1981). *Mind, mood, and medicine: A guide to the new biopsychiatry.* New York: New American Library; Woodman, M. (1982). *Addiction to perfection.* Toronto: Inner City Books.

14. Murray, M. T., & Pizzorno, J. E. (1991). *The encyclopedia of natural medicine.* Rocklin, CA: Prima.

15. Hayes, D., & Ross, C. E. (1993). Body and mind: The effect of exercise, overweight, and physical health on psychological well-being. *Journal of Health and Social Behavior, 27,* 387-400; Stetson, B., Schlundt, D. G., Sbrocco, T., Hill, J. O., Sharp, T., & Pope-Cordel, J. (1992). The effects of aerobic exercise on psychological adjustment: A randomized study of sedentary obese women attempting weight loss. *Women and Health, 19*(4), 1-14.

16. Claire, T. (1995). *Bodywork: What type of massage to get and how to make the most of it.* New York: Morrow.

17. Claire (1995).

18. Kaplan, H. S. (1987). *The illustrated manual of sex therapy.* New York: Brunner/Mazel.

19. Boston Women's Health Book Collective. (1979). *Our bodies, our selves.* New York: Simon & Schuster; Julty, S. (1979). *Men's bodies men's selves.* New York: Delta; Rathus, S. A., Nevid, J. S., & Fichner-Rathus, L. (1993). *Human sexuality in a world of diversity.* Boston: Allyn & Bacon.

20. Carnes, P. (1983). *The sexual addiction.* Minneapolis, MN: CompCare; Goodman, A. (1993). Diagnosis and treatment of sexual addiction. *Journal of Sex and Marital Therapy, 19,* 225-246.

21. Oki, M. (1979). *Zen yoga therapy.* Tokyo: Japan Publications.

22. Fu, H. H. (1984). *Therapeutic breathing exercise* (L. Ping, Trans.). Hong Kong: Hai Feng.

23. Gummerson, T. (1992). *Training theory for martial arts.* London: A & C Black.

24. Finn, M. (1988). *Martial arts: A complete illustrated history.* Woodstock, NY: Overlook.

25. Berrol, C. F. (1992). The neurophysiologic basis of the mind-body connection in dance/movement therapy. *American Journal of Dance Therapy, 14*(1), 19-29.

26. Serlin, I. (1993). Root images of healing in dance therapy. *American Journal of Dance Therapy, 15*(2), 65-76.

27. Payne, H. (Ed.). (1992). *Dance movement therapy: Theory and practice.* London: Tavistock.

28. Maxmen, J. S. (1991). *Psychotropic drugs: Fast facts.* New York: Norton; Miller, S. I., Frances, R. J., & Holmes, D. J. (1989). Psychotropic medications. In R. K. Hester & W. R. Miller (Eds.), *Handbook of alcoholism treatment approaches* (pp. 231-241). New York: Pergamon.

29. Gach, M. R. (1981). *Acu-yoga: Self help techniques to relieve tension.* Tokyo: Japan Publications.

30. Lowen, A. (1977). *Bioenergetics.* New York: Penguin.

31. Duff, K. (1993). The alchemy of illness. *Common Boundary, 11*(3), 40.

32. Hendricks, G., & Hendricks, K. (1993). *At the speed of life: A new approach to personal change through body-centered therapy.* New York: Bantam.

33. Duff (1993).

34. Kaplan, H. S. (1974). *The new sex therapy: Active treatment of sexual dysfunctions.* New York: Brunner/Mazel.

35. Peaceworks Center for the Dances of Universal Peace. (1990). *Dances of universal peace: Movement and music to enliven and unify* (Vol. 1). Available from: SIRS Publications, 65 Norwich Street, San Francisco, CA 94110.

Chapter 15

36. Jackson, J. (1971). Unnamed address for Operation Breadbasket. Chicago.

37. Burghardt, S. (1982). *The other side of organizing: Resolving the personal dilemmas and political demands of daily practice.* Cambridge, MA: Schenkman.

38. Freire, P. (1989). *The pedagogy of the oppressed.* New York: Continuum.

39. Peck, M. S. (1993). Stages of community building. In C. Whitmyer (Ed.), *In the company of other: Making community in the modern world* (pp. 37-45). New York: Jeremy P. Tarcher/Perigee.

40. Fox, W. (1990). *Towards a transpersonal ecology: Developing new foundations for environmentalism.* Boston: Shambhala.

41. Garbarino, J. (1988). *The future as if it really mattered*. Longmont, CO: Bookmakers Guild.

42. M. Fox, personal communication, July 1997.

43. Caldicott, H. (1992). *If you love this planet: A plan to heal the earth*. New York: Norton.

44. Murray, J. (1995). A few beautifully made things. *Common Boundary, 13,* 42-43.

45. Campbell, P. A. (1989). *Bio-spirituality: Focusing as a way to grow*. Chicago: Loyola University Press.

46. Halifax, J. (1993). *The fruitful darkness: Reconnecting with the body of the earth*. San Francisco: Harper San Francisco.

47. Marx, J. D. (1988). An outdoor adventure counseling program for adolescents. *Social Work, 33,* 517-520.

48. Devall, B. (1988). *Simple in means, rich in ends: Practicing deep ecology*. Salt Lake City, UT: Peregrine Smith.

49. Hartmann, A. (1993). Award acceptance speech at annual program meeting, Council of Social Work Educators, Atlanta, GA.

50. Garbarino (1988).

51. M. Fox, personal communication, February 1994.

52. Spretnak, C. (1993). The other: Community's shadow. In C. Whitmyer (Ed.), *In the company of other: Making community in the modern world* (pp. 169-174). New York: Jeremy P. Tarcher/Perigee.

53. Whitmyer, C. (1993). Making community: The task. In C. Whitmyer (Ed.), *In the company of other: Making community in the modern world* (pp. 31-36). New York: Jeremy P. Tarcher/Perigee.

54. Murray (1995).

55. Boal, A. (1992). *Games for actors and non-actors* (A. Jackson, Trans.). London: Routledge.

56. Kozeny, G. (1993). Intentional communities. In C. Whitmyer (Ed.), *In the company of other: Making community in the modern world* (pp. 117-123). New York: Jeremy P. Tarcher/Perigee.

57. Dass, R. (1993). Service: The soul of community. In C. Whitmyer (Ed.), *In the company of other: Making community in the modern world* (pp. 89-92). New York: Jeremy P. Tarcher/Perigee.

58. Brown, J. (1993). The corporation as community. In C. Whitmyer (Ed.), *In the company of other: Making community in the modern world* (pp. 130-137). New York: Jeremy P. Tarcher/Perigee.

59. Hanh, T. N. (1993). Awareness: The consciousness of community. In C. Whitmyer (Ed.), *In the company of other: Making community in the modern world* (pp. 101-104). New York: Jeremy P. Tarcher/Perigee.

60. Murray (1995).

61. O'Sullivan, W. (1995). What makes a place sacred? *Common Boundary, 13,* 25.

62. Garbarino (1988).

63. Morgan, A. E. (1993). Homo sapiens: The community animal. In C. Whitmyer (Ed.), *In the company of other: Making community in the modern world* (pp. 16-19). New York: Jeremy P. Tarcher/Perigee.

64. R. Russel, personal communication, December 1, 1995.

65. Duff (1993).

66. Campbell (1989).

Professional Self-Development

The key hypotheses in this section are that (a) effective conscious use of self requires ongoing professional self-development; (b) in professional self-development, the worker continues to develop in all of the dimensions of self, including the affective, physical, spiritual, cognitive, and social; and (c) professional self-development also involves the development of knowledge, skills, and values necessary to effectively manage transference and countertransference reactions in the helping relationship.

From the inclusive perspective, professional development includes both the development of the multidimensional self and the development of technique (based upon increasing skills, knowledge, and values in managing the helping relationship). Both of these processes are, of course, interrelated. Both are necessary. As Maslow[1] suggested, technique without the use of self is "mechanistic" and "reductionistic." Similarly, use of self without the application of skills, knowledge, and values also limits effectiveness. The use of various techniques of assessment and intervention was examined in Parts I, II, III, and IV. In this section, the development of the professional self is described, and the application of the use of self in working with transference and countertransference reactions is illustrated.

The effective social worker is committed to her own continuing self-development. As the social worker learns how to grow, he learns more about how to help other people grow and becomes a positive role model for his clients.

CHAPTER 16

Affective Development

The social worker needs to be involved in three ongoing, interrelated processes of emotional development: (a) self-awareness, (b) self-acceptance, and (c) capacity to feel. These processes are all important to effective use of self in practice. The social worker who is developing self-knowledge, self-acceptance, and depth of feeling is increasingly effective in conscious use of self and as a model for clients.

Self-Awareness

The effective social worker strives to become more aware of herself. Without self-awareness, the social worker cannot differentiate well between the client and herself; aspects of the self that are still unknown may be projected onto others. Without self-awareness, the social worker cannot fully accept himself or other people; one can only accept what one is first aware of. Without self-awareness, the social worker may make errors in assessment and intervention. Awareness of countertransference reactions enables the worker to use her self to help the client.

Self-awareness is required for empathic response. The social worker uses his own self-awareness to sense or intuit the affect of a client: He must listen to his own self in order to read the client. Although such intuition may seem extrasensory, it is actually a quite ordinary and common human experience (e.g., the social worker at a suicide phone line center who uses well-developed intuition to detect or tune in to the affect of clients over the phone). Such a social worker is often able to assess the client's affect quite accurately and to relate empathically in interventions.

For each person, the work of a relationship is, in large part, a process during which she becomes more aware of where she ends and the other person begins. In other words, the boundaries between people gradually become clearer as a relationship matures. Without such awareness, people can become so close (enmeshed) or distant (disengaged) that interpersonal boundaries and interrelationships become confused. For example, in a very enmeshed marriage, a woman may expect her husband to always anticipate her needs (because he is an extension of herself). In a very disengaged marriage, a man may assume that his frequent drinking has absolutely no effect on his wife.

Such development of clear boundaries is important in conscious use of self in practice. The effective social worker strives to be aware of the personal needs that brought her into social work. If a social worker is not aware of such needs, he is less likely to know what motivates his practice decisions. For example, a tendency for a social worker to be active and responsive in the environment may often serve to help clients who need these qualities from their worker. However, if a social worker has a lack of awareness about having this tendency, that worker may assume that all clients need her to act this way. The worker may not help and may even harm clients who need a less active and responsive style.

Each social worker needs to be aware of the price he may pay for being a helper. For example, many social work students find that they cannot turn off their need to help when they leave work. They are often unable to ask for help themselves and may even be unaware of their own needs in their personal lives. Each social worker also has her own unique personality, which may include such lifelong traits as activity level, adaptability, mood, distractibility, and persistence.[2] Awareness of such innate qualities enables the social worker to differentiate more clearly the client's needs from her own.

A good percentage of graduate students and practicing social workers who are asked to consider their life experiences at first tend to idealize their pasts. They ignore or diminish the importance of the painful experiences that are associated with their vocational choice, and they exaggerate the importance of the more positive experiences. Thus, one student might write about how she chose social work because her mother was a positive model of a giving person. She did not report, however, that her father was an alcoholic and her mother had many codependent tendencies. She did not discuss how she had to give up much of her self, particularly of her childhood, as she began caring for her father and younger siblings at an early age. Such lack of awareness can lead to difficulty appreciating similar loss and pain in clients.

Often, a social worker develops cognitive awareness or growth first, and only months or even years later develops affective (or deeper, "cellular") awareness or growth. Although emotional growth is often more gradual than cognitive growth, workers frequently expect their emotions to change rapidly. For example, a social worker takes an assertiveness class and starts to realize that he has been letting others manipulate him constantly. He is frustrated with himself that, despite his new cognitive awareness, he still gets intimidated by others.

Experiential Exercises

1. Consider your own affective development. Which emotions are you most aware of (e.g., the five basic feelings of being sad, glad, mad, scared, excited)? Which emotions are you least aware of? Why do you think that is?

2. Now, consider which emotions in yourself you accept most easily. What emotions are the most difficult for you to accept? Why do you think that is?

3. Now decide which is easiest for you to do: (a) Feel and show compassion for the pain of a friend or client, or (b) feel and celebrate the joy of a friend or client. Why do you think that is?

4. Which emotions in other people are the hardest for you to accept? Why? How could you learn to better accept such human diversity of emotion?

5. Consider at what point in your life you first began acting as a helper for others. Consider the circumstances at that time. How did helping others also serve to help yourself? What price did you pay for helping (i.e., in what ways did helping others also hurt you)? How does helping others continue to help you now? What price do you now pay for helping others (e.g., how does helping others now somehow harm you)?

The development of awareness is often greatly accelerated by sharing with others. As social workers explore who they are and what they think or feel, new insights often emerge. These insights often expose those aspects of self about which social workers feel the greatest shame. Our pathology (what we believe are our problems) often leads us to the most profound growth; the symptoms about which we are most concerned can be viewed as clues about our souls, about who we are. As the street expression "get your s— together" implies, emotional development requires the ongoing integration of all aspects of our selves, particularly those aspects about which we feel the most shame ("like s—").

Another person, particularly a caring, intuitive, and skilled helper, can assist a social worker in gaining insights into herself. The process of exploring new aspects of ourselves, of sharing new visions, is most effectively encouraged within an atmosphere of empathy, warmth, and genuineness. Each social worker should have the right, of course, to select the unique way in which she wishes to work on her own personal development. For example, some workers may want to participate in individual or group psychotherapy, others may choose to work with a supervisor, and still others may work within a spiritual or religious discipline.

Effective sharing cannot occur in an unsafe atmosphere. A social worker needs, perhaps most of all, to feel that she can explore herself without any fear of judgment or punishment, and only as quickly as she is ready to. Such safety may not exist in various work or educational settings. Social workers who teach or supervise other workers may especially need to work on personal development before they can effectively model and support acceptance for other social workers.

There are feelings that may arise in the moment that occur when the social worker is actually working with clients. These feelings may include anger, fear, attraction, repulsion, and even love. When the social worker is aware of them, such feelings can be powerful tools and healing visions in the helping process. When the social worker is unaware of them, these feelings can also interfere with assessment and intervention.

For example, a male social worker who is working with an abusive mother and her son may become aware of an intense dislike of the mother and equally strong affection for the son. As the social worker reflects on these feelings, he may realize that he is overidentifying with the boy and underidentifying with the mother. He is overidentifying with the child in this case because as a child, this social worker had been abused by his own mother. Therefore, he has a lack of awareness about who this boy really is. Instead of seeing the boy's unique past and present characteristics clearly, the social worker imagines instead that the boy's development has been and is currently similar or identical to his own. He also has a blind spot about the mother, underidentifying with her and thus not seeing her realistically either. As this social worker processes (works to understand) these feelings, he becomes more aware of the specific needs of both the mother and son.

Many social workers work almost exclusively with very difficult client populations, such as sexual abuse victims and perpetrators, serious substance abusers and addicts, or chronic and violent criminals. Doing social work can be tremendously rewarding; the work can lead to personal actualization and feelings of fulfillment and satisfaction. However, this kind of work can also cost the social worker, who may become emotionally drained, pessimistic about human nature, and increasingly filled with chronic frustration and even despair. The social worker who does this work needs to become aware of this cost, and aware of what she needs to rebalance in her life. Few social workers are (or should expect themselves to be) like Mother Teresa, able to serve selflessly across a lifetime. Instead, most workers need to regularly replenish themselves, often through their own chosen forms of re-creation.

The rewards of increased self-awareness are many. Personal growth and fulfillment depend on increased self-awareness; the ancient dictum "know thyself" is as valid today as ever. Self-knowledge can provide the social worker with an important possession: the knowledge of what she wants and loves to do. The social worker's clients benefit too. Many social workers find that their clients can only go as deeply into their emotional awareness as they themselves have gone. Workers may also find that their clients seem to move emotionally deeper following movements in their own emotional growth.

Experiential Exercises

1. Consider how and when you made the decision to be a social worker. Can you describe that process?

2. To what extent did your own biogenetic makeup (e.g., needs, personality tendencies) contribute to the decision? To what extent did your life experiences contribute to the decision?

3. In the process of this vocational choice, which was most important overall—nature or nurture?

4. What rewards has social work brought you in your life? What has been the cost? Of the two (rewards and cost), which are you most aware of and least aware of? Why do you think this is?

Self-Acceptance

Self-acceptance is perhaps the most fundamental and most radical change that the social worker can make. As the social worker accepts herself, she becomes a free person who is capable of loving and fostering the freedom of others.

Self-acceptance is as important to social worker effectiveness as self-awareness. One cannot accept one's whole self without being aware of who one is, and self-knowledge without self-acceptance can lead to difficulties in accepting others. Self-acceptance is a generally compassionate and approving attitude toward oneself that evolves over time as new self-awareness grows. Self-acceptance is not the denial or minimization of personal imperfections, nor is it the denial of responsibility for personal choices. Rather, self-acceptance is a forgiving perspective toward where one happens to be in one's own developmental process.

Self-acceptance is as necessary as self-awareness in the development of empathic understanding and attunement. The social worker who does not accept his own inner signals and reactions to the client is unlikely to be able to use these important data in his assessments and interventions. When those inner signals and reactions are accepted, then the worker does not need to hide his inner workings from himself or the client. For example, a social worker may notice anger at a client. If the worker is ashamed of her own anger, the worker may deny it to herself and to the client. If the worker accepts the anger, he can now perhaps discuss it with a supervisor, consider its significance, and make practice decisions.

When the worker can accept her own emotional process, her emotional growth tends to accelerate.[3] Nonacceptance of emotional process, however, tends to retard growth.[4] For example, one social worker had difficulty letting people care for her. For years, she felt guilty that she pushed people away from her when they started to love her. It was only when she started to accept the fact that she was very frightened to let love into her life that she was able to let go of her defensiveness and allow someone to care for her. Thus, in the psyche, what one resists does indeed tend to persist. The aspects of the worker's self about which she feels shame and tries to hide tend not to heal or change.[5] For example, a worker started to wonder whether his caring personality was just a coping style that he learned as a child to protect himself from hostile parents. He discussed this issue with a therapist and realized how ashamed he was about the abuse he had suffered as a child. The therapist helped him overcome his shame about his past. Gradually, he started to become aware that he reacted to others with anger or fear more often than he thought. He began to feel and accept the emotions, and he started to express more of his feelings in safe situations.

The social worker who accepts herself is better able to accept her clients and to model self-esteem for them. Positive self-esteem and acceptance may be the foundation of individual and family mental health.[6] The psychosocial importance of self-esteem is well-documented; self-esteem has been shown to be associated with such social problems as child maltreatment, school failure, teenage pregnancy, crime, and addiction.[7]

Without self-acceptance, the social worker is disabled in his ability to help self and client.[8] In part, this is because his attention must be focused on defending, protecting, or hiding from the shame he feels about any still unaccepted aspects of self. Thus, less attention is available for personal growth, expansion, or awareness. In addition, a social worker cannot easily help a client become more self-accepting when the worker is not also striving to become more self-accepting.

As social workers attend graduate school and later make the transition to begin practice, they may experience lowered self-acceptance as they realize that they have limited knowledge and skills for practice.[9] The worker can, however, be aware of his own limitations and still feel that he is good enough in the present moment. Self-acceptance does not necessarily have to be shaken during and after professional education. With support and positive modeling, students and young professionals can develop their skills and knowledge and, at the same time, experience enhancement of self-esteem.

The most effective worker realizes that she is always learning new knowledge and behaviors, and must occasionally go through a developmentally necessary period of moderate discomfort and experimentation with success and perceived failure. Just as children who are learning to ride a bike must sometimes fall, social workers have to make mistakes to learn. Learning may be made more difficult in part because social workers often feel that they are expected to be more perfect than they could possibly be. Unrealistic expectations usually result in feelings of failure. When expectations are more realistic, failure becomes appropriately reframed as just being human.

Social work students and practitioners often focus almost exclusively on what they need to know rather than on how much they already know. Developmental science suggests that people learn best when they are allowed to build upon their strengths, rather than constantly forced to work in their more limited areas of development.[10] The education of a social worker should ultimately result in increasing self-awareness and self-acceptance.

Clients do not need social workers who are perfect as much as they need social workers who are willing to see and accept their imperfections. Such perfectionistic attitudes may persist in the workplace. Although limitations are natural, social workers often expect themselves to have literally no limitations. Every social worker is tired some days, may have weeks during which she feels worse about herself, or even months and years when personal life crises occupy most of her consciousness. Every social worker makes mistakes, misses signals of abuse in a family, projects qualities onto one client, or tries a technique with a client that is unhelpful or even harmful. The social worker does not necessarily have to be transparent with the client about her own imperfections, but she does need to be personally aware and accepting of these imperfections.

However, as South African leader Nelson Mandela has said, the part of ourselves that people usually have the most difficulty accepting is not our personal limitations (which are difficult enough), but the very best (or highest) parts of ourselves. The highest self represents the most developed dimensions of a person's development and is capable of awe, love, compassion, forgiveness, and connection. In an adolescent culture, where being cool is often preferred over displaying the higher self, the social worker may not accept her higher self out of fear of being seen as boastful or even a little crazy.

The effective social worker realizes that boastfulness, or narcissism, is often confused with self-acceptance in our culture. They are, in fact, opposite processes. Narcissism is associated with the lack of self-acceptance; people boast and become overinflated because they do not think that the way they really are is enough. As a person learns to loves himself, he can accept his highest qualities, as well as his limitations.

For example, one social worker at a particular social work setting seems to irritate many people around her. She monopolizes the conversations in meetings and seems to think that she never makes a mistake. Another worker complains about her to the director, saying, "She seems to feel too good about herself." The director replies, "Actually, she does not like herself at all. That's why she constantly has to seek our attention and praise."

Experiential Exercises

1. How safe do you feel in your workplace or in the classroom? Specifically, do you feel that you can openly examine your strengths and limitations with others? Are these obstacles to safety internal (e.g., related to your own fears or shame) and/or external (e.g., related to the norms of the institution or the judgmental nature of a supervisor)?

2. What could be done to make these environments safer? What other informal or formal support systems do you have in your life where you may feel safer?

3. To what extent do you think you accept your own limitations? To what extent do you accept your highest self? If your primary goal in the next year was to increase your acceptance of both your own limitations and your highest self, what would you do differently in your life?

The social worker's professional strengths are also her limitations. For example, a particular social worker is an excellent listener; she is able to be quiet and listen to people and really hear what they are saying. This ability to listen may have a flip side that can be, at times, a limitation: The same social worker in his quietness may be unable to speak out assertively and give clients feedback when necessary. When the social worker accepts such combinations of strength and weakness in herself, she is better able to build upon personal strengths and reduce the impact of personal limitations. As this worker accepts the way she is in the present moment, she is likely to both further develop her ability to listen and be assertive.

An unaccepting attitude toward any aspect of the self can lead to errors in practice. When a social worker does not accept an aspect of himself, he often loses some of his energy (which is focused upon denial and hiding) as well as some of his self-awareness and awareness of others (because he is focused upon strategies of hiding). For example, a social worker feels sexually attracted to one of her clients. She refuses to accept her feelings and tries hard to be distant and unloving with her client. The client feels that the worker does not like him, and the helping relationship is damaged. The worker finally tells her supervisor what is happening, and the supervisor helps the worker accept the attraction. As the worker accepts her feelings, she is able to relax and to care about the client and concentrate upon helping him.

Any aspect of self is acceptable. Acceptance of who the social worker is in the moment does not imply that the worker's behaviors are necessarily healthy or destructive. For example, with the current professional and public concern about codependency, some social workers may be concerned that any motivations for entering social work are unhealthy. Currently, the inclination to serve others is viewed less favorably than it might have been viewed a generation ago; being helpful has become unhealthy.

An alternative way to think about helping involves avoiding dualities and thinking in terms of balance. The need to be helpful to others is, in itself, neither good nor bad, right nor wrong, and can be balanced with a commitment to self-care. Those who help others are some of society's most talented individuals. Often, the most gifted child is the one who learns to help others (with such gifts as sensitivity to self and others, intelligence, wisdom, inner strength, and emotional maturity).[11]

Similarly, concern for self, or selfishness, is also neither bad nor good. In fact, one could argue that every human act is selfish in some way. Because selfishness is inevitable, perhaps the best a social worker can do is be selfish in a way that benefits or at least does not harm others. Both care for self and care for others are necessary, in varying degrees of relative emphasis, in every life situation.

How does a social worker accept himself more? The process may include four interrelated subprocesses. First, the social worker, by acting to accept clients (and others) more, tends to eventually learn to accept herself more. Said differently, it becomes increasingly difficult for a social worker to avoid hearing what he keeps telling his clients. Second, the social worker benefits from having others accept her, so she seeks out mentors, therapists, friends, and others who can model greater self-acceptance for her.

Third, the worker can act as if he feels better about himself. Often, it may be easier for the social worker to act her way into new ways of feeling than to feel her way into new ways of acting. Finally, because the dimensions of development are interrelated, the social worker may also improve self-esteem through work in any of the dimensions of development (see exercises below).

Ultimately, self-acceptance is required if the social worker hopes to escape what Fritz Perls called the "endless torture of self-improvement" that our culture's many self-help psychologies have perpetuated.[12] A both/and position is possible; social workers can include both planning for future change and self-acceptance in the here and now in their practice. Change and acceptance are not mutually exclusive; in fact, self-acceptance usually facilitates change.

Experiential Exercises

1. If you felt better about yourself, how would you act differently around other people this next week? Offer specific examples. (This exercise is focused on the social dimension of development.)

2. What new ways of thinking would you have if you felt better about yourself? Consider specific examples. (This exercise is focused on the cognitive dimension.)

3. Which areas of your spirituality might you explore and express differently if you felt better about yourself? (This exercise is focused on the spiritual dimension.)

4. How might you take better care of your body if you felt better about yourself? (This exercise is focused on the physical dimension.)

5. How could you learn to enjoy yourself more in your life? (This exercise is focused on the affective dimension.)

The Capacity to Feel

The effective social worker is able to both suffer and celebrate with the client. The word *compassion* literally means "to suffer with." Although the importance of compassion itself is well recognized in the literature,[13] the process of becoming compassionate is relatively ignored in the current literature. Indeed, all therapeutic work could be viewed as a process of getting through the pain of life's losses with the whole self intact. It is interesting to note how both Eastern and Western psychologies agree on the vital connection between being able to feel both sadness and joy, and optimum human development.[14]

A social worker's ability to have compassion for the client is substantially related to her ability to feel her own personal pain. Although each of us, of course, has emotional pain in life, our society tends to promote the avoidance of pain. Most of us have many socially acceptable distractions available to help us avoid pain (e.g., cable television, videos, drugs, music).

Ironically, attempts to avoid pain never ultimately lead to a painless life, and they are likely to create new problems and suffering. These new problems were called "neuroses" by Sigmund Freud,[15] a "substitute for legitimate suffering" by Carl Jung,[16] and "pseudo-pain" by Virginia Satir.[17]

The new pain may be worse than the initial suffering. For example, an addiction might be a substitute for pain. As John Bradshaw said, "An addict is like a man on fire who jumps into the water and then begins to drown."[18]

The legitimate suffering to which Jung referred (sometimes called "real pain" by Satir) can lead to the further development of the human spirit. The discipline required to deal with suffering in a healthy way requires a number of tools, including delaying gratification, taking responsibility, making dedication to reality, being open to challenge, problem solving, and balancing.[19]

Experiential Exercises

1. Think about a person in your life who was (or is) compassionate with you. What did it feel like to be with that person? How was that person able to be so compassionate? (You may want to ask him or her.)

2. Think of a time when you felt you were unusually compassionate toward someone else. Why were you able to do that? Could you recreate that compassion again? How?

3. Think of a time when you felt you were unusually unable to be compassionate. Again, consider why you were unable to be compassionate then. How could you overcome whatever obstacles you identified?

Clients often seem to intuit, as we all do, the extent to which a social worker has become comfortable with her own pain. Clients are most likely to work on their own pain when their social worker has done the same kind of personal work. The process of feeling one's own pain and working through it can lead to increased *affective surplus* (the capacity to experience compassion), *connection* (the ability to feel empathy for the client's affect), and *ability to disclose* (the capacity to demonstrate compassion and empathy). Without affective surplus, connection, and ability to disclose, the social worker's interventions tend to be only technical, and her effectiveness may become much more limited. The work of suffering thus includes three steps:

1. The social worker strives to increase awareness of his own emotional story and landscape. The emotional story is the individual's history of emotional experiences. The emotional landscape includes all of the feelings that the

person currently is experiencing. There are many ways to increase such awareness, including various forms of psychotherapy, meditation, and classroom study.

2. The worker strives to increase acceptance of her own emotional story and landscape. Such work often requires receiving the acceptance of another person.

3. The worker strives to find ways to forgive himself and others, as well as remove other obstacles to bringing compassion toward himself and others. The worker may need to learn how to gradually let go of feelings of hurt and anger that may remain in her emotional landscape. In this process, the worker may need to experience being forgiven by another person.

Thus, social workers who do their own work of suffering tend to become more compassionate toward themselves and their clients. The work of suffering often requires quiet, inward time when the worker reflects on his own pain. As the worker feels and expresses his pain, at his own rate and in his own way, he becomes more open and more sensitive to his inner and outer world. Perhaps Rick Field described the process most concisely when he wrote about how, after a person is hurt, her heart may actually become more receptive to life and love.[20]

The ability to celebrate with a client is as important as the ability to suffer with a client. Whereas many of us may find it difficult to suffer with the client, probably even more of us find it especially challenging to celebrate with the client. Just as it is difficult to have compassion if one cannot feel one's own pain, it is also difficult to feel happy for a client if one cannot enjoy one's self.

The ability to feel joy and pain is an interdependent process, just as the two opposite directions in the swing of a pendulum are related (see Figure 16.1). When the swing of the pendulum is restricted in either direction, it cannot swing as far back in the other direction. When a social worker is unable to feel personal pain, the worker is usually restricted in her ability to feel joy, and when a social worker is unable to feel personal joy, the worker is usually restricted in her ability to feel pain.

When the social worker can feel joy, he models that for the client. When the social worker can share in the client's happiness, this is usually experienced by the client as an act of caring and tends to further the client's process. Joy is also diagnostic: It could be said that joy is the surest sign that someone is on his or her multidimensional developmental path.

Scientists have identified three strategies that tend to make experiences more enjoyable (or to create what they call "flow"): "getting caught up in what one is doing, controlling what is happening, and creating variety and stimulation so as to make activities novel and challenging enough to stay caught up in them" (p. 172).[21] Social workers can experiment with these strategies in their own personal and professional lives.

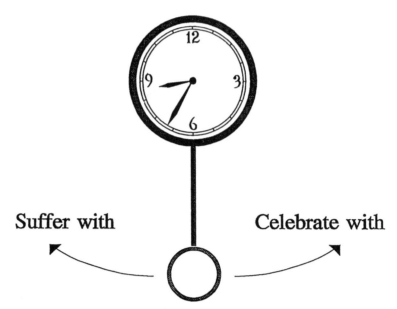

Figure 16.1. The Pendulum of Ability to Feel

Experiential Exercises

1. How much joy do you have in your life? What brings you joy? What are the primary obstacles to you having joy in your life?

2. When you have had a happy event in your life, how did your family or friends react? How did you feel about their reactions?

3. What mixed emotions are you aware of having when someone tells you about a happy event in his or her life? Why do you think you have these feelings? How do you want to behave in the future when you hear a happy story?

CHAPTER 17

Physical and Spiritual Development

Physical Dimension

Krueger's[22] theory of development suggests a movement toward gradually increasing sensitivity of and care for one's body. Thus, physical development includes an increasing ability to create healthy patterns of self-care and self-expression that may be associated with exercise, diet, self-care, sleep, relaxation, or the use of various medicinal drugs.

Sensitivity to the physical self is essential at times to the process of assessing clients. The healthy social worker is aware of her own body and the interconnections between her physical, emotional, and spiritual health. The worker can use her body awareness to help her assess the well-being of herself and clients. For example, a social worker might feel sick to his stomach when he is around a particular client. This reaction may provide information about the client. Perhaps many people have a similar reaction to the client, or perhaps the client reminds the worker of someone else in her life that affected her stomach similarly.

Many social workers experience their intuition as physical sensations. These sensations may also include tension in the jaws, tingling in the spine, sexual feelings, or headache. Satir[23] observed that social workers often do not trust their own body sensations and perceptions. She noticed that workers usually do not believe that their own internal experience (or intuition) is a legitimate way of knowing. Instead, workers have been taught to trust only external sources of knowledge (e.g., opinions of experts, published findings, and responses to assessment instruments). Internal perceptions are usually ignored, and discussion of their meaning discouraged in the classroom and supervision office. The use of such sensations is discussed further in Chapter 19.

Many social workers, perhaps as a result of both the larger society and their profession's culture, tend to trust their minds much more than the sensations in the rest of their body. A more effective strategy is to *also* listen with the heart, the spinal cord, the intestines (guts), the sexual organs, and all of the other parts of the body. The social worker's body is an important source of information in assessing the client. The more aware and accepting the social worker is of such sensations, the more able he is to assist the client in learning to trust himself. Conversely, the lack of such awareness and acceptance tends to reinforce less functional ways of thinking and acting in the social worker and client.

For example, most people occasionally notice a shiver down their spine or goosebumps on their skin when they have certain kinds of life experiences. People often ignore or dismiss such sensations. The effective social worker is curious when she has any physical sensation and examines ways to use bodily sensations in practice. For example, a social worker notices that she has a tightness in her throat when she sits down to talk with a new client. The worker is curious about the sensation and realizes that she is afraid. She decides to ask the client, "How do you feel now?" The client shrugs, so the worker then asks, "Is it a little scary to be here?" The client nods and starts to sob.

Sensitivity to the physical self is also essential to social work interventions. The social worker serves as a model to her client. The worker often asks clients to discipline themselves in various ways. The word *discipline* has the root word "disciple" within it, which literally means "follower." The social worker's own lifestyle speaks louder than spoken words. The worker is learning how to relax, exercise, eat and sleep, and recognize personal physical needs and limitations in a nurturing and balanced manner.

Modeling can, of course, be negative as well as positive. Social workers are not immune to a variety of physical problems, including those related to alcoholism, drug addiction, poor diet, and lack of exercise. When professional helpers become relatively unaware of their bodies, they may give their clients mixed messages about healthy physical development. Some clients have noted the irony of being encouraged to learn stress reduction techniques from a professional who is obviously living under chronic distress. The mixed message is, of course, do not do as I do, do as I say.

The developing social worker also is aware of the connection between body, mind, and spirit and is learning how to use the consciousness of the body more effectively. The interrelationship between the body and the mind and spirit is increasingly described in the literature.[24] Indeed, the word *health* is derived from the original root "hal," which means "whole." Thus, physical health is associated with the extent to which a person is connected to her whole self—her body-mind-spirit connection.

The body is an instrument of consciousness, and it often reminds us of who we are and remembers past events that the mind may no longer remember. In Wilber's[25] theory of the development of consciousness, the physical body represents the first structure of consciousness, characterized by the realms of sensation, matter, and perception. This structure is not replaced by higher structures of consciousness, but remains an integral part of being human. Therefore, the body is connected with the mind and spirit in all human beings. Thus, the social worker strives for holistic health, which is not just the absence of disease but a level of well-being associated with optimum physical, emotional, mental, social, and spiritual functioning.

Experiential Exercises

1. Explore the life experiences that have particularly interfered with and/or fostered your physical development. How well do you accept your own body?

2. In what ways do you take care of your body? In what ways do you not?

3. Are you able to listen to your body when it needs healing, rest, food, fasting, sex, or exercise? What physical needs are most unmet this month?

Spiritual Development

Spirituality is probably the dimension of human development that is most ignored and least defined in the social work literature. In addition, spirituality is often confused with religion and sometimes carries powerful positive or negative connotations for people. The following definitions are offered for the purposes of this discussion.

Spirituality (literally, the "breath of life") is an essential process of human development toward realization of such goals as the highest levels of well-being and consciousness; a sense of meaning and purpose in life; appreciation of the sacred and transcendent; and a sense of idealism, acceptance, and connectiveness with self and the world. By this definition, each one of us has a spiritual dimension, just like each one of us has a cognitive dimension or an emotional dimension. The spiritual dimension may be the dominant dimension in some people, and a rather dormant or underdeveloped dimension in others.

Spirituality involves not only moving up toward the highest levels of well-being, but also down to explore and remember the shadow (unknown) aspects of self. Our culture's traditional view of spiritual growth has been that it is an uplifting voyage, an inspiration of the breath of life, as the root word "spirit" (air) suggests. In this view, one is moved toward one's higher nature until one reaches the ideal state of well-being or salvation.

Another view of spiritual growth, suggested by the Jungian psychologists,[26] involves a journey downward into darkness, shadow, and the depths of the soul. The goal of shadow work is the integration of all of the aspects of self, particularly those aspects of self of which people are unaware and about which they are often uncomfortable. Knowledge of one's dark side includes awareness of feelings that are less socially acceptable (e.g., anger, jealousy, revenge, sexuality, and fear).

According to Wilber,[27] spiritual development includes three primary levels of functioning, which were described in Part II. Wilber's model suggests that the social worker must first develop a personality (personal-level functioning) before she can move beyond it (to transpersonal functioning). Other theories of spiritual development tend to support Wilber's models and suggest such goals as affirmation of life and true self, development of a central life philosophy, dealing with death and other losses, shedding previous roles, and gaining wisdom.[28]

Religion (literally, to "bring together") involves socially shared beliefs, doctrines, and rituals, usually institutionalized as a form of worship, that may include reverence for a supreme creator of the universe. Fowler[29] has suggested that the religious person gradually becomes more open to viewing reality from multiple perspectives as she matures. From that perspective, a key goal of religious maturity for each individual is an attitude of openness and tolerance for religious and spiritual diversity.

Spirituality and religion are not mutually exclusive. A social worker's attendance in a religion may or may not foster his spiritual development. One could say that religion is to spirituality as education is to learning. Just as most educational institutions can either foster or obstruct learning, most religions can either foster or obstruct spirituality.

Experiential Exercises

1. Explore the religious experiences you have had in your life. How have they interfered with or fostered your spiritual development?

2. Explore your own spiritual development. What was your earliest spiritual experience? How has your spirituality changed through your childhood, adolescence, and adulthood? What do you anticipate will be the next stage in the development of your spirituality?

3. What religious traditions or spiritual paths are the hardest for you to tolerate? Why? How could you learn to accept such elements of human diversity better?

Today there appears to be a renewed public and professional interest in spirituality and religiosity. The Society for Spirituality in Social Work, currently still housed at the School of Social Work at the University of Nebraska at Omaha, conducted its first national conference in 1995 at the University of Utah's Graduate School of Social Work. Increasing church attendance in the United States may be related to a worldwide rise in religious fundamentalism that may not peak until the first years of the next millennium.[30] As the Baby Boom generation of the United States ages and faces the inevitability of death, an increasing percentage of our population may become more interested in spiritual development. For these reasons, social workers can expect that they will probably see increasing numbers of clients who have issues related to spirituality and religion.

The importance of spirituality in practice, a subject that only now is being recognized again in some of the professional journals, has been well identified in decades past. Many leading theorists have written about the connection between spirituality and the helping professions.[31] For example, throughout much of his career, Freud[32] wrote about "soul making" and a "collective mind" or "mass psyche" that is the underlying reality of human consciousness. Satir stated simply, "I believe that the first step in any change is to contact the spirit."[33]

In modern times, social workers and other professional helpers gradually assumed the roles of premodern shamans and modern religious leaders. Social work was initially one of the most spiritual professions, with roots in religious, charitable organizations. Although the term *vocation* literally means "divine calling," the social work profession, like most Western professions, no longer embraces the spiritual aspects of work.[34]

The effective advanced generalist social worker is committed to working on his own spiritual path. When a social worker is in touch with her own spirituality, she is employing what could be called *conscious use of higher self*. In conscious use of higher self, the worker uses her own spirituality to help the client. For example, a social worker starts working with a homeless man who also happens to be an alcoholic. Before the worker sees the client, she sits alone in her office and focuses a brief meditation on the idea that her work helps foster the highest good of her client. When she sees the man, she focuses on having compassion for him. The client seems to sense that she cares about him. It is the first time he has felt that another person cared about him for as long as he remembers.

In order to help others develop their spirituality, social workers need to develop their own spiritual dimension. The spiritually developing social worker acts as a model as well as a catalyst and guide for the client. The worker strives to be open to alternative spiritual viewpoints, and she also recognizes and accepts her current, personal, and unique spiritual development. Conscious use of higher self is fostered by five interrelated elements of professional development:

1. Following one's bliss. Campbell's[35] studies of comparative religion suggest that most wisdom traditions teach the importance of what he called "following one's bliss" when making vocational choices. Bennett and Sparrow[36] have defined bliss as the ability to follow one's own power, or soul, and have likened it to the spiritual concept of "oneness with universe," the psychological concept of "peak experience," the business concept of "peak performance," and the concept in athletics of "sweet spot in time." The social worker who has the courage to identify and practice her true vocation becomes a powerful model for her client's spiritual development.

The process of discovering one's bliss is different for every person. Often, social workers will discover that it is easier to first determine what they do *not* want to do, and then determine what it is they *do* want to do. For some workers, this process of self-discovery may be likened to Frankl's[37] idea of systematically exploring one's own existential concerns. As in all self-growth experiences, processing such internal concerns with other people (such as friends, colleagues, or supervisors) may be helpful.

For example, one social worker was discouraged because she had tried three jobs in the 3 years since she earned her MSW. She was an excellent worker, but she told her supervisor that she was feeling like a failure because she had discovered that the work she was doing now (in school social work) was also not very enjoyable for her. The supervisor wisely reframed the situation and told the worker that she was smart to have identified so quickly some of the areas in which she did not want to work. She added, "Sooner or later, I think you will discover the work you love today . . . and then perhaps 5 or 10 years later, you will find it necessary to move on again."

2. Openness to spiritual diversity. Another element of conscious use of higher self is the worker's ability to tolerate a variety of spiritual perspectives. Fowler's[38] developmental theory suggests that the maturing individual becomes gradually more open to alternative ways of viewing the universe. Beginning social workers may particularly feel the need to adopt a particular spiritual or religious model and hold tightly to it for support, much like a shipwrecked sailor might hold on to a section of floating wood, in the "stormy seas" of professional helping. Although this may well be a necessary stage in the development of a social worker, the social worker strives to enlarge her ability to accept the spirituality and religiosity of both her clients and herself.

Regardless of his own spiritual or religious beliefs, each social worker can approach his clients with both tolerance and passion. For example, James and James[39] called for a path with "passion for life":

> It is the commitment to life that motivates us to do our best and strive to make a positive difference in other people's lives. It is the determination to fight for what we believe in and to fight against suffering, injustice, and the waste of natural resources. It is the decision to transcend barriers that inhibit out best efforts. It reflects a commitment to be and to do more than we believed was possible. (p. 12)

3. Reconnection with the natural environment. One often neglected aspect of spiritual development is the developing sense of connection with the earth and the natural environment. The name of our species, *homo sapiens,* comes from the root word "humus," which means "earth." The widespread alienation of people today from their connection with the earth not only threatens our ultimate survival as a species (because of pollution and destruction of resources), but may well be associated with many of our biopsychosocial problems.[40]

Mounting evidence that the quality of the natural environment affects biopsychosociospiritual health (the mind-body-spirit connection) suggests that increasing numbers of social workers will be considering such environmental factors in their assessments and interventions in the next century. For example, most people living in overcrowded and heavily polluted urban environments are somehow affected by those environments, but each person is affected uniquely. The social worker will realize that those with biogenetic tendencies toward depression may experience depressive symptoms as local environmental decay creates more stress. Others with antisocial tendencies may become more violent.

The effective social worker strives to reconnect herself with the earth. She pays attention to the sources and quality of the food she eats, the water she drinks, and the air she breathes. Many people living in urban locations in the United States have little idea where the food they buy at the grocery store comes from. Most people do not realize that the air they breathe may be mixed with chemicals emitted from smokestacks hundreds and even thousands of miles away.

The effective social worker also tries to become more connected with the earth's seasons and the gigantic universe through which our relatively tiny planet sails. For example, because there are probably few people who are not affected by seasonal change in some ways, one social worker tried to pay attention to exactly how the seasonal changes affected her. Another social worker tried to notice his reactions to the night sky, which included an increased reverence for the specialness of earth and his own life.

The social worker is aware that many people in the culture still consider environmental connection to be a fad or even unpatriotic. However, connection to the natural environment is actually not a fad but an ancient tradition that has been valued highly by the vast majority of cultures that have lived on the earth. Connection with the environment is not unpatriotic but can be viewed as being very public spirited and consistent with traditional social work values.

4. *Setting aside contemplative time.* Each social worker will need support and encouragement to work her own unique spiritual path (developmental process). Without regular opportunities for unscheduled, unstructured time, it is difficult for a social worker to contemplate what her spiritual path actually is. Social workers may need regular time off from clinical, administrative, or academic positions to create the conditions necessary for spiritual work. Each social worker may also need daily or weekly time to contemplate and look inside of herself to recognize her own route to "inner transformation."[41] Without contemplative time, the worker's ability to foster the spirituality of herself or other people is limited. It can be said that "if a social worker gets too far off her path, she gets pathology."

5. *Shadow work.* The effective social worker is committed to continually working on himself. This work includes increasing awareness, acceptance, and healthy expression of those aspects of himself with which he is least comfortable. Each worker faces her own unique challenges, but her work may typically focus

upon sexual, aggressive, or spiritual aspects of herself. As the social worker works on himself, he not only loves more of himself, but he is also capable of loving his clients more.

For example, one social worker was employed at an agency where she was working with clients who were court-referred for counseling because they had physically abused their children. These clients were difficult for her to accept. Although she was normally a very self-controlled person, one day she lost her temper in a conversation with her mother. She had never acted so angry before, and she realized that she needed to work on this angry part of her that had surfaced. In therapy with another social worker in town, she gradually discovered that she had more anger at her own parents than she had wanted to believe. As she understood, accepted, and expressed her anger, she found that she could work more effectively with the angry parents at the agency. She also felt more connected with herself and the world, and she modeled that way of being for her clients.

Moral Development

Moral development is the individual's evolving formation of her own principles of right and wrong behavior. Moral development is related to the affective, spiritual, cognitive, physical, and social dimensions of development. Kohlberg's[42] theory of moral development suggested a movement from reliance upon external authority (e.g., family rules, legal laws, religious doctrine) toward development of and reliance upon internal authority. Kohlberg's stages thus parallel Wilber's theory of spiritual growth, which also postulates movement from a "prepersonal" stage toward a "personal" stage of consciousness.

Gilligan[43] has suggested that the development of females in our society may differ significantly from Kohlberg's schema. Modifications of Kohlberg's stages may be particularly necessary in currently developing population cohorts. For example, a lifelong issue for many women may be the development of autonomy while remaining sensitive to other people's needs.[44] Similar modifications have yet to be created that are sensitive to the expanding roles that many men play in our culture.

From its inception, social work has traditionally taught morality through its code of ethics. Some social workers do function at the beginning levels of moral development and need external codes to help them make decisions. Most, however, operate at more advanced levels and need opportunities to talk about the complex ethical practice dilemmas with which social workers usually struggle on a daily basis. In the field, social workers must often struggle alone with some of society's most critical and controversial issues (e.g., the protective removal of maltreated children, the care of people with AIDS, implementing living wills for the terminally ill).

The effective social worker knows where she stands on ethical issues, but she also affirms the right of others to have moral perspectives that are different from hers. She is willing to wrestle with ethical dilemmas, rather than to merely accept external authority or her own biases as the final word.

Experiential Exercises

1. Consider which values are most important to you in your life. Are they the same values that underlie your social work practice? Why or why not?

2. How did you develop your current values? Are you still open to changing your values?

3. Which values of other people are the hardest for you to tolerate? How could you learn to better accept such moral diversity?

CHAPTER 18

Cognitive and Social Development

Cognitive development includes the gradual formation of life-enhancing beliefs about self, others, and the universe; effective problem-solving, decision-making, and conflict resolution skills; and full use of the various forms of intelligence. Ivey[45] suggested that as the individual becomes able to understand the complexity of systems and "systems of systems," she gradually takes on a more multifaceted view of the world. The effective social worker strives to understand many viewpoints of reality and is able to use his imagination to "walk in another person's shoes." The cognitively mature worker also does not reduce people to simplistic generalizations, but appreciates how complex and unique every person really is.

The effective social worker realizes that she can continue to learn across her lifespan. As she learns more about herself and the world, her humility increases as she better understands the limits of her own knowledge. The social worker also develops an evolving sense of humor about herself and the world, realizing that humor requires the often healing ability to view life from new perspectives. Mental flexibility is another goal: The worker appreciates the viewpoints held by both herself and others.

Experiential Exercises

1. How have you developed cognitively since you were 13 years old (about the time when most humans have developed the maximum number of neurons)? What influences were most important in this process?

2. What beliefs do you now have that are similar to those of your parents, childhood culture, and religion (if any)? Which are different? How do you explain these similarities and differences?

3. Which beliefs that are held by other people are the most difficult for you to tolerate? Why? How could you become more accepting of such cognitive diversity?

The ability to understand and be sensitive to human diversity is related to cognitive development. The social worker who has strived to understand alternate viewpoints is much more likely to be sensitive to issues of diversity, whether they have to do with culture, race, sex, age, development, sexual preference, or any other factor. Cognitive development does not mean that the effective worker no longer has biases; most of us may always have some biases about ourselves and the world. Rather, the effective worker is well aware (and accepting) of her existing biases and is always vigilant to discover any additional biases that may interfere with practice.

The way the social worker views himself, other people, and the universe has a powerful effect on practice. The cognitive map of reality that each person develops is formed as that person tries to make sense out of various life experiences. Sometimes, these beliefs, which tend to persist through time, can act to get in the way of effective living. The cognitive map that social workers have can also serve to either help or hinder the therapeutic process. The effective social worker is always reviewing (and, when necessary, replacing) personal beliefs about self, people, and the universe, and their impact on practice.

For example, a social work student remarked in a class that "poor people choose to live in poverty." This student's belief (which is not based upon existing evidence) could contribute to her decision to avoid working with the poor, to underidentify with poor people, or to ignore community-level interventions with the poor.

The effective social worker also does not value one form of cognitive development over all other forms. Gardner[46] suggested that there are seven forms of intelligence: body/kinesthetic, intrapersonal, interpersonal, mathematical/logical, linguistic, musical, and spatial/visual. Our society and the helping professions tend to devalue body/kinesthetic, intrapersonal, interpersonal, musical, and spatial/visual intelligence. Instead, we tend to most emphasize the value of mathematical/logical and linguistic intelligence, both in the classroom and in the workplace.

The developing social worker strives to develop her own most gifted forms of intelligence and builds upon this success as she develops her more limited forms. The worker accepts her own strengths and limitations; recognizing that limitations often can become strengths, and those strengths are often also limitations. For example, solid linguistic intelligence may be a strength when the worker is writing reports but it may be a limitation when the worker intellectualizes with threatening clients.

As the worker develops a more accepting attitude toward his own intellectual strengths and limitations, he is more likely to accept the diverse gifts that each client has. The tendency of many social workers is to particularly value the linguistic (perhaps because of our many years spent developing our reading and writing in school) and the intrapersonal (perhaps because many of us are interested in feelings). However, many clients may not value these same forms and may need their social worker to accept their unique intellectual qualities.

Mahoney[47] has suggested that the experience of being a professional helper requires development in four key areas, including awareness of (a) the many motives for and meanings of helping (e.g., the "wounded healer" or "guru" metaphors); (b) the responsibilities and risks of the work; (c) the privileges and enrichments of doing counseling; and (d) the importance of taking care of the "serving self." Each social worker may choose to focus on these kinds of issues not only when initially choosing the profession, but also periodically throughout her career.

Although cognitive development is not usually thought of as being directly related to issues of the heart and spirit, the argument could be made that the worker's love and commitment for others is associated with cognitive development. As May has argued, love is interrelated with will, which is "the capacity to organize one's self so that movement in a certain direction or toward a certain goal may take place" (p. 218).[48] In other words, one chooses to love another human being; there is "intentiality" in loving another, and our intent (our meaning or purpose) always "has within it commitment" (p. 230).[49]

Peck[50] defined love as "the will to extend one's self for the purpose of nurturing one's own or another's spiritual growth" (p. 82). The ability to make that choice, and to continue to make that choice, is a reflection of cognitive maturity. Ellis[51] suggested that we tend to feel the way we think. Although Ellis provides insufficient evidence to prove that thinking always precedes feelings, his theories at least suggest that emotional and cognitive maturity are interrelated.

Although love is not usually mentioned as a key aspect of social work effectiveness, it may well be that it is one of the most important aspects of conscious use of self. Some social activists, inspired by the life of Mahatma Gandhi, have indicated that active commitment to service to others is a key element in their success.

> Love is really sacrifice. It's actually not vocal. Although it can be enunciated, it has to be practiced. You need both. . . . Part of Gandhi's greatness was that he didn't want to be a servant, he wanted to be of service. (p. 108).[52]

"The spirit of Gandhi summons us to *satyagraha,* truth's insistent call, in the service of the Earth *now*" (p. xiv).[53]

How does the social worker develop intentionality and will? May suggests that both "eros" and the "daimonic" are necessary in this growth process. The function of eros is to suggest the "ideal forms" of what we might become.

The function of the daimonic is integrative; like the Jungian concept of shadow, the daimonic represents "man's struggle with forces from his own unconscious" (p. 170).[54] Therefore, the worker develops love and will through the exploration of her own personal potentialities (higher self) and shadow characteristics. For example, one social worker found that he could love his clients much more after he learned that he could forgive himself for being a heroin addict in his early adulthood.

Experiential Exercises

1. Which forms of intelligence (body/kinesthetic, intrapersonal, interpersonal, mathematical/logical, linguistic, musical, and spatial/visual) do you value the most? Which do you devalue? Why?

2. How could you learn to accept the intellectual diversity of other people better?

3. Which person in your life would you like to learn to love more? What obstacles (e.g., lack of will, challenging shadow characteristics in yourself) do you need to overcome to increase your love for this person?

Social Development

Social (psychosocial) development includes maturation in the individual's interpersonal patterns (a) in her intimate relationships, (b) in her family, (c) with her friends, (d) with co-workers and supervisors, and (e) with others in society. The ego and self psychologies have theorized a development of the self that includes the stages of bonding and attachment, symbiosis, separation/individuation, and rapprochement.[55] Selman's[56] social role-taking theory describes the process whereby the developing child learns to take another's point of view into account.

Social development is interrelated with the other dimensions of development and includes gradual maturation in the areas of trust, individuation, and identity. As a social worker becomes more of an individual, she creates a boundary inside of which she can discover herself. The worker no longer has to give up self when in relationship with others. Many client systems have boundary dysfunctions, including either enmeshed or disengaged relationships.[57] The social worker who has a healthy boundary, a separate self, is much less likely to be triangulated into dysfunctional family relationships.

The worker strives for healthy individuation, in which the worker is neither too enmeshed nor too disengaged with family, friends, and community. In their search for their own healthy boundaries, clients may challenge the social worker's boundaries, sometimes by inappropriately intrusive or helpful behavior. The social worker cannot give his client an identity, but he can model the process for the client. The social worker who has found a way to develop trust can also model this quality for clients.

Experiential Exercises

1. Describe your own social development. What major influences helped shape this process?

2. In your own relationships, do you tend to become too enmeshed or too disengaged with others? Why do you think? How would you like to be?

3. Consider which social traits are the hardest for you to tolerate in other people (e.g., mistrust, pushiness, withdrawal, etc.). Why do these traits bother you? How can you learn to better accept such social diversity?

Social goals include the development of effective communication, mutual respect, a balance of power, a balance of give and take, a balance between healthy competition and cooperation, a balance between the welfare and interests of the individual and the society, the ability to have an impact on the environment, and the ability to locate and obtain resources from others. Social development also includes the gradually increasing ability to choose one's own actions in an age-appropriate and functional manner. Therefore, such behavioral goals as impulse control, self-discipline, the ability to relax, full range of affective expression, and assertive skills are included in the social dimension.

As the worker interacts with clients, the worker models effective social skills. When social workers work together, they also model these skills through their interactions with each other as well. The social worker who, for example, is learning to be more assertive may help her clients learn similar behaviors. Social workers who co-lead groups can demonstrate such behaviors as assertiveness, effective communication, problem solving, and conflict resolution as they interact with each other in front of the group.

Conscious use of self can often increase one's effectiveness in working with difficult clients. For example, hostile and aggressive clients often respond more positively to and are more calmed by the social worker who consciously acts calmly, despite the fear and anger that the worker may be feeling inside. The social worker realizes that she would not want to be calm all of the time with every angry person, because some angry people may need their worker to show angry emotion at times. The worker also realizes that his calmness could be a habitual pattern of behavior that has more to do with his early experiences as a child with a hostile father than his conscious choice in the present to try to reach a difficult client.

Thus, the actions of the effective social worker with her client are increasingly conscious *choices* rather than less conscious responses or habitual patterns. The ability to assess the client's needs, accept internal countertransferences, and then choose a specific intervention is a sophisticated, high level of functioning that most social workers will gradually develop over time.

As Satir[58] has suggested, the quality of the interactions between the social worker and the client is very important in practice effectiveness. She encouraged social workers to develop what she called "horizontal" relationships with their clients. A horizontal relationship can be understood as one characterized by mutual respect, equality of power, mutual ownership of self, and genuineness.

In a vertical relationship, the social worker assumes more power than the client, assumes that she is better situated to assess the client than the client himself, and solely controls the assessment and the selection and implementation of interventions. There may be times when elements of both horizontal and vertical relationships are required to help client systems best. For example, although the social worker will always want to respect clients, some clients may be so immature or disabled that they require more direction and control from the worker. As discussed in Parts III and IV, some intervention models encourage horizontal relationships with clients, and other models encourage vertical relationships.

From the social worker's perspective, mutual respect means that the social worker acknowledges and values the unique qualities, perspectives, and visions of the client and of self. Equality of power means that the social worker gives the client the maximum autonomy, control, and choice that the client is developmentally ready to assume. Mutual ownership of self means that as two people communicate with each other, they can also relate to the many aspects of their own selves. The social worker does not, for example, relate only from a "parental" ego state to the client's "child" ego state; such a relationship would be limiting, static, and would be labeled "vertical" by Satir.

Transferences, Countertransferences, and the Multidimensional Development of the Social Worker

The social worker's multidimensional development of self is critical to professional effectiveness. Self-development is particularly important in preparing a social worker to deal effectively with transference and countertransference issues. The developing social worker tends to be better prepared to tune in to the client's transference reactions and the client's underlying needs. The developing social worker also tends to be better prepared to tune in to countertransference reactions, to intervene effectively, and to model growth for the client. In this section, transference and countertransference are further defined and described from the perspective of each of the four forces (or major paradigms) of psychology.

Transference

Transference is defined to include *any* reaction of the client to the worker, on the cognitive, affective, physical, social, and/or spiritual dimensions. These thoughts, feelings, and behaviors may be simple or complex, consistent or contradictory. Usually, a transference reaction is rooted both in the past and present; the here-and-now reaction is often distorted or modified by similar past experiences in the client's life. The client's reaction is thus about both the client and the worker; the client responds to the worker from her own perspective and history. Because an individual always has at least one reaction to another person, at any given time there is *always* a transference reaction between a client and worker.

For example, a father may become quite angry with his Child Protective Services worker when the worker removes his child into protective custody. He screams at the worker on the phone, refuses to see her, and says that he will get a lawyer and sue the state. This reaction is, of course, partly rooted in the here and now; most fathers would be upset with a worker for removing his child. However, the anger is quite intense and is accompanied with the thought that "this worker is out to get me." It turns out that the client has had authority figures in the past who really were out to get him (e.g., his own abusive father, his hostile second-grade teacher, etc.). So, although the reaction is quite normal, the client's transference was intensified by his victimization in the past.

Experiential Exercises

1. How does your culture and the social work profession seem to feel and think about transference reactions (e.g., do we acknowledge or accept them)?

2. Identify some transference reactions you now have toward a social worker, teacher, or other professional helper in your life. Explain why you have those reactions. Do you accept those reactions? What do you think you do not see clearly about that helper because of the transference?

3. Describe a transference that a client (or someone else) seems to have toward you now. How does it feel to have someone react to you with that transference? What would be the best way to handle the reaction?

Different paradigms of practice view transference differently and incorporate different treatment techniques. Regardless of the model she uses, the social worker needs to be able to effectively handle a variety of very challenging transference reactions, including intense anger, love, and fear. There is no evidence that any one theoretical approach to dealing with transference is more effective than any other.[59] Within each model, there is a variety of different ideas about transference. In assessing and intervening in transference reactions, social workers can consider the following guidelines and outlines of the basic differences between the practice paradigms.

1. Awareness. The social worker strives to become more aware of the client's feelings, thoughts, and behavioral intentions/impulses. There are many ways of discovering transference, including using (a) internal clues, (b) external clues, and (c) verbal communications. Usually, the social worker wants to consider all three sources of information when possible. No one way of knowing is necessarily more legitimate than the others.

With *internal clues,* the social worker experiences the client's transference in her own body. For example, we feel anger inside of us when the client is angry, fear when the client is afraid, and so on. Sometimes, internal clues come in the form of visual pictures (for social workers who are visually dominant) or cognitions (for clients who are more cognitively dominant). The social worker may also have intuitive hunches. Some social workers also use their logic to deduce or induce the client's transferences. The social worker may combine logic with intuition and observation of self. Obviously, the social worker who is more aware of self will be more likely to use internal clues effectively and to distinguish such clues from countertransference reactions and biases. All such clues may be checked out directly with the client, as appropriate.

Often, there are also *external clues* from the client's body language. Body language may include many aspects of expression; for example, the client may avoid eye contact, sit still, or hold her shoulders quite stiffly. The client may always choose to sit in a particular chair in group or individually. Other professionals or family members may give the social worker information about the client. The history of the client, collected in assessment, may be another source of external information. The social worker should check out these clues further by directly talking with the client about them.

Some clients will be both able and willing to tell the social worker about their transference reactions. If it occurs at all, such *direct communication* often develops gradually in the therapeutic relationship. Many clients will, of course, be unable and/or unwilling to disclose such information. The social worker cannot always trust direct communications; clients will sometimes give inaccurate information because they are either unaware of or uncomfortable with their transference reaction. There will also be clients who will use disclosure of transference reaction as a coping mechanism. One client who was a sex offender, for example, told the social worker how angry he was at her whenever they got close to talking about his sexuality. Another client always fell in love with her social workers, but also always left therapy and found a new social worker before she got into her core issues.

2. Acceptance. The social worker works to become more accepting of all of the client's feelings, thoughts, and behavioral intentions and impulses. Self-acceptance, just like self-awareness, is a gradual process that continues throughout the lifespan. The social worker tries to accept the client's own level of self-acceptance; impatience with the process tends to impede it. Every transference reaction of the client is acceptable, although some of the client's behaviors may not be appropriate or desirable. Thus, for example, any angry or sexual feeling is acceptable, but murder or rape are, of course, unacceptable expressions of these impulses. The goal is not to change the transference, but rather to understand and accept the transference and then use it to foster client development.

3. *Interventions.* The social worker selects differentially an intervention response to the client's transference. In selecting interventions, the worker considers her own comfort level, the client system, and any constraints of the practice setting.

Theories of Transference

Some approaches to dealing with transferences, drawn from the Four Forces of psychology, are described below.

Psychoanalytic theory. In psychoanalytic theory, work with transference is seen as a central aspect of therapy. The worker uses the transferences as sources of information about the client and as material with which to work in the sessions. Freud described the transference neurosis, in which certain clients transferred problems associated with their psychosexual development or their Oedipal conflict to their therapists.[60] Therapy was designed to explore how clients project their unresolved conflicts about past relationships into the present therapeutic relationship. The social worker uses interpretations to help the client make old conflicts more conscious and gradually reduce the client's anxiety. In this process of working through, the client deals with the pain of insight and makes the often slow process of reworking old conflicts in his relationships. When a client reacts negatively to a suggestion of the worker, for example, the worker might make an interpretation such as, "Perhaps your anger toward me is actually displaced anger that really belongs with (is felt toward) your overcontrolling mother."

Although they incorporate some psychoanalytic theory, the ego psychologists and self psychologists generally look at transference somewhat differently from Freud. They tend to view most or all clients as having transferences. Kohut[61] has, for example, developed a general classification of transferences that links formal, Freudian psychoanalysis to less intensive forms of psychotherapy. Instead of using interpretations, Kohut teaches social workers to empathically respond to where the client actually is. Instead of encouraging change, the worker accepts the client as he is in the present. In the process of transmuting internalization, the client integrates the empathic responses of the worker and strives toward greater competence and self-esteem.

Kohut noted three common transferences.[62] The first is the *mirroring transference.* In this transference, the client may act as if he does not need the worker's help. In this case, one appropriate empathic response would be, "It must have been difficult for you all these years, feeling like you had to go it alone because no one else was responsive to you." The client might also continually seek validation from the worker. In either case, the client may not have received adequate mirroring, or validation and approval, as an infant.

In the *idealizing transference,* the client may panic when the worker is leaving for a short vacation. One appropriate empathic response might be,

"It must be hard having to always worry about people leaving you, maybe because you have never felt like you had anyone you could rely on." The client is still idealizing the social worker, just as an infant often idealizes the parent.

The third is the *alter ego transference*. For example, the client asks if the worker has felt the same way. One appropriate empathic response might be, "What has it been like, always feeling like you were so different from everyone else?" The client is seeking a twin or alter ego to be like, much as young children often do.

These three transferences each reflect a different psychic wound that occurred in one of the early developmental stages in the client's infancy and childhood. Therefore, the nature of the transference helps the worker identify the developmental stage in which the client was emotionally damaged. A client can have one or more of these different transferences.

Cognitive/behavioral/communications theory. In the various cognitive/behavioral/ communications psychologies, transference is often either addressed indirectly or ignored. The past is largely disregarded, and here-and-now strategies are used, often without explanation to the client. Transference may be minimized by screening out resistant clients or by stressing mutual responsibility for problems. In addition, client strengths and positive goals are emphasized. Sometimes, various nonfunctional cognitive beliefs that may be in the way of behavioral change are challenged and replaced.[63]

Using the paradoxical approach of Erickson,[64] the worker might welcome the transference instead of viewing it as something to overcome. With a client who is overcontrolled and unwilling to allow the worker to help, the technique might be to ask the client to exaggerate the symptom and act even more overcontrolled and isolated. The client then might respond by relaxing. This technique is not recommended in situations involving potential violence or harm; you should not recommend to an abusive client that she go home and be more abusive. Similarly, other social workers who use strategic strategies might overcome resistance through the use of relabeling and reframing techniques.

For example, if a parent angrily and defensively states that he is tired of his son spending so much of his time playing video games, the worker might say, "I am impressed that you care so much about your child that you are willing to try so hard to help him develop himself in a well-balanced manner" or "Your son must have gotten quite a bit of intelligence from his father to be able to master such a difficult game." Structural family social workers expect transferences and resistance and may modify their timing, style, and interventions to accommodate what the client is ready and capable of using.[65]

Experiential/phenomenological theory. In the various experiential/phenomenological therapies, transference is often handled openly in the context of the here-and-now therapeutic relationship. Perls[66] might, for example, challenge the hostile client to act out in an exaggerated way her anger toward the social worker in a role-play so as to increase awareness and ownership of the resistance. Rogers[67] might respond to the client's hostility with empathy, warmth, and genuineness.

Transpersonal theory. The transpersonal social worker's goal in working with transference is to facilitate the client's growth toward more optimal states of consciousness and levels of well-being. The meaning that the client gives to the transference may be discussed. For example, Albert Einstein is often quoted as having said that the most important thing to decide about the universe is whether it is friendly. A client who is hypervigilant in sessions with the social worker may believe that the universe is an unfriendly place and may expect the social worker to hurt him. The social worker helps the client own that belief and accept the fact that he feels that way now. In that process of self-acceptance, change becomes more possible. The client may also work with the social worker to disidentify with that belief, realizing that he is more than just his beliefs and associated thoughts and behaviors. As Jungian[68] psychology suggests, some of his reactions to the social worker may be both individual experience and archetypes of a "collective unconscious" that all people share.

Process-oriented psychotherapy. In process-oriented psychotherapy,[69] the worker might see client resistance as part of a process of which the client is relatively unaware ("a secondary process") and that needs to be identified and owned. The social worker might ask the client who is placating to act out the related primary process (that which is ego-congruent) and secondary process (that which is less ego-congruent) alone or with a group of clients in the office.

Many clients will have strong biases either for or against a particular religion (or for or against religion in general). The worker needs to assess such biases and to be aware of how these biases can lead to the client either idealizing or devaluing the worker (depending upon whether the client perceives the worker's religion or spirituality as being similar or different from that of the client). Often, the most important intervention that the worker can make is to simply ask the client to tell her story of spiritual and religious development and to listen in an accepting manner.

Inclusive social work with transference. The Four Forces are not necessarily mutually exclusive; there is no reason why a social worker cannot use all of these techniques, even with the same client. Thus, for example, a social worker might use empathic responses (First Force), reinforcement (Second Force), and disclosure (Third Force), as well as work with religious history (Fourth Force), in the same session.

Countertransference

Countertransference is similar to transference, except that it includes any reaction of the *worker to the client* on the cognitive, affective, physical, social, and spiritual dimensions. The social worker always has a countertransference reaction to the client. Examples of such reactions include a worker who is (a) hostile with the client, (b) afraid of the client, and (c) sexually attracted to a client. The countertransference can be associated with a pattern or can be a one-time occurrence.

Experiential Exercises

1. How does your culture and the social work profession seem to feel and think about countertransference reactions (e.g., do social workers talk freely about their countertransference reactions)?

2. Identify some countertransference reactions you now have toward a client or someone else in your life. Explain why you have those reactions. Do you accept those reactions? What do you think you do not see clearly about that person because of the countertransference?

3. Describe a countertransference that a helper (or someone else) seems to have toward you now. How does it feel to have someone react to you with that countertransference? What would be the best way for you to handle their reaction to you?

The social worker may not even know what the deeper work with a client will be until she has an inappropriate (undesired) countertransference with the client. In other words, the most powerful and least desired countertransference reactions often provide the worker with important information about what the client needs. As will be explained further, countertransferences often suggest how others have treated and experienced the client and how the client now feels about herself.

Effective use of countertransference has been recognized as an important aspect of social work practice.[70] If the worker is unaware of countertransferences, she may well put personal needs ahead of the needs of the client without even being aware of what is happening. For example, suppose that a female worker came from an abusive home. When her father beat her mother, she learned as a child to try to diffuse the conflict by calming her father down and trying to distract him. When she sees an abusive family system as a professional, even years later, she easily slips into the same familiar coping style, calming down the abusive father and distracting him. This strategy may not be helpful to a particular family, however, in part because the father's lack of control and anger is never directly dealt with in the sessions.

All countertransference reactions involve characteristics of both the social worker and the client. The worker's reaction to some characteristics of the client activates some preexisting characteristics of the worker. Often, what is activated in the worker are complex patterns of emotion, thought, and behavior that were first induced by life trauma(s) in the worker's own past. For example, one social worker got angry at a mother who neglected her son. The worker's own mother was also neglectful of him, and his angry reaction to the mother was intensified because some of the anger he had toward his own mother was displaced onto his client. Countertransference reactions thus are related to both the worker's own past experiences and to his present experience of the client.

Forms of Countertransferences

Various countertransferences that can occur include the following common forms.[71]

Triangulation occurs when a worker joins an often unconscious and involuntary alliance with one or more clients. Objectivity and the ability to intervene freely are often lost. Instead of responding from an objective assessment of the unique case, the worker may be capable of only one response. Triangulation can be caused by either overidentification or underidentification with a client. In both cases, the issues involved have been and/or are of such great importance in the worker's life that the worker is unable to see the client(s) and situation realistically.

Underidentification occurs when a worker is unable to clearly see who the client is because the client reminds the worker of (a) a person the worker did not like, and/or (b) an aspect of self that the worker does not like. The worker then responds from personal experience and needs instead of out of a sensitivity to the client's experience and needs. An example of underidentification is when the female worker who was beaten by her father as a child tends to ignore the experience of and withdraw empathy and warmth from the physically abusive father with whom she is now working. In this situation, the abusive father may well sense the lack of empathy and even hostility of the worker, and he may become more defensive and unwilling to change.

Overidentification occurs when a worker is unable to clearly see who the client is because the client reminds the worker of (a) a person the worker likes, and/or (b) an aspect of self that the worker likes or desires to have. The worker then responds from her own experience and needs instead of out of sensitivity to the client's experience and needs. The male worker who was beaten by his father may overidentify with the little boy, also beaten by his father, with whom he is now working. In this case, the overidentification with the boy by the worker might result in the worker assuming that the boy feels the same way he did as a child, instead of seeing him as a separate and unique individual.

A worker can and often does have both overidentification and underidentification with different members of the same family. Using the same example above, the worker could overidentify with the abused girl and underidentify with the abusive father at the same time.

Working With Countertransference

In general, several steps can be recommended in working with counter-transference issues.

1. Awareness. The social worker strives to become more aware of her personal feelings, thoughts, and behavioral intentions/impulses. Behavioral intentions/impulses are our first knee-jerk reactions that we tend to express verbally and/or physically. Most social workers gradually become more and more aware of their own countertransference reactions. Accompanying this increase in awareness is usually also an ability to identify such reactions more quickly after they first begin. Although the ultimate goal is to eventually be aware in the moment, the social worker is aware that self-understanding is an ongoing, lifelong process.

2. Acceptance. The social worker works to become more accepting of all of his personal feelings, thoughts, and behavioral intentions/impulses. Self-acceptance, just like self-awareness, is a gradual process that continues throughout the lifespan. The social worker tries to accept his personal level of self-acceptance; impatience with the process tends to impede it. There is nothing unusual or bad about a worker having a strong countertransference with a client. According to Anderson and Stewart,

> All family social workers have issues with their own parents, spouses, or children which are unresolved and which predispose them to see situations in a distorted way. Rather than feeling inferior for not being perfect, dwelling on inadequacies, or trying to hide them, the task for social workers is to know and accept their own peculiar vulnerabilities. Only in this way can they use their assets and minimize their liabilities. Family social workers, like any other social workers, have few answers. No personal or professional factor guarantees competence. There are advantages and disadvantages to every personal characteristic (be it age, sex, or marital status) and every professional characteristic (be it discipline, style, or years of experience). (p. 123)[72]

3. Using countertransference in the assessment. With *underidentification* reactions, the social worker considers a series of questions:

- What am I feeling? To which client characteristic(s) (activating characteristics) am I reacting? Which past experiences in my life may be distorting or modifying my current reaction to the client?

- What other people in the client's life (e.g., lovers, family members, friends, colleagues, etc.) have or had similar reactions to the client?

- Does the client feel the same reaction toward herself and/or others?

- What experiences may the client have had that could have contributed to him having the activating characteristics? For example, have significant people in the client's past (e.g., parents, siblings, lovers, etc.) often expressed the same reaction to the client?

- Given these hypotheses, what is it probably like to be this client? Therefore, what does this client need? How can I show this client empathy for her affective state?

For example, a female social worker is working with a father, mother, and their 8-year-old son. The father has physically abused the son, and the father was physically abused by his own father when he was a child. The father blames the child for the abuse, stating that the boy "asked for it" and "does not understand anything else besides a spanking." The boy is very intelligent, but he is quite shy and socially withdrawn. The social worker notices that she is very uncomfortable around the father. In supervision, she realizes that she is quite angry at the father, and that she is especially reacting to his denial of responsibility. The social worker is also aware that her own mother blamed her for the spankings she gave her.

The father's history shows that he was often blamed and criticized by his own parents. The worker realizes that the mother and the son also seem to dislike the father's tendency to blame others for his behavior. She believes that the father tends to dislike himself for his blaming behaviors. She guesses that the father likely feels quite isolated in the family and is probably alienated from most people in his life. She decides that the father needs to start to feel what he has lost because of the way he relates to his family and others (he has lost any connection with them). She tries to show him empathy for his disconnected and alone affective state by talking with him about what it is like to have his family dislike him.

With *overidentification* reactions, the social worker considers another series of questions:

- What am I feeling? To which client characteristic(s) (activating characteristics) am I reacting? Which past experiences in my life may be distorting or modifying my current reaction to the client?

- Which aspects of the client may I be missing because of this overidentification?

- What other people in the client's life (e.g., lovers, family members, friends, colleagues, etc.) may also be missing (or, in the past, missed) important aspects of the client?

- Does the client also tend to underrecognize these aspects?

- What experiences may the client have had that could have contributed to him having the activating characteristics? Have significant people in the client's past (e.g., parents, siblings, lovers, etc.) expressed the same reaction to the client?

- What advice or other interventions do I want to give to this client that may not reflect what the client actually needs?

- Given these hypotheses, what is it probably like to be this client? Therefore, what does this client need? How can I show this client empathy for this affective state?

Using the example of the abusive father, mother, and their 8-year-old son introduced above, the social worker may notice that she has an overidentification with the son. She realizes that she feels sorry for the boy and has the impulse to tell him to forget about his father and to concentrate on his schoolwork and other interests. She believes that he may remind her of herself as a child; she was also very intelligent, like him, and chose to withdraw into her work to protect herself. The social worker may be missing the boy's need to have a loving relationship with his father and other adults, as well as the cost of social withdrawal. She believes that the boy's parents, as well as the boy himself, may all be underestimating his social needs and painful loneliness.

4. Interventions. The social worker differentially selects an intervention response to the client's transference. In selecting interventions, the worker considers personal comfort level, the client system, and any constraints of the practice setting. There is no evidence that any one theoretical approach to dealing with countertransference is more effective than any other.[73] Some approaches to dealing with transferences, drawn from the Four Forces of psychology, are described below.

Psychoanalytic theory. In psychoanalytic theory, work with countertransference is seen as a central aspect of therapy. From the traditional psychoanalytic perspective,[74] in a countertransference reaction, the worker does not see the client realistically in the here and now, but unconsciously reacts to her as if she is the person who originally traumatized the worker (often a parent or parents). The traditional psychoanalytic approach had the social worker become a blank slate that would not reveal any countertransferences directly to the client. Instead, in this approach, the worker focuses on the client's transferences and behaviors. The social worker does try to be aware of the countertransference, but the worker discloses the material only to another social worker or a supervisor. For example, if the social worker is angry at the client, the worker may decide to make the interpretation, "Perhaps you want to make people angry with you for some reason."

Cognitive/behavioral/communications theory. In the various cognitive/behavioral/communications psychologies, countertransference is often addressed indirectly or ignored. The social worker does not tell the client what the countertransference is, but she may use the context of the countertransference as additional data that may be useful in planning goals, tasks, and behavior modification strategies. For example, if the client always makes the social worker angry, the social worker may decide to try to help the client act in new ways with people that are less likely to make them angry.

Experiential/phenomenological theory. In the various experiential/phenomenological therapies, countertransference is often handled in the here-and-now therapeutic relationship. The experiential/phenomenological social workers tend to be more transparent about their countertransferences. They may gently reveal their reactions to a client or, in some cases, even become rather confrontational with their countertransferences. For example, if the social worker is angry with the client, she may simply say, "It makes me angry when you make those kinds of comments to me."

Transpersonal theory. The transpersonal social worker's goal in working with countertransference is facilitating the client's growth toward more optimum states of consciousness and levels of well-being. Some transpersonal social workers regularly provide their clients with information about all of their countertransference reactions. For example, some social workers using eidetic imagery[75] will tell clients what visual image comes up for them as the client works during a session.

Effective social workers strive to pay particular attention to their own religious and spiritual countertransferences. Most social workers have experienced religion as being either supportive, nonsupportive, or even abusive in relation to their own spiritual development. Such past experiences can lead to strong biases toward clients who seem to have religious and spiritual experiences that are either similar or different from the worker's. For example, a worker who felt that she was abused by the XYZ church may have a blindspot about how anyone could possibly benefit from being involved with XYZ rituals and beliefs. Another worker who remains an XYZ fundamentalist may have the opposite countertransference (e.g., a blindspot about how anyone who was not XYZ could possibly reach salvation or see truth).

Inclusive social work with countertransference. Again, the Four Forces are not necessarily mutually exclusive; there is no reason why a social worker cannot use all of these techniques, even with the same client. Thus, the social worker might use interpretation (First Force), cognitive restructuring (Second Force), disclosure (Third Force), and Eidetic Imagery (Fourth Force) within the same session.

Notes

Part V Introduction

1. Maslow, A. H. (1971). *The further reaches of human nature.* New York: Viking.

Chapter 16

2. Chess, S., & Thomas, A. (1986). *Temperament in clinical practice.* New York: Guilford.

3. Olny, R. (1991, July). *Self acceptance training.* Paper presented at the Summer Institute, Graduate School of Social Work, University of Utah, Salt Lake City.

4. Kaufman, G. (1988). *The psychology of shame: Theory and treatment of shame-based syndromes.* New York: Springer.

5. Bradshaw, J. (1988). *Bradshaw on: The family.* Deerfield Beach, FL: Health Communications.

6. Satir, V. (1988). *The new peoplemaking.* Mountain View, CA: Science and Behavior Books.

7. Mecca, A. M., Smelser, N. J., & Vasconcellos, J. (Eds.). (1989). *The social importance of self-esteem.* Berkeley: University of California Press.

8. Friedman, D., & Kaslow, N. (1986). The development of professional identity in psychotherapists: Six stages of the supervision process. In F. W. Kaslow (Ed.), *Supervision and training models, dilemmas, and challenges* (pp. 29-49). New York: Haworth.

9. Wilson, S. J. (1981). *Field instruction: Techniques for supervisors.* New York: Macmillan.

10. Horowitz, F. D. (1987). *Exploring developmental theories: Toward a structural/behavioral model of development.* Hillsdale, NJ: Lawrence Erlbaum.

11. Miller, A. (1990). *The drama of the gifted child.* New York: Basic Books.

12. F. Perls, as quoted in Olny (1991).

13. Satir, V. (1972). *Peoplemaking.* Palo Alto, CA: Science and Behavior Books.

14. Satir (1988); Trungpa, C. (1987). *Shambhala: The sacred path of the warrior.* Boston: Shambhala.

15. Freud, S. (1913). *Totem and taboo.* New York: Hogarth; Freud, S. (1921). *Massenpsychologie.* London: Hogarth.

16. Jung, C. J. (1968). *Archetypes of the collective unconscious.* Princeton, NJ: Princeton University Press.

17. Satir (1988).

18. Bradshaw, J. (1988, July). Workshop, Oakland, CA.

19. Peck, M. S. (1978). *The road less traveled: A new psychology of love, traditional values and spiritual growth.* New York: A Touchtone Book.

20. Ingram, C. (1990). *In the footsteps of Gandhi: Conversations with spiritual social activists.* Berkeley, CA: Parallax.

21. Logan, R. D. (1992). Flow in solitary ordeals. In M. Csikszentmihalyi & I. Csikszentmihalyi (Eds.), *Optimal experience: Psychological studies of flow in consciousness* (pp. 150-172). New York: Cambridge University Press.

Chapter 17

22. Krueger, D. W. (1989). *Body self and psychological self.* New York: Brunner/Mazel.

23. Satir (1972, 1988).

24. Cousins, N. (1989). *Head first: The biology of hope.* New York: Dutton.

25. Wilber, K. (1986). The spectrum of development. In K. Wilber, J. Engler, & D. P. Brown (Eds.), *Transformations of consciousness: Conventional and contemplative perspectives on development* (pp. 65-106). Boston: New Science Library.

26. Hillman, J. (1975). *Re-visioning psychology.* New York: HarperColophon.

27. Wilber (1986).

28. Seeber, J. J. (1990). *Spiritual maturity in the later years.* New York: Haworth.

29. Fowler, J. F. (1981). *Stages of faith.* San Francisco: Harper & Row.

30. Naisbitt, J., & Aburdene, P. (1990). *Megatrends 2000.* New York: Morrow.

31. Coles, R. (1990). *The spiritual life of children.* Boston: Houghton Mifflin.

32. Freud (1913, 1921); Freud, S. (1937). *Moses and monotheism.* London: Hogarth.

33. Satir (1988).

34. Fox, M. (1994). *The reinvention of work: A new vision of livelihood for our time.* San Francisco: Harper San Francisco.

35. Campbell, J. (1988). *The power of myth.* New York: Doubleday.

36. Bennett, H. Z., & Sparrow, S. J. (1990). *Follow your bliss.* New York: Avon.

37. Frankl, V. (1959). *From death camp to existentialism.* Boston: Beacon.

38. Fowler (1981).

39. James, J., & James, M. (1991). *Passion for life: Psychology and the human spirit.* New York: Penguin.

40. Roszak, T. (1978). *Person/planet: The creative disintegration of industrial society.* New York: Anchor/Doubleday.

41. Anthony, D., Ecker, B., & Wilber, K. (1987). *Spiritual choices: The problem of recognizing authentic paths to inner transformation.* New York: Paragon House.

42. Kohlberg, L. (1981). *The philosophy of moral development.* San Francisco: Harper & Row.

43. Gilligan, C. (1982). *In a different voice.* Cambridge, MA: Harvard University Press.

44. Nemiroff, R. A., & Colarusso, C. A. (Eds.). (1990). *New dimensions in adult development.* New York: Basic Books.

Chapter 18

45. Ivey, A. E. (1986). *Developmental therapy.* San Francisco: Jossey-Bass; Ivey, A. E. (1991). *Developmental strategies for helpers: Individual, family, and network interventions.* Pacific Grove, CA: Brooks/Cole.

46. Gardner, H. (1983). *Frames of mind: The theory of multiple intelligences.* New York: Basic Books.

47. Mahoney, M. J. (1991). *Human change processes: The scientific foundations of psychotherapy.* New York: Basic Books.

48. May, R. (1969). *Love and will.* New York: Norton.

49. May (1969).

50. Peck (1978).

51. Ellis, A. (1962). *Reasons and emotion in psychotherapy.* New York: Lyle Stuart.

52. Chavez, C. (1990). Cesar Chavez. In C. Ingram (Ed.), *In the footsteps of Gandhi: Conversations with spiritual social activists.* Berkeley, CA: Parallax.

53. Ingram, C. (1990). *In the footsteps of Gandhi: Conversations with spiritual social activists.* Berkeley, CA: Parallax.

54. May, R. (1975). *The courage to create.* New York: Norton.

55. Johnson, S. M. (1987). *Humanizing the narcissistic style.* New York: Norton.

56. Selman, R. (1971). Taking another's perspective: Role taking development in early childhood. *Childhood Development, 42,* 1721-1734.

57. Minuchin, S. (1974). *Families and family therapy.* Cambridge, MA: Harvard University Press.

58. Satir (1972).

Chapter 19

59. Garfield, S. L., & Bergin, A. E. (1986). *Handbook of psychotherapy and behavior change.* New York: Wiley.

60. Freud (1913).

61. Kohut, H. (1977). *The restoration of the self.* New York: International Universities Press; Kohut, H. (1984). *How does analysis cure?* Chicago: University of Chicago Press.

62. White, M. T., & Weiner, M. B. (1986). *The theory and practice of self-psychology.* New York: Brunner/Mazel.

63. Ellis (1962).

64. Haley, J. (1973). *Uncommon therapy: The techniques of Milton H. Erickson.* New York: Ballantine.

65. Anderson, C. A., & Stewart, S. (1983). *Mastering resistance: A practical guide to family therapy.* New York: Guilford.

66. Perls, F. S. (1969). *Gestalt therapy verbatim.* Moab, UT: Real People Press.

67. Rogers, C. R. (1965). *Client-centered therapy.* Boston: Houghton Mifflin.

68. Jung, C. J. (1968). *Archetypes of the collective unconscious.* Princeton, NJ: Princeton University Press.

69. Goodbread, J. H. (1987). *The dreambody toolkit: A practical guide to the philosophy, goals, and practice of process-oriented psychology.* New York: Routledge and Kegan Paul.

70. Hepworth, D. H., & Larsen, J. A. (1990). *Direct social work practice: Theory and skills.* Belmont, CA: Wadsworth.

71. Anderson and Stewart (1983).

72. Anderson and Stewart (1983).

73. Garfield, S. L., & Bergin, A. E. (1986). *Handbook of psychotherapy and behavior change* (3rd ed.). New York: Wiley.

74. Freud, S. (1915). The unconscious. In *Standard edition* (Vol. 14, pp. 159-204). London: Hogarth.

75. Ahsen, A. (1977). *Psyche self analytic consciousness: A basic introduction to the natural self analytic images of consciousness eidetics.* New York: Brandon House.

Author Index

Subject Index

About the Author

David S. Derezotes is currently Associate Professor and Chair of the Practice Committee at the Graduate School of Social Work, University of Utah. He is also currently Clinical Director at the Pacific Resource Center in Salt Lake City and is involved in private practice and consultation. Derezotes received a PhD in social work from the School of Social Welfare, University of California, Berkeley and a PhD in clinical psychology from International College in Los Angeles. He has 27 years of practice experience, working primarily with troubled and disadvantaged children, youth, and families in a variety of settings.